CONTINUITIES
IN
PSYCHOLOGICAL
ANTHROPOLOGY

CONTINUITIES IN PSYCHOLOGICAL ANTHROPOLOGY

A HISTORICAL INTRODUCTION

PHILIP K. BOCK

University of New Mexico

W. H. Freeman and Company
San Francisco

Sponsoring Editor: Richard J. Lamb
Project Editor: Pearl C. Vapnek
Manuscript Editor: Suzanne Lipsett
Designer: Sharon Helen Smith
Production Coordinator: William Murdock
Illustration Coordinator: Cheryl Nufer
Compositor: Interactive Composition Corporation
Printer and Binder: The Maple-Vail Book
Manufacturing Group

Library of Congress Cataloging in Publication Data

Bock, Philip K
    Continuities in psychological anthropology.

    Bibliography: p.
    Includes index.
    1. Ethnopsychology.   I.   Title.
GN502.B62   155.8   79-23200
ISBN 0-7167-1136-2
ISBN 0-7167-1137-0 pbk.

For Barbara,
at last

Contents

Preface   xi

PRELUDE
ALL ANTHROPOLOGY IS PSYCHOLOGICAL   1

ONE
THE PSYCHOLOGY OF PRIMITIVE PEOPLES   7

Perception, or "Do You See What I See?"   10

Motivation, or "The Natives Are Restless Tonight"   17

Cognition, or "Thinking Can Make It So"   24

TWO
PSYCHOANALYTIC ANTHROPOLOGY   31

Elements of Psychoanalysis   32

The Origins of Psychoanalytic Anthropology   38

Totemism and Exogamy   43

Psychoanalysis and Clothing   49

Summary and Critique   52

THREE

**CONFIGURATIONS OF CULTURE
AND PERSONALITY   57**

Configurations of Culture   63

To and From the South Seas   74

Summary   79

FOUR

BASIC AND MODAL PERSONALITY   85

Basic Personality Structure   86

The Modal Personality Approach   93

Projective Tests: Rorschach and Thematic
Apperception   96

Applications of Projective Tests   100

Summary   105

FIVE

NATIONAL CHARACTER STUDIES   107

The Yellow Peril   109

On the Western Front   112

The Slavic Soul   114

The Lonely Crowd   119

And Elsewhere   127

Summary   128

INTERLUDE

THE CRISIS IN CULTURE AND PERSONALITY   131

Quo Vadis?   137

SIX

CROSS-CULTURAL CORRELATIONS   141

The Yale Synthesis   141

Correlations and Customs   145

Galton's Problem   153

Male Initiation Rites   155

Brotherly Love   158

Summary   162

SEVEN

THE RETURN OF THE REPRESSED   165

Instinct and Culture   166

Symbolic Wounds   168

Insight and Identity   172

Psychohistory and the Interpretation of Myth   177

Psychosocial Adaptation   180

Summary   182

EIGHT
SOCIAL STRUCTURE AND PERSONALITY   185

Materialist Approaches   186

Positionalist Approaches   189

Interactionist Approaches   196

Summary   203

NINE
FOCUSING ON THE HERE AND NOW   207

Six Cultures   208

Human Ethology   212

Attachment, Separation, and Crowding   215

Alternative States of Consciousness   219

Of Human Thought   224

TEN
COGNITIVE ANTHROPOLOGY   227

Ethnosemantics   228

Cognitive Development: Stages, Styles, and Maps   235

Race, Culture, and Intelligence   242

Toward a New Synthesis   245

POSTLUDE
ALL PSYCHOLOGY IS CULTURAL   247

References   251

Index   279

Preface

Psychological anthropology can be understood best from a historical perspective. As an interdisciplinary field, its development has been influenced by the interplay between anthropological problems and the psychological theories that were current when these problems were being formulated. Contemporary psychological anthropology is the product of nearly a hundred years of research, during which, all too often, investigators failed to learn from the errors of their predecessors. I hope this survey of major schools and approaches will help to prepare the way for a much needed new synthesis.

This book is intended for use in courses on psychological anthropology, cross-cultural psychology, and the history of anthropology. It should be read together with some of the classics that are discussed or with one of the comprehensive anthologies now available (for example, Hunt 1967; LeVine 1974). In advanced classes or seminars, George Spindler's recent collection, *The Making of Psychological Anthropology* (1978), would be an excellent supplement.

I have tried to explain important concepts when they first appear in the text to enable the student to follow discussions of their applications and modifications in later chapters. For example, I have introduced basic notions of perception, motivation, and cognition in the very first chapter, and included in the chapter on Psychoanalytic Anthropology, Chapter Two, extra material on the defense mechanisms that is relevant to several later approaches. Similarly, I have discussed projective tests at length in Chapter Four to aid students in understanding their application in later studies. Occasionally, I have included long quotations to give the reader a sense of the style of certain leading figures. In most cases, I have presented each approach in its own terms before offering any critical remarks. I am sure that my own preferences and prejudices are quite clear.

While this book was in press, Richard Shweder's two-part article, "Rethinking Culture and Personality," appeared in the journal *Ethos* (Fall/Winter 1979). His thoughtful essay is essential reading for concerned students of psychological anthropology. Although his terminology is different from mine, our views on the "crisis in Culture and Personality" are quite similar, and we agree that present methods of cross-cultural analysis are not the remedy for this crisis.

I am grateful to the following colleagues for reading and commenting on the manuscript: Theodora Abel, Harry W. Basehart, Bruno Bettelheim, Patricia Draper, Steven Piker, and David H. Spain. My daughter, Marian Bock, typed part of the manuscript and assisted in clarifying the thought and language of the text. My editors at W. H. Freeman and Company, Richard J. Lamb and Pearl C. Vapnek, were always courteous and efficient. I appreciate the efforts of manuscript editor Suzanne Lipsett and of Freddie Heitman, who supervised the final stages of manuscript preparation.

My thanks also go to my students at the University of New Mexico and Stanford University, who listened patiently and responded vigorously to the lectures on which this book is based.

January 1980   Philip K. Bock

CONTINUITIES
IN
PSYCHOLOGICAL
ANTHROPOLOGY

PRELUDE

All Anthropology
Is Psychological

Psychological anthropology comprises all anthropological investigations that make systematic use of psychological concepts and methods. The goal of such studies is to understand
the relationship between individual and sociocultural
phenomena. This book traces the history of anthropological
studies that have made *explicit* use of psychological ideas. Beginning with early speculation about the psychology of
"primitive peoples," we will examine the development of
the discipline, including the impact of Freud's psychoanalytic theories and the rise of several approaches (configurationalist, basic and modal personality, national character, cross-cultural, and neo-Freudian). After surveying
the school of Social Structure and Personality and describing
some recent work in human ethology, we will return to contemporary studies of "the savage mind."

The statement "All anthropology is psychological" is a deliberately provocative one. Depending on one's conception
of the two disciplines, it might be taken as plausible, debatable, erroneous, or simply absurd. I propose to take it seriously and to offer four kinds of arguments in its support.
The first is an argument of logical inclusion. If we briefly

define anthropology as "the science of humanity" and psychology as "the science of behavior," it would appear that psychology, which deals with the behavior of all organisms, from protozoa to humans, includes anthropology as a special case. Certainly, if humans did not "behave," there would be no point to anthropology. Even those anthropologists concerned with fossil humans attempt to reconstruct the behavior of our extinct ancestors, and contemporary archeologists use the material remains of past societies to understand such behaviors as subsistence practices, settlement patterns, and political relationships.

Many anthropologists who adhere to the goal of understanding behavioral systems show little interest in current psychological theories. They prefer to operate with a "common-sense psychology" of human motivation and learning, using these ideas to account for changes or continuities in cultural systems. This preference is surprising, for they would certainly despise anyone who used a "common-sense chemistry" or "common-sense geology" in scientific research. A few ethnologists even argue that anthropologists *should* disregard the theories of other behavioral sciences and freely adopt "naïve assumptions" if these help to define limited problems (Gluckman 1964:168). Thus, while all anthropology may logically be psychological, to paraphrase George Orwell, some anthropologists are more psychological than others.

The most radical attempt to eliminate psychological considerations from anthropology is found in the work of Leslie A. White. White argued that the entire discipline should be redefined as *culturology,* that is, the study of culture independent of the individuals and societies with which it is associated. He viewed culture as a material system of objects and symbols that determines human behavior so completely that differences among individuals can safely be ignored (White 1949:121–145). The idea that individual differences are irrelevant to cultural processes is actually a most radical psychological assumption, which rules out, by definition, any study of the relationship between social and individual phenomena. However, as Anthony F. C. Wallace wisely pointed out,

> if people are going to essay explanations of institutionalized human behavior without reference to individual psychological processes, the psychology had better be pruned away by a sharper knife than simple denial or neologism; and if, as is more likely, explanation does have recourse to psychology, more use should be made of the resources psychology has to offer. (Wallace 1966a:1255)

Wallace's statement leads to my second argument for the proposition that all anthropology is psychological. If we ask what a nonpsychological anthropology would be like, a *reductio ad absurdum* follows, for anthropologists within such a field would have to avoid any reference to perception, motivation, cognition, learning, or related topics. No consideration could be given to individual differences in performance or to the ways in which children (or adults) learn the culture of their society. The individual would be a mere "black box" exposed to certain inputs (culture) and responding with determinate outputs (behavior). But this is an image of humanity that satisfies only the narrowest behaviorists, and then only when they are writing about other people.

The only anthropologist I know of who seriously advocated this viewpoint is Marvin Harris. In his book *The Nature of Cultural Things*, Harris outlined a program for cultural description that used only externally observable, nonverbal actions, and that aimed at "laws" that would have no reference to individuals or their properties. Harris has since retreated from this extreme positivism, but even in that book he was forced to use an implicit, common-sense psychology of perception and motivation to write about human interaction at all (Harris 1964:23–35).

Another argument for the psychological nature of all anthropology is methodological: We cannot actually separate cultural from psychological phenomena because ethnologists and psychologists make use of identical kinds of data. Both sciences start from the observable behavior of individuals, but each analyzes these data with different *operations* and for different *purposes*. For example, a "life-history interview" might produce the same information whether conducted by an anthropologist or by a clinical psychologist. The anthropologist, however, would use the data to gain an understanding of the typical life cycle in a given society, or of the social factors affecting marital or occupational choice. The psychologist, on the other hand, might use the same data to make inferences about the personality of the subject: how he or she handles anxiety or relationships with authority figures, need for achievement, and so forth. If a linguist now arrived on the scene, she might use the same material to make inferences about rules of syntax in the subject's language.

At least where human organisms are involved, the operations performed, not the data employed, make the difference between a psychological and an anthropological study. A given "slice" of behavior is subject to multiple interpretations. When Jack asks his mother for food by saying "I'm hungry," he may be expressing dependency *as well as* conforming to the norms governing mother–son interactions in his society. (Our linguist would point out that he is simultaneously following the phonological and grammatical rules of his language.) Every bit of human behavior is influenced by a host of cultural and noncultural factors, from climate to hormone levels. All of these "influences" join together to produce the unified *experience* of the individual and the *purposive behavior* that flows from that experience.

A final argument for my position is obvious but nevertheless important: Anthropology is psychological because anthropology is a social enterprise carried out by all-too-human individuals who possess varying degrees of self-awareness and quite diverse personalities. Clyde Kluckhohn believed that every ethnologist should be psychoanalyzed before beginning fieldwork. We do not have to go this far to recognize the part played by individual differences in the observation and interpretation of ethnographic data. Included here are differences in motivation, sensitivity, intelligence, and sheer energy level. On the practical side, qualities of personality may affect any anthropologist's ability to get along with people under study. This point is important because people are quite capable of refusing assistance or accurate information to investigators who personally offend them. As Bertrand Russell once observed, "All the data upon which our inferences should be based are psychological in character; that is to say, they are experiences of single individuals."

If I have not yet convinced you that all anthropology is psychological, no matter. The following chapters will illustrate the range of psychological concepts and methods that have been used in anthropological studies. By the end of the book, we will be ready to consider the converse proposition, "All psychology is cultural." And you may by then have become aware that, in anthropology as in all human affairs, the more things change, the more they remain the same.

William James

ONE

The Psychology
of Primitive Peoples

Anthropology is the product of three great historical movements: the Age of Exploration, the Enlightenment, and Evolutionism. The first of these brought European civilization into contact with alien cultures both of great complexity and of great simplicity. Exploration of the Orient, Africa, and the New World revealed peoples of diverse physical types living in a bewildering variety of ways. During the centuries that followed, many European nations carved out colonial empires around the world, subjugating and often enslaving the native peoples while expropriating their land and exploiting their labor and resources (Bodley 1975).

The European nations often found theological rationalizations for imperialism: The *souls* of the natives had to be saved, even if their bodies and their societies were destroyed in the process. Europeans even questioned whether "savages" were capable of understanding the revealed truth of Christianity. Missionaries usually took little interest in the superstitions they attempted to suppress, though some religious orders (especially the Jesuits) wrote extensive reports on the customs and beliefs of the peoples they ministered to.

Accounts written by early explorers, traders, and missionaries provide essential data on conditions of primitive peoples in earlier times, but they must be read and interpreted with care. These accounts often include statements and speculations about the psychological abilities and needs of native peoples: anecdotes report the bizarre, childlike, or uncomprehending behavior of non-Europeans. In most cases, cultural differences were assumed to indicate mental inferiority. Stereotyped images of "the savage" emerged, most of which were highly negative, as reflected in Shakespeare's phrase "dull and speechless tribes" (Sonnet 107), or Kipling's description of the native as "half devil and half child" (in "The White Man's Burden").

As Eliot Aronson has observed, stereotypes (past or present) are usually "ways of justifying our own prejudices and cruelty." Thus,

> it is helpful to think of blacks or Chicanos as stupid, if it justifies our depriving them of an education, and it is helpful to think of women as being biologically predisposed toward domestic drudgery, if we want to keep them tied to the vacuum cleaner. (Aronson 1976:175–176)

The stereotypes that Europeans held during the Age of Exploration concerning primitive peoples were used to justify exploitation and indifference. They also contained many contradictory elements. Thus, the savage was considered to be "dull" but "crafty," "lazy" but "impulsive," and "superstitious" but "lacking in true religious feeling." Obviously, such contradictory notions made it possible for European observers to explain any kind of primitive behavior after it had occurred, and to rationalize any oppressive action on their own parts.

During the Enlightenment, philosophers such as Hobbes and Rousseau drew selectively on the early accounts to document their opposing views of human nature. The Classical (or Hobbesean) view was that human nature is fundamentally evil and violent and thus in need of constraint by the State. The Romantics maintained that humans (in a state of nature) were basically good but that they have been corrupted by artificial institutions. Attempts to imagine a universal human nature independent of culture are based on a fallacy, for a human being is "not only a social animal, but an animal which can develop into an individual only in society" (Marx 1904:265).

In modern anthropology, the concept of human nature refers to the entire range of human adaptations in all cultures that ever have existed and that ever will exist. Human organisms achieve articulate speech, satisfying interaction, and a secure sense of identity only when they encounter, at each stage of development, a cultural tradition transmitted with enough consistency to permit the unfolding of their potentials. Since we cannot know the form future cultures will take, we do not know what *Homo sapiens* may become. (See Geertz 1973:33–54; M. Mead 1953:165; and Erikson 1950.)

The rise of evolutionary thought in the mid-nineteenth century brought with it a new view of human development. Charles Darwin wrote of natural selection as "the preservation of favoured races in the struggle for life." Social Darwinism applied this idea to human affairs and interpreted the contemporary dominance of Europeans in evolutionary terms. The "inferior" races were destined to be thrust aside by the more highly evolved (white) race. Racial groups were ranked according to their resemblance to white Europeans, and their physical differences were related to levels of cultural development. Social Darwinists such as Herbert Spencer developed a deep faith in the inevitability of progress, and they saw human society as evolving to higher and higher levels through conflict and survival of the fittest.

The field of anthropology was born in this milieu. Some early anthropologists rejected the racist explanations of cultural differences, but most retained the concept of levels or stages of culture and tried to understand the historical processes of development from lower to higher levels. Often, they assumed that peoples at any given level shared common psychological characteristics, including ways of experiencing the world, distinctive needs, and modes of thinking. Even today, students (and anthropologists) come to the study of primitive peoples with many irrational prejudices and contradictory stereotypes. It is important that we become aware of our own unconscious assumptions and critical of our common-sense knowledge. In the remainder of this chapter, we will consider some early anthropological studies of primitive psychology while simultaneously introducing basic concepts of perception, motivation, and cognition that will be important throughout the book.

PERCEPTION, OR "DO YOU SEE WHAT I SEE?"

The term *perception* refers to all the processes by which an organism acquires information about its environment and about its own internal states. We cannot directly experience the perceptions of another organism, but we can *infer* its perceptual abilities by finding whether changes in some stimulus can be linked to consistent differences in overt behavior. For example, if you can always push a button or say a word when a light goes on or a soft tone is heard, I infer that you can perceive these stimuli. Experiments of this type have shown that dogs can perceive high-frequency sounds that are inaudible to most humans, and that bees perceive ultraviolet light that the human eye cannot see. Still other animals (fish and insects) are sensitive to certain chemical compounds dissolved in water or diffused in the air.

The members of each species live in a perceptual world (*Umwelt*) different from that of all other species. They receive different kinds of information due to differences in their size and sense organs, and their respective nervous systems interpret the information in different ways. An odor that is sexually stimulating to male muskrats may be repellant to members of another species (or quite imperceptible to them) while a sign of food to one animal is a danger signal to

another. Even within a species, considerable individual variation in perceptual ability may exist.

As a result of our evolutionary history, human beings live
in a rich world of colors and shapes, a somewhat narrower
(though still diverse) world of sounds and tastes, and a
rather impoverished world of smells. Each human nervous
system performs the remarkable job of *integrating* these sensory inputs so that each of us experiences a colorful, three-
dimensional world of familiar objects, meaningful sounds,
and coherent events, rather than a "buzzing, blooming confusion" of color patches and random noises. Our reliable
perceptual world is all the more remarkable, considering
that it is in fact a *reconstruction* from information that has
been coded into electrical impulses. As these impulses travel
to the brain, they differ only in their relative frequency and
in the paths they take. (See W. T. Powers 1973.)

But do all humans live in the same perceptual world?
How can we tell whether they do or not? And if differences
exist, where are they located? In the sense organs? In the
nervous system, which interprets sensory input? In both? Or
are still other factors at work? And how are these differences
distributed among human populations—where are they
found and in what frequencies? Finally, are perceptual differences genetically determined, or are they due to differences in group experiences (such as learning and culture)?
We are just beginning to answer these important questions.

For example, many people are unable to distinguish colors that others can easily discriminate. There are several
kinds of color blindness. Some types involve only a weakness
of vision in limited areas of the spectrum; others involve the
total inability to see certain colors (red and green or yellow
and blue). And in a rare condition called *monochromatism* all
color vision is eliminated. We now know that these perceptual differences are primarily produced by inherited defects
in the cone-shaped receptors of the retina, though blue-
yellow blindness can also be caused by eye disease. Due to
the way in which they are inherited, all types of color blind-

ness are more common in males than in females. Rates also differ among racial and national groups, but this does not indicate any general group inferiority. Disturbances of color vision can also be produced by mental illness and hypnotic suggestion, indicating that the central nervous system may sometimes be involved as well as the retina.

Do people in primitive cultures have better or worse vision than "civilized" persons? Color blindness does not appear to be any more frequent in simple than in complex societies. Nevertheless, early investigators believed that primitives *must* have poor color vision because their languages have relatively few color terms; for example, many groups have a single word for the colors we call "blue" and "green." But recent studies indicate that the number of basic color terms in a person's vocabulary bears no relationship to his or her ability to perceive the full spectrum, although it may affect classification and recall. (This issue will be discussed further in Chapter Ten.)

Another kind of stereotype involved the "sharp-eyed savage," who could supposedly detect objects (or hear sounds) that escape the civilized eye (or ear). People in every society develop culture-specific perceptual skills that enable them to detect subtle cues that outsiders are unlikely to notice. Beyond this, there is some evidence that hunters have better distance vision (on the average) than do settled agricultural peoples. Natural selection against poor visual acuity is probably relaxed for agriculturalists, since they perform fewer tasks requiring good sight: Nearsighted people probably succeed better with a plow than with bows and arrows! Industrial civilization creates new hazards for the nearsighted (for instance, speeding automobiles), but it also provides corrective lenses that compensate for poor vision, thus relaxing selection still further. *Overlapping distributions* between populations occur for all such perceptual differences, however, so that some agriculturalists see as well as (or better than) some individual hunters.

Since we cannot directly experience other persons' perceptions, we must find ways of inducing subjects to respond to differences in stimuli, thus providing us with data that can be compared with those from other cultures. However, evoking such responses can present many difficulties in a strange society. Visual acuity, for example, is a fairly simple characteristic to measure, but this does not mean that one can simply grab an eye-chart and dash off to New Guinea or Alaska to test people's vision: "Okay, fellas, just line up over there and let's have you read off the third line from the top . . . the big guy first." Such an approach will not produce reliable data even in our own society, where people are used to being "processed." Some reasons for difficulties in cross-cultural testing of perception are these:

1. *Unfamiliarity with the test situation.* The novelty of the situation may produce fear and confusion rather than cooperation. It is essential that an investigator establish rapport with test subjects first, if the responses are to have any consistent relationship to the subjects' perceptions. (See Triandis et al. 1971.)

2. *Unfamiliarity with the test materials.* Even with good rapport, subjects may respond erratically if they have never before encountered materials such as those used in the test. As an extreme example, they may be illiterate, or literate in an alphabet different from that used in the test materials. (How would *you* respond to a chart printed in Hebrew or Arabic?) Subjects may be unable to understand or to follow the instructions.

3. *Insufficient motivation.* Subjects may not see any reason to cooperate or to do their best. They may be too amused by the investigator to take the test situation seriously. Rewards for participation can help, but they can also cause problems: A strong desire for the reward

may divert attention from the task or encourage fake responses.

4. *Differing values.* In many societies it is considered poor manners to stand out in any kind of performance, so subjects may hold back in order to stay within group norms. Extreme cooperation or competition may lead some subjects to cheat on a perceptual test, either to do better than others or to help those who would otherwise fail. (See Price-Williams 1975:95–108.)

Additional problems arise due to conditions of investigation in the field. An eye-chart, for example, is only a rough screening device, but it does require standardized conditions and constant illumination. More elaborate testing devices that might be more accurate require electricity, which is not always available. For these and many other reasons, data on even basic perceptual abilities are hard to come by.

As early as 1900, the British psychologist and ethnologist W. H. R. Rivers compared Europeans with various "native" groups to determine what proportion of each group experienced various *optical illusions,* and how strongly individuals were affected. For example, in the familiar Müller-Lyer illusion (see Figure 1-1), most Europeans see Line A as longer than Line B, though the two horizontal lines are in fact of equal length. Rivers used a device that allowed him to adjust the length of one of the lines until the subject reported the two as equal; this yielded an objective measure of the strength of the illusion. When he tested Melanesian natives with this device, Rivers found that (1) most of them were not affected by the illusion at all, and (2) those few who were affected made smaller adjustments than did the Europeans (in other words, the illusion was weaker for the Melanesians).

Such findings mean very little by themselves, although people who are already convinced that "primitives" have better (or worse) visual perception than "civilized" persons may use these facts to support their prejudices. Simple notions of "how savages perceive" will not do, for Rivers also discov-

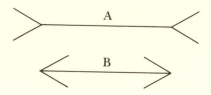

Figure 1-1 The Müller-Lyer illusion, in which most Western subjects judge line A to be longer than line B, although the lines are of equal length.

ered that populations that are barely susceptible to the Müller-Lyer illusion may be highly susceptible to certain forms of the horizontal-vertical illusion (see Figure 1-2). It appears that different classes of illusions exist, and a person (or group) strongly affected by one will not necessarily be affected by another.

One plausible explanation for differential susceptibility to illusions is the "carpentered-world hypothesis." This hypothesis states that if one lives in a highly carpentered environment (in which buildings have rectangular floorplans, many straight lines, and right angles between floors, walls, and parts of windows), one unconsciously *learns* to use angles as cues for distance. When these perceptual habits are applied to certain two-dimensional figures (illusions), they produce systematic under- and overestimates of length. People who have grown up in environments lacking these features (say, in houses with round or oval floorplans), or who have had no experience with two-dimensional representations of reality, have not acquired these perceptual habits, and their estimates of length will therefore be different.

Recent research has demonstrated that differences in illusion susceptibility exist between rural African natives who live in round houses and their urban relatives who have lived—if only for a few years—in a more carpentered world. Segall, Campbell, and Herskovits (1966) did tests in a number of societies, showing a standardized series of visual illusions to people of various ages, both sexes, and different degrees of modernization. Like Rivers, they found that Western samples were more susceptible than non-Western

Figure 1-2 The horizontal-vertical illusion, in which most subjects judge the vertical line to be longer than the horizontal one, though the lines are actually of equal length.

peoples to the Müller-Lyer illusion, and that Western samples were less susceptible to the horizontal-vertical illusion than some non-Western peoples. They conclude that

> these and other differences are *not* "racial" or "primitive." They are differences produced by the same kinds of factors that are responsible for individual differences in illusion susceptibility, namely, differences in experience.... For all mankind, the basic process of perception is the same; only the contents differ, and these differ only because they reflect different perceptual inference habits. (Segall et al. 1966:214)

Finally, what about the "special senses" that have often been attributed to primitive peoples? The anecdotal nature of most of the evidence should make us suspicious, yet many explorers have reported that "the natives have some kind of sixth sense" that allows them, for instance, to track game over barren ground, to find their way home "instinctively," or to navigate out of sight of land without a compass or other instruments.

Careful study of these alleged special senses has usually shown them to be romantic or racist nonsense. This is not to deny that peoples who have lived for generations in a given environment often develop abilities that puzzle outsiders. They do. Polynesian sailors routinely cross hundreds of miles of open water, and Algonquin trappers do find their way home in areas that strike non-Indians as featureless, but anthropologists such as Thomas Gladwin and A. I. Hallowell have shown that no "homing instinct" or other sixth sense is involved. Rather, these peoples possess large amounts of practical knowledge (of astronomy, topography and ecology), and they give careful attention to detail (for instance, noticing changes in the direction of the wind or the displacement of a few pebbles). As Hallowell states, "It is not only the direct experience of the terrain which assists the individual in building up his spatial world; language crystallizes this knowledge through the customary use of place names" (Hallowell 1955:193; Bock 1974:174–178). The relation of perception to motivation and cognition will be dealt with later in this chapter.

MOTIVATION, OR "THE NATIVES ARE RESTLESS TONIGHT"

The study of *motivation* is concerned with the biological needs and psychological drives that influence the behavior of organisms. Human motivation is a complex topic that generates many points of view and little agreement. Some psychologists write of hierarchies of needs, while others deal with biological tensions or unconscious complexes. Still others feel that "motivation" is a useless concept, because it lumps together several different types of phenomena, each of which requires a different approach (Wolman 1973:673–733). Here we shall consider motives simply as those *needs* that have been claimed to influence human behavior, with special attention to alleged differences between those of primitive and civilized peoples.

The writings of early explorers and anthropologists often attribute brutish motives to native peoples. Comparisons with civilized men are usually uncomplimentary, and the contradictions and ambiguities often found in stereotypes are included in the picture. In 1771, John Millar wrote of "the savage" that "his wants are few, and in proportion to the narrowness of his circumstances. His great object is to be able to satisfy his hunger; and, after the utmost exertion of labour and activity, to enjoy the agreeable relief of idleness and repose" (quoted in Harris 1968:48). More than a hundred years later, L. H. Morgan wrote of the "inferiority of savage man in the mental and moral scale, undeveloped, inexperienced, and held down by his low animal appetites and passions" (1877:41). Morgan also felt that primitives lacked a strong *desire for property*, a "passion" whose dominance over all other motives "marks the commencement of civilization" (1877:6).

The notion of "savage passions" implies strong, uncontrolled urges that may at any moment erupt into violent action. It is understandable that such ideas might develop in the minds of European settlers and colonial officials who had good reason to fear the outbursts of the peoples they had displaced and exploited. The natives had to be controlled— prevented from "gorging" themselves in pagan feasts, from "slaughtering" one another in combat, or from "foolishly" giving away all their possessions. Their sexual desires had to be curbed—though the exaggerated tales of orgies and wife-sharing make one suspect the presence of wishful thinking on the part of missionaries and other reporters. As Frantz Fanon has shown, the increasing anxiety of settlers is expressed in repressive measures, which in turn provoke hostile outbursts among the natives that lead in a vicious circle to further anxiety (Fanon 1965).

The same natives whose violent passions had to be restrained and whose "undue generosity" had to be curbed were, under other circumstances, said to be incurably lazy and uncooperative. Their "laziness" had to be overcome—by force if necessary, but preferably by schooling and the development of new needs—for instance, for cash and consumer goods. Peoples who had lived close to a subsistence level for generations, working only long enough to provide themselves with food and the instruments of survival, quickly acquired a taste for canned fruits, brightly printed cloths, bicycles, metal tools, and rifles. If these desires did not sufficiently "motivate" them, a tax payable only in cash effectively forced them into wage labor (see Bodley 1975:127–131).

How can we measure motivation? Like perception, motivation can only be inferred from observable behavior. In animal experiments, we make such inferences indirectly, for example, by noting the number of hours since the animal last ate, or the level of electric shock it will endure to reach a goal (food, water, or a receptive mate). One infers positive and negative motives (desires and avoidances) by observing the overt responses of individuals to opportunities for gratification. However, making such observations is much more difficult when one is working with humans in a natural setting, though intensive observational studies do provide data relevant to assessing motives (see Chapter Nine).

One way that motives influence behavior is by lowering *thresholds*, that is, by making us more sensitive to certain kinds of stimuli, even to the point of distorting them. When we are very hungry, we notice smells, sights, and sounds (such as the opening of a refrigerator door) that might go unnoticed at other times. We may, if hungry enough, fantasy or "perceive" things that are not actually present. For example, one evening as I was driving along with my young daughter, who had not eaten for many hours, I pointed out the beautiful sunset; she replied, "Yes, it looks just like a big red enchilada on a blue plate." The degree to which individual needs distort perception provides a measure of the strength of motives; it is basic to the so-called "projective tests," discussed in Chapter Four.

Lists of human motives go back at least to Aristotle. Saint Thomas Aquinas systematically analyzed the human "passions" of the body and soul in his *Summa Theologica*. These philosophers were more concerned with universals than with group differences. The plays of Shakespeare are filled with

keen analyses of individual motivation, although his statements about groups—Jews, Moors, and Frenchmen—
embody the stereotypes of his age (Bock 1976). The Swedish
naturalist Carl Linnaeus divided *Homo sapiens* into four
"major races," each characterized by physical and motivational features: Americans were copper-colored, erect, and
"choleric"; Europeans were fair, brawny, and "sanguine";
Asiatics sooty, rigid, and "melancholy"; and Africans black,
relaxed, and "phlegmatic." Unfortunately, racist theories
that attribute motivational differences to group inheritance
are still with us today.

Another venerable theory of differential motivation attributes social differences in activity to the direct influence of
climate. Constant rainfall, for instance, is claimed to make
people melancholy, whereas intense heat makes them lazy,
and temperate climates stimulate creativity. (It is easy to
guess what climactic zone the author of such a theory comes
from.) While climate certainly does influence our moods and
behavior, theories that try to explain cultural achievements
or national character on such grounds invariably oversimplify the issue. They certainly cannot account for individual differences or for changes through time in a given
climatic zone. Environmental factors can go a long way toward explaining cultural variability, though not by way of
their direct effects on individual motivation (see Vayda
1969).

Still another type of motivational theory attributes differences in present motivational states to differences in childhood experiences. Thus, if the members of a society seem
preoccupied with food and eating, it is because early experience produced in most of them strong anxieties about getting enough to eat. If they frequently behave in what an observer interprets as a highly "aggressive" manner, this too is
attributed to early training (socialization) that either encouraged or failed to control aggressive impulses (Dollard et al.
1939; Gladwin and Sarason 1953).

Most such theories are able to explain behavior fairly well after the fact. Given an individual or group preoccupied with food or with headhunting, a creative observer can discover (or postulate) past events that plausibly account for present actions. (The Freudian theory to be examined in the next chapter is a good example of this kind of reasoning.) Inherent in such reasoning, however, is the danger of a logical fallacy of the following type: Johnny is aggressive; therefore, he *must have had* early experiences (teasing, frustration, and the like) that instilled the motives that produce this behavior. All too often, the early experiences are assumed rather than demonstrated to have occurred, and no proof is given of the *continuity* between those early experiences and present motives or behavior. This chain of reasoning contains too many debatable links to be very reliable in the absence of independent evidence. Furthermore, behavior that one observer calls aggressive might be considered normal assertiveness by another, and attributed to quite different circumstances.

We shall return to the relationship between child training and motivation in several later chapters, but even in this introduction it is important to note the contradictory nature of many common ideas about primitive child training. True, primitive peoples do not bring up their children as civilized peoples do, but great variability exists in child-training customs in both simple and complex societies. Early European explorers in North America were surprised that native Americans seldom used physical force to discipline children. Their reactions ranged from approval of the Indians' great love of children to horror at the "spoiling" that took place. For their part, most American Indians were shocked to see adult Europeans "beating" defenseless youngsters. (See Briggs 1970.)

Human societies hold widely differing conceptions of what infants and children need. The child-training practices of primitive peoples range from little to much discipline,

early to late weaning, ice-cold to scalding hot baths, much
verbal instruction to almost none, and constant supervision
to great freedom (Bock 1979, Chap. 3). Some societies consider babies almost sacred, while others practice infanticide
(child killing) during the early days of life with little apparent remorse. Childhood may be a time of freedom and independence or of important and increasing responsibilities.
(See Lee 1959:59–77.)

Societies (and subgroups within societies) affect the motivation of their members in three general ways:

1. *Recognition.* By giving public recognition to a motive,
culture "codifies" it, making it available to people who
can then attribute their experience to it (Schacter and
Singer 1962; Aronson 1976:176–181). Every human
society recognizes "hunger" as a motive; that is, all
people have hunger available as an explanation for
their own or another's behavior. But certain motives
are limited to specific cultures. The need to "defend my
sister's honor" or to "save face," the desire for "union
with the Eternal" or for "self-actualization," are quite
unknown as motives in many societies. Other "needs"
(such as those for whiter teeth and fresher breath) are
even more obviously created by social recognition,
while some motives that we might presume to be universal have been reported as absent among certain
peoples. (For example, sexual jealousy is reportedly
quite unknown among the Toda of central India.)

2. *Emphasis.* Both simple needs and complex social motives receive different emphasis in various societies.
The very fact that a culture defines something as
"worth doing" or "worth having" demonstrates that
certain desires (for wealth, wisdom, or many wives) are
valued more highly than others. The need to excel as
an individual, usually referred to as "need for achievement," is by no means universal; it is probably em-

phasized less strongly in American culture today than it was even one or two generations ago. Some cultures put so much emphasis on people's "spiritual needs" that large proportions of their populations regularly withdraw from secular society into lives of devotion and contemplation (Spiro 1965). Other cultures place the communal needs of the group above those of the individual, requiring people to subordinate their personal desires to the good of the family, the fatherland, or the revolution. Culture, in a sense, creates motives, but as Abram Kardiner has noted, "no culture can interdict an emotion; it can only create conditions which render the emotion unnecessary; it can make the suppression of the emotion acceptable; or it may interdict its manifestation. The rest is a problem for the individual" (1939:87).

3. *Canalization.* Even where societies recognize similar needs and give them equal emphasis, the needs may be directed toward quite different *goals.* For example, two societies may recognize sexual satisfaction as important, but one may channel this motive into monogamous marriage while the other encourages its members to seek many partners of both sexes. The term *canalization* refers to the learning of specific types of satisfactions for a general drive (Murphy 1947:161–191), as when one is "thirsty for a cold beer" or "hungry for spaghetti." The staple foods that members of one society consider necessary to complete a meal (for example, rice, bread, manioc, tortillas) may be unknown or treated as occasional side dishes in another society. The canalization process applies to all types of motives.

We still have a great deal to learn about why human societies recognize and emphasize different needs and how these needs are directed, or canalized, toward diverse goals. In later chapters, we shall consider some theories that have been advanced to account for differential motivation. Let us now turn to a third area of primitive psychology: the comparative study of thought processes.

COGNITION, OR "THINKING CAN MAKE IT SO"

Whatever their views on primitive perception or "savage passions," many people assume that primitives must think differently from civilized people. Up to a point, this is true. Modern science has left its mark on all of us who live in complex societies. We may speak of the sun "rising and setting," but we know better. For us, the stars are other suns vast distances away from our planet, though we may reserve judgment about their effects on human affairs. We determine matters of fact by empirical test, even if we choose to keep certain areas open to speculation or private faith.

The qualifications noted with respect to these characteristics are essential to my argument, for while one may distinguish civilized from primitive mentality by determining whether members of a society hold views anchored in scientific thought, one cannot thereby assume that all members of a complex society are equally rational in all areas of their thinking. The scientific part of modern culture is carried by a relatively small corps of highly trained thinkers, many of whom still exhibit large areas of irrationality in their own thought (for example, in believing in astrology or unsupported notions concerning reincarnation).

Probably more has been written about primitive thought than about perception and motivation combined. Cognitive differences have been inferred from language, ritual, mythology, and a large variety of psychological tests. Remember, though, that differences in thought processes— among individuals or groups—can only be inferred from observable behavior or its products, and behavior is affected by many kinds of factors, including those discussed above in relation to cross-cultural tests of perception.

The characteristics of primitive thought were of great concern to early anthropologists and "folk psychologists." Many of these scholars attempted to trace the development of ways of thinking by the same historical and comparative methods that others were using to study the development of technology and social organization. For example, Lewis H. Morgan postulated a series of evolutionary stages from savagery through barbarism to civilization. These stages were based primarily on technological features (subsistence, metallurgy, housing), but Morgan also associated specific mental developments with each stage. He wished to demonstrate "the growth of the ideas of government, of the family, and of property," for he believed that modern institutions "have been developed from a few primary germs of thought" (Morgan 1877:6; 18).

The concepts of *animism* (belief in spirits) and of "animistic thinking" were the contribution of Sir Edward Tylor. Tylor was less of a stage-builder than Morgan, but he did try to show that culture evolved from simple to complex forms, and to demonstrate the steps by which humans slowly arrive at a valid understanding of the universe. Tylor considered animistic thinking—the attribution of spirits or souls to animals, objects, and natural phenomena—to be the earliest type of religious thought. He argued that early people reasoned their way to a belief in spirits on the basis of dream experience, and then generalized this belief to any other phenomena that were difficult to understand (Tylor 1958, Chaps. 11–17).

The eminent German psychologist Wilhelm Wundt had as one of his many interests the study of *Völkerpsychologie* (folk psychology). Wundt defined its goal as "the psychological explanation of the thought, belief, and action of primitive man on the basis of the facts supplied by ethnology" (1916:7). Like Tylor, he attempted to link particular thought processes, whose existence he inferred from ethnographic reports, with specific stages of cultural evolution. Wundt contrasted the early "totemic stage" with an "age of heroes and gods," leading to the enlightened "age of humanity," and he associated each of these ages with a characteristic type of thinking. However, Wundt held that "the intellectual endowment of primitive man is in itself approximately equal to that of civilized man. Primitive man merely exercises his ability in a more restricted field; his horizon is essentially narrower because of his contentment under these limitations" (Wundt 1916:113). (Among Wundt's students were Émile Durkheim, Franz Boas, and Bronislaw Malinowski. His indirect influence on anthropology may have been far greater than is generally recognized.)

Many writers have considered primitives to be incapable of abstract thought. In his *Principles of Psychology* (1880), William James wrote that

> men, taken historically, reason by analogy long before they have learned to reason by abstract characters. . . . In all primitive literature, in all savage oratory, we find persuasion carried on exclusively by parables and similes (i.e., concrete rather than abstract thinking).

With his usual good sense, though, James recognized that "over immense departments of our thought we are still, all of us, in the savage state. Similarity operates in us, but abstraction has not taken place" (1952:688–689).

Sir James Frazer researched extensively into mythological themes throughout the world; he combined ethnological sources with his great knowledge of Greek and Roman mythology in his classic fourteen-volume work, *The Golden Bough*. Frazer also wrote four huge volumes called *Totemism and Exogamy,* in which he sought to explain the origins and meanings of various primitive belief systems. Though Frazer constantly revised his conclusions, making a brief summary difficult, his basic approach was to infer the content of primitive peoples' thought from a study of their myths and customs.

Frazer believed that primitive people could reason as well as civilized people, but that since primitives invariably started from false premises, their conclusions were necessarily in error. For example, if one starts from the premise that a person's discarded clothing, hair, or nail-clippings retain some spiritual connection with him, it is quite rational to conclude that one can affect the person by doing something to these objects. Frazer called the procedures related to this belief "contagious magic," and documented their practice all over the world.

Frazer is often called a "rationalist" because he insisted that differences existed not in the reasoning abilities of different peoples, but only in the assumptions that underlay reasoning. If this position is taken as one end of a continuum, the other extreme is best represented by the French philosopher Lucien Lévy-Bruhl, who in his early works argued for a distinctive primitive mentality. Lévy-Bruhl called this mentality "prelogical," by which he meant that primitives are not usually concerned with logical contradictions. Their thought, he said, was organized in terms of "collective representations" (socially derived complexes of thought and emotion), and anything unusual called forth in them an attitude of "mystical participation" rather than rational analysis. In a recent study, Jean Cazenueve summarizes Lévy-Bruhl's position as follows:

> Certainly the "savage" has concepts, but they are less systematized than ours. The knowledge of primitive people is not classified rationally—it is "unpackaged." Since items of knowledge remain thus simply juxtaposed, the field stays open to mystical preconnections, and contradictions have little hope of being disclosed or rejected. Finally, it is the emotional element which compensates for logical generality. (Cazeneuve 1972:12–13)

Lévy-Bruhl's position has often been ridiculed, and it does have racist overtones, but he was an original and careful scholar whose ideas deserve serious attention. (For an appreciation, see Needham 1965; for an early critique, see Bartlett 1923:282–286.)

In American anthropology, the question of cognitive differences between primitives and civilized peoples was considered settled—or at least irrelevant to the proper goals of the discipline—for nearly forty years. The man most responsible for this attitude was the influential Franz Boas. Boas was not opposed to psychology; indeed, having studied with Wundt, he knew more about the psychology of his time than did most anthropologists. But he fought against facile interpretations of culture that reduced complex historical phenomena to a few "elementary ideas" or common-sense "laws of association." Above all, he opposed all forms of racism, insisting that "there is no fundamental difference in the ways of thinking of primitive and civilized man" (1939:v). In his widely read book *The Mind of Primitive Man* (first published in 1911), Boas stated his program as follows:

> If [anthropologists] can show that the mental processes among primitive and civilized are essentially the same, the view cannot be maintained that the present races of man stand on different stages of the evolutionary series and that civilized man has attained a higher place in mental organization than primitive man. (1939:130)

Boas pointed out the extraordinary self-control required by many taboos and the persistence shown by natives when engaged in work that *they* considered important. Claims that "savages lack strong powers of attention" were shown to derive from situations in which the native people could hardly be expected to take much interest. Boas worked long hours with native informants, and he confessed that when the topic was one that interested them, *he* was usually the first to tire. His conclusions on this point are worth quoting for, as we shall see, they sound very modern:

> Perseverance and control of impulses are demanded of primitive man as well as of civilized man, but on different occasions. If they are not demanded as often, the cause must be looked for, not in the inherent ability to produce them, but in the social structure which does not demand them to the same extent. (p. 133)

Boas also criticized the ideas and methods of Lévy-Bruhl; for example, concerning mystical participation, he wrote:

> This conclusion is reached not from a study of individual behavior, but from the traditional beliefs and customs of primitive people. . . . However, if we disregard the thinking of the individual in our society and pay attention only to current beliefs [we shall] reach the conclusion that the same attitudes prevail among ourselves that are characteristic of primitive man. (p. 135)

Actually, Boas and Lévy-Bruhl agreed more closely in their later work than either realized. In his posthumous publications, Lévy-Bruhl abandoned the notion of prelogical thought and came to agree with Boas that "the functions of the human mind are common to the whole of humanity" (Boas 1939:143). Boas in turn drew close to the Frenchman's concept of the "affective category of the supernatural," which is "rationalized" by civilization, when he wrote of "the emotional, socially determined associations of sense-impressions and of activities, for which intellectual associations are gradually substituted" (p. 226).

Primitive mentality was never a "taboo topic" in the United States (see M. Mead 1932; Radin 1957), but little original research was done on the subject until the late 1950s. At about that time, a rebirth of interest in comparative thought processes gave rise to the subfield of *cognitive anthropology*. Discussion of these developments will have to wait until Chapter Ten. My goal in the present chapter has been to indicate the kinds of psychological assumptions made by early anthropologists as a background for later developments. We turn now to the school of *Psychoanalytic Anthropology* and the work of its founder, Sigmund Freud.

Sigmund Freud

TWO

Psychoanalytic Anthropology

The importance of Sigmund Freud to twentieth-century psychology can hardly be overestimated. From his early work in neurology, hypnotism, and drug therapy to his founding and leadership of the psychoanalytic movement, Freud's genius illuminated virtually every aspect of human behavior. Whether they accepted, modified, or rebelled against his ideas, most workers in psychological anthropology from 1920 to the present were stimulated and influenced by Freud.

As we saw in the preceding chapter, the problems of "human nature" and of "primitive mentality" were central to early anthropology. But whether scholars used common-sense psychology (as did Frazer) or the latest academic theories (as did Wundt), their attempts to reduce the data of ethnology to general psychological principles were seldom illuminating. Rivers' studies of primitive perception and Lévy-Bruhl's speculations on prelogical thought identified important problems and developed some useful methods, but until about 1910, when Freud began work on "the culture question," no one had formulated a general theory that brought these ideas together in a coherent way and pointed the direction for further research.

In his clinical practice, Freud had already created his unique *dynamic theory of mental processes.* By means of this theory, the thoughts and behavior of children and adults, normal and insane, primitive and civilized, could be brought together and explained by general principles as far removed from common-sense psychology as is molecular biology from folk notions of heredity. In Freud's dynamic theory, all behavior is viewed as the result of *conflict.* His work also included a scheme of individual development and a hypothetical "anatomy of the mind" consisting of "mental organs" (id, ego, and superego) that battle for control over behavior.

ELEMENTS OF PSYCHOANALYSIS

Perhaps the most important element of psychoanalysis for a beginning student is Freud's insistence that we take seriously all kinds of mental phenomena: Nothing is irrelevant to a psychoanalytic explanation. Seemingly trivial phenomena such as dreams, slips of the tongue, lapses of memory, or minor accidents are all clues to dynamic processes and hidden motives. Of course, this principle can be abused ("party psychologists" who eagerly interpret dreams or *faux pas* probably reveal more about themselves than about their unwilling clients); but in the hands of a skilled clinician, psychoanalytic theory provides a link between experience and imagination, motive and behavior, that has not been surpassed.

Let us begin with some generally accepted facts about memory, and then see what Freudian theory says about them. Human memory is highly variable and unpredictable. Most people retain few if any memories from the early years of their lives, and those few are often highly inaccurate. Still, we are occasionally favored with an exceptionally vivid memory, triggered by a smell, sound, or taste; and hypnotism or electrical stimulation of the brain can yield flashes of supposedly long-forgotten memories (Schachtel 1959; Penfield 1975). Furthermore, we do not walk about repeating important names, addresses, or phone numbers to ourselves; yet when we need them, they are usually available. Where have these memories been stored? How do we retrieve them when needed? And, more important, why do perfectly familiar facts sometimes elude our attempts to remember them, only to "pop into our minds" at another time, "for no good reason"?

Psychoanalysis assumes that lapses of memory, be they momentary or extended (as in hysterical amnesia), always take place for a good reason, though not one that is immediately obvious. Like others before him, Freud distinguished between conscious and unconscious mental processes (Whyte 1960). He maintained, however, that consciousness was only a tiny part of our mental life—like the tip of an iceberg—and that it developed out of the unconscious, both in the early life of each individual and in the evolution of our species. Forgetting must be understood as a dynamic process occurring within this context, not merely as the passive "decay of memory traces." One forgets, for example, because a memory is too damaging or too painful to enter consciousness, or because it is associated in some way with other unpleasant experiences. But a "forgotten" memory remains in the unconscious.

In Freud's view, every person strives constantly for pleasure—the immediate satisfaction of physical and psychic needs. We are born with a number of such needs, and these become more and more differentiated with experience. Freud referred to the inborn strivings for pleasure as *instincts*; in his later writings he grouped these into two categories: *eros* (life or sexual instincts) and *thanatos* (death or destructive instincts).

Some discussion of *eros* is necessary to prevent common

misunderstandings, for Freud used the terms "sex" and "sexual" in a much broader sense than most people realize. Sexual pleasure in psychoanalytic theory includes all the gratifications that an individual derives from his or her own body, through many different organs. Freud shocked many of his contemporaries (including his medical colleagues) with his insistence that despite their obvious dependency and presumed "innocence," babies are capable of experiencing a variety of sexual pleasures.

In psychoanalytic theory, each child is said to mature through a series of psychosexual stages. These stages are universal and rooted in human biology. The pleasures of the newborn child center on its *oral zone* (the lips and mouth), and are related to the nursing situation. Then for a time the *anal zone* becomes the center of pleasure; it also becomes a center of conflict during toilet training, when cultural constraints are imposed on the natural rhythm of the child's bowels. Still later, pleasure becomes centered in (and largely narrowed to) the *genital zone*. This stage occurs at about age five—long before sexual maturity for reproductive purposes is achieved in our species. In most cases (for reasons to be discussed), this genital stage is followed by a period of "latency," during which little overt sexual expression takes place. Genital sex has not vanished: It has only been repressed until it again erupts with the onset of adolescence.

The concept of *repression* is central to psychoanalytic theory. It refers to the dynamic process whereby an impulse, thought, or experience is kept from becoming conscious. In this process, a constant expenditure of energy is required to keep contents out of awareness. "Since the repressed continues to exist in the unconscious and develops derivatives, repression is never performed once and for all. . . . the repressed constantly tries to find an outlet" (Fenichel 1945: 150).

Why do we bother to repress thoughts and feelings, especially since to do so is costly in terms of mental energy? Repression is one way in which individuals "defend themselves" (their conscious egos) against unpleasant experiences, as when we "forget" a painful memory or a dentist appointment. The notion of *defense mechanisms* that protect the ego from pain or anxiety is central to psychoanalytic theory. It received its most influential formulation in a book by Anna Freud, the daughter of the founder. She distinguished a number of different mechanisms of defense (A. Freud 1946). The following are the most important for our purposes:

1. *Repression.* The mechanism by which, as we have seen, painful experiences are kept out of consciousness by unconscious forces. Repression may be accompanied by *denial* of a thought or feeling.

2. *Projection.* A process by which unacceptable impulses are attributed to external persons or objects, as when the unconscious hostility felt toward a parent or teacher is converted into the conviction that "he hates me." Freud recognized the positive functions of projection in each individual's construction of the external world (Freud 1950:64).

3. *Introjection.* Through this process, external objects or persons are "incorporated" into the ego. A common form is *identification,* in which the individual introjects and adopts the characteristics of a loved or hated person, especially a parent.

4. *Displacement.* By this mechanism, impulses and feelings are transferred from their actual (unconscious) objects onto other, less threatening objects, as when a man who has been frustrated by his boss yells at his wife or child. In dreams, displacement is one way in which a latent wish may be disguised.

5. *Regression.* This mechanism is the tendency to return to earlier types of satisfaction when one meets with frustration; for example, a child may regress to thumbsucking (oral) during toilet training (anal) or as a

substitute for masturbation (genital). "Any disappoint-
ment in or threat to adult sexuality may influence a
person to revert to those levels of his infantile sexuality
to which he is unconsciously fixated; in other words, to
levels that have been repressed and remained un-
changed in the unconscious" (Fenichel 1945:160).

6. *Sublimation.* By definition, sublimation is a "successful" defense in which an unacceptable impulse is transformed and directed toward an acceptable substitute
goal, often bringing the individual social rewards and
recognition. This generally involves a "desexualization"
of the impulse, as when an individual with a strong
need for oral gratification becomes an announcer or a
food-taster. Sublimation can involve a variety of
mechanisms, including displacement and *reaction formation*, "a change from passivity to activity [or] a reversal
of an aim into its opposite" (Fenichel 1945:141). For
example, excessive cleanliness may mask an anal desire
to play with dirt or feces.

Although Freud believed that society rightfully required
people to find substitute gratifications for most of their
erotic impulses, he also recognized the great pleasure to be
found in direct satisfaction of needs. Best of all, thought
Freud, would be a world in which individuals could become
aware of all their impulses and then consciously decide
which to gratify and which to sublimate, rather than being at
the mercy of unconscious conflicts. (Under present forms of
society, this goal can be achieved only through long-term
psychotherapy; see Marcuse 1955.)

In work with his own patients, Freud developed ways of
understanding and treating the symptoms of *neurosis.*
Neurotic patients suffer as much as any patient with a physical disease—perhaps more, since they are told that "it's all in
your mind." The fears and the headaches, the inability to eat
or sleep, the morbid fantasies, the paralysis or impotence,

the compulsion to repeat a word or gesture—such typical neurotic symptoms do not yield to drugs or to pep talks. Neurotics can become increasingly withdrawn from a normal social life; often they are fired from jobs, abandoned by friends, in conflict with family members, and too "nervous" (anxious) to engage in ordinary relationships.

Freud's approach to such symptoms (as to all mental phenomena) was to take them seriously and to interpret them symbolically in terms of his dynamic theory. He understood a given neurotic symptom to be the result of conflict between opposing impulses—an effort made by the patient's ego to defend itself against threats from within and without. Freud's "talking cure" was an attempt to trace the roots of the conflict and to make the patients aware of the defenses they had erected against their problems. By encouraging them to "free associate" to words and dream events, he could discover the unconscious significance of symptoms. Freud saw that merely treating symptoms was ineffective, since the underlying conflict would only be expressed in a different form.

Before we turn to Freud's influence on anthropology, we should look briefly at his contribution to the study of dreams. When Freud published his first great book, *The Interpretation of Dreams,* in 1900, he was challenging a prejudice in Euro-American society which held that dreams were trivial and any interest in them frivolous. For Freud, dreams were the "royal road to the unconscious." In dreams, the repressions and constraints of adult life are relaxed, not destroyed. Here our minds are flooded with scenes and figures of strange and fantastic kinds: Monsters mingle with old friends in wondrous landscapes, and events we fear are mixed with those we most desire. Psychoanalysis takes the *manifest content* of a dream (the images and words reported by the dreamer) and uses free association to arrive at the *latent content* (the symbolic meaning and unconscious conflicts concealed within the dream). The formula "every dream represents a wish fulfillment" underlies the Freudian strategy of dream interpretation.

Freud believed that "repressed infantile sexual wishes provide the most frequent and strongest motive forces for the construction of dreams" (Freud 1952:107). These wishes must be disguised in symbolic forms, for even in sleep we do not allow ourselves to become aware of such socially unacceptable desires as incestuous object choices or pregenital satisfactions. Dream messages are condensed and distorted: Hostile or erotic impulses toward a parent or child are displaced onto other persons, animals, or inanimate objects; one part of the body is symbolized by another.

Not only dreams and neurotic symptoms, but also myths, legends, fairy tales, jokes, and much of our daily behavior are symbolic substitutes for what we unconsciously desire (1952:107–111). These data must be interpreted to reveal their true meaning. A basic principle of such interpretation is that things are seldom what they seem to be.

THE ORIGINS OF PSYCHOANALYTIC ANTHROPOLOGY

Throughout his life, Freud was fascinated by art, literature, history, and anthropology. He was well acquainted with the archeological and ethnological theories of his time. Around 1910, stimulated by the work of Wundt and of Carl Jung, Freud turned his mind to "the cultural question." In a series of books and papers, he attempted to show how psychoanalysis could help to explain the origins and functioning of cultural institutions. The problem occupied him for the next thirty years. His five major works dealing with social and cultural issues are *Totem and Taboo* (1913), *Group Psychology and the Analysis of the Ego* (1921), *The Future of an Illusion* (1927), *Civilization and Its Discontents* (1930), and *Moses and Monotheism* (1939).

In the Freudian view, culture is to society as neurosis is to the individual. If we accept this proposition, it follows that institutions may be analyzed to reveal their latent content and the conflicts that they at once mask and are meant to resolve. Freud used his understanding of neurotic symptoms to interpret cultural institutions.

I use the term *Psychoanalytic Anthropology* to designate attempts by Freud and his followers to apply psychoanalysis to a wide range of societies and cultural phenomena. Some of these followers, such as Ernest Jones, Erich Fromm, and J. C. Flügel, were practicing psychoanalysts who took an interest in cultural matters. Others, such as Géza Róheim, George Devereux, and Erik Erikson, were trained as psychoanalysts and also carried out ethnographic fieldwork. Still others were primarily anthropologists who were later analyzed and trained in psychoanalysis, for example, Geoffrey Gorer, Clyde Kluckhohn, William Caudill, and Robert LeVine.

Freud's own pioneering effort is entitled *Totem and Taboo*. Most brief accounts of this book emphasize (and criticize) Freud's treatment of totemism. However, in my opinion, his analysis of taboo carries much greater conviction and has greater anthropological value.

The word *taboo* refers to a great variety of prohibitions against eating, touching, or otherwise contacting certain objects or persons. Something or someone—especially a high-ranking person—may be considered inherently taboo, or a person who has the necessary power may impose a temporary taboo by performing the required ritual. Individuals may also become temporarily taboo due to contact with a taboo or polluting object (such as a corpse). Such pollution is usually highly "contagious," being spread by contact to other persons or objects, and it can only be removed by rituals of purification (see Figure 2-1).

In anthropological usage, the term taboo has been extended to cover all types of prohibitions, from the "incest taboo" to the Jewish rule against eating pork or shellfish. In his book, Freud makes reference principally to the Polynesian types of taboo, hoping to illuminate them by showing

Taboo   violation   Pollution   requires   Purification
(prohibition) $\xrightarrow{\text{results in}}$ (contagion) $\xrightarrow{\hspace{2cm}}$ (renunciation)

Figure 2-1 Taboo and some related concepts.

"Some Points of Agreement between the Mental Lives of Savages and Neurotics" (the subtitle of *Totem and Taboo*). He begins with the observation that every psychotherapist "has come across people who have created for themselves individual taboo prohibitions of this very kind and who obey them just as strictly as savages obey the communal taboos of their tribe or society" (p. 26). After warning that the similarities *may* be only external, Freud proceeds to offer a dynamic hypothesis to account for both kinds of prohibitions.

Since a neurotic's self-imposed obsessional prohibitions are just as extensive and restrictive as taboo prohibitions, Freud suggests that both are produced by deep *emotional ambivalence*. For example, a typical "touching phobia"— whereby an individual fearfully avoids touching some common object or substance—is claimed to have originated when the patient's childhood desire to touch his or her own genitals was met by a parental prohibition. The prohibition was accepted—in part, because of the child's love for the parents; however,

> the prohibition does not succeed in *abolishing* the instinct. Its only result is to *repress* the instinct (the desire to touch) and banish it into the unconscious. Both the prohibition and the instinct persist . . . and everything else follows from the continuing conflict between the prohibition and the instinct.
>
> The principal characteristic of the psychological constellation which becomes fixed in this way is . . . the subject's *ambivalent* attitude towards a single object, or rather towards one

act in connection with that object. He is constantly wishing to perform this act (the touching) . . . and detests it as well. . . . (p. 29)

Using obsessional neuroses as a "model" (his term), Freud infers that taboos prohibit desires that are still strong. Just as the person who has given up masturbation may still unconsciously desire it, primitive peoples have highly ambivalent feelings toward their taboos:

The desire to violate it persists in their unconscious; those who obey the taboo have an ambivalent attitude to what the taboo prohibits. The magical power that is attributed to taboo is based on the capacity for arousing temptation; and it acts like a contagion because examples are contagious and because the prohibited desire in the unconscious shifts from one thing to another. The fact that the violation of a taboo can be atoned for by a renunciation [ritual of purification] shows that renunciation lies at the basis of obedience to taboo. (p. 35)

Thus far, Freud has only offered an *analogy* between (1) a dynamically motivated type of neurotic behavior and (2) a class of social customs with a possible basis in ambivalence. He recognized that the value of this hypothesis depended on whether it resulted in "a clearer understanding of taboo than we could otherwise reach" (p. 35). He therefore proceeds to examine evidence from many cultures, dealing with three particular types of taboos. In each case, the hypothesis of ambivalence contributes to an explanation of the customs. Let us look briefly at each of these.

1. *The treatment of enemies.* Ample evidence exists to show that tribal peoples throughout the world observe similar customs with regard to a slain enemy. The dead person is "appeased" with gifts and prayers, whereas the victorious slayer is placed under restrictions, notably isolation from social contact, food taboos, and

rules against touching or being touched. These prohibitions persist for a certain period of time, or until rites of purification have been performed. Freud relates all of these customs to "emotional ambivalence towards the enemy" (p. 41). That is, in addition to hostility toward the dead person, unconscious feelings of remorse and admiration are also present, and these conflicting impulses account for both the fearful appeasement of the enemy ghost and the taboo restrictions on the killer.

2. *The taboo upon rulers.* Following Frazer, Freud tells of the various customs by which people attribute to their rulers far-reaching powers over nature, even as they impose many unpleasant restrictions on the rulers' lives. To the psychoanalyst, the "excessive solicitude" represented by the taboo rituals indicates the existence of an unconscious current of hostility or ambivalence toward the rulers. Freud suggests that the importance of the rulers is greatly exaggerated precisely in order that rulers may be blamed for any disappointments: "The ceremony is *ostensibly* [consciously] the highest honor and protection for them, while *actually* [unconsciously] it is a punishment for their exaltation, a revenge taken on them by their subjects" (p. 51).

3. *The taboo upon the dead.* Taboos on bodily contact with the dead are widespread, and purification ceremonies are required following such contact. Many of these restrictions also apply to those who have had such contact "only in a metaphorical sense: the dead person's mourning relations, widowers and widows" (p. 53). Freud relates both these customs and the prohibitions against using the dead person's name to *fear of the dead*, as did Wundt; but Freud goes further by asking the important question: Why should a "dearly loved relative" change upon death "into a demon, from whom his survivors can expect nothing but hostility and evil" (p. 58)? His answer is that this fear is a reaction to the

mourners' projecting their own hostility onto the dead, for survivors often deny their ambivalent feelings toward the deceased, as reflected in our own admonition against "speaking ill of the dead." Here too we find that "the taboo has grown up on the basis of an ambivalent emotional attitude ... the contrast between conscious pain and unconscious satisfaction over the death that has occurred" (p. 61).

In each of these examples, we see Freud reaching beyond the superficial or piecemeal explanations offered by others toward a more dynamic and comprehensive understanding of social customs. Whether we accept his conclusions or not, we must acknowledge the validity of these goals. His method here and elsewhere is to "submit the [ethnographic] facts to analysis as though they formed part of the symptoms presented by a neurosis" (pp. 48–49). Just as individual neuroses result from compromises between unconscious erotic and hostile impulses, many taboo customs may be understood as expressions of ambivalent emotions. In a most suggestive passage, Freud states that "the neuroses are social structures [that] endeavor to achieve by private means what is effected in society by collective effort" (p. 73). He never confounds neurosis with culture, but remarks that neuroses are like "distortions" of the great social institutions:

> It might be maintained that a case of hysteria is a caricature of a work of art, that an obsessional neurosis is a caricature of a religion and that a paranoic delusion is a caricature of a philosophic system. (p. 73)

TOTEMISM AND EXOGAMY

As noted earlier, I consider Freud's analysis of taboo much more successful than his treatment of *totemism*—the use of an animal as an emblem of a kinship group; yet most anthro-

pologists who have dealt with *Totem and Taboo* have focused on the part of the book that attempts to explain the
origins of certain ill-defined totemic institutions. In this attempt, Freud was following the most eminent anthropologists of his day, all of whom tried to elucidate totemism and
its relationship to marriage prohibitions. (See Lévi-Strauss
1963.)

A *totem* is an animal species after which a kinship group is
named and from which the group claims descent. Members
are normally forbidden to eat the totem animal, but in certain circumstances, the members of a totem group (clan) are
required to kill and ritually consume their totem animal.
Freud asked why it is that "poor, naked cannibals," whom
one should hardly expect to find observing rules of morality,
go to the greatest lengths to avoid "incest," and even prohibit
marriage with any member of their totem clan. The combination of the characteristics of clan exogamy with animal
name, belief in descent, and ritual consumption of the usually taboo species stimulated Freud to produce an account
that has been called variously a "hypothesis," a "myth," and a
"just-so story." (See Brown 1966, Chap. 1.)

Freud first sought a type of neurosis to serve as a model
for the customs to be explained. In this case, he chose children's "animal phobias," that is, the irrational fears and
avoidances that are frequently "attached to animals in which
the child has hitherto shown a specially lively interest" (p.
127). Analyzing several cases in which young boys were terrified of large (but quite harmless) animals, Freud concluded
that "their fear related at bottom to their *father* and had
merely been *displaced* on to the animal" (p. 128; italics
added). To understand why this displacement occurs, we
must first consider a central concept of psychoanalysis as yet
unexplained in this account: the Oedipus complex.

Most people are familiar with the myth of King Oedipus,
who unknowingly (that is, unconsciously) killed his father
and later married his mother, thus bringing disaster to himself and his city. When he finally discovered the truth about

his ancestry, Oedipus blinded himself and went into exile. Freud used the term *Oedipus complex* to denote the constellation of unconscious tendencies affecting children at about the age of five—intense love for the parent of the opposite sex coupled with hatred of and desire to replace the parent of the same sex. Young boys and girls frequently express their intention to marry "mommy" or "daddy," and show, in various ways, their wish that the other parent should "go away" (die). Their feelings toward the rival are necessarily *ambivalent:* The same-sex parent stands between them and the love object, but he or she is also admired and feared. The child is frequently frightened by his or her own hostile fantasies, for these may provoke fear of retaliation. In Freud's day, threats of castration were common deterrents to masturbation, and the sight of female genitals might have convinced a boy that "it could happen to me, too!" (The blinding of Oedipus is interpreted as a symbolic equivalent of castration, a punishment he incurs for loving his mother too well. For another interpretation, see Bock n.d.)

In normal individuals, the Oedipus complex is "resolved" at about age six or seven by (1) *renunciation* of the mother (or father) as an erotic love object, and (2) *identification* with the same-sex parent, who is taken as an ego-ideal, partly out of guilt for the former feelings of hostility. This initiates the latency period discussed above, under "Elements of Psychoanalysis." Even in the best of families, renunciation is based on repression of unconscious desires. Thus, when overt sexuality again appears, the young person seeks out a partner who is, in some respects, like the beloved parent. (In pathological cases, an unresolved Oedipus complex may contribute to regression, hostility, homosexuality, and various character disorders.)

Freud believed that the Oedipus complex was *universal,* and he made it a central part of psychoanalytic theory. The universality of Oedipal feelings has been argued back and forth for many years, but psychoanalysts always have the last word, for anyone who rejects the concept is accused of *resis-*

tance: "You only oppose the idea because you never resolved your own Oedipus complex." Though the alleged castration fears may be difficult to accept, many people find that the Freudian notions of emotional ambivalence and early object-choice do correspond with their own experiences. Few can reject this *minimal* formulation of the Oedipus complex: Children's erotic and hostile impulses are frequently directed toward family members, and this fact can complicate their later relationships. (See Erikson 1950:83.)

We have seen that some children displace their fear of the jealous parent onto animals. For example, Little Hans (in a famous case study) was terrified that a horse would come into the house and "bite" him; Freud concluded that he was symbolically expressing his castration anxiety. If Hans had lived in a totemic society rather than nineteenth-century Vienna, he might have identified himself with the animal-parent (totemism) and renounced his desire for his mother or sisters as sex objects (thus demonstrating the incest taboo and exogamy).

We come here to Freud's myth. He asks us to envision, at the dawn of human society, a "primal horde" (the idea is Darwin's) dominated by a "violent and jealous father who keeps all the females for himself and drives away his sons as they grow up" (p. 141). Freud immediately admits that such a society has never been observed among humans, but he invites us to take it as a hypothetical starting point. Guided by psychoanalysis, we are to derive from it the equalitarian band that practices totemism and exogamy, which he believed to be a primitive form of human society.

Recalling the ritual meal in which the totem is solemnly killed and eaten by the group as a whole, Freud suggests the following sequence of events:

> One day the brothers who had been driven out came together, killed and devoured their father and so made an end of the patriarchal horde. . . . The violent primal father had been the feared and envied model of each one of the company of brothers: and in the act of devouring him they ac-

complished their identification with him. . . . The totem meal
. . . would thus be a repetition and a commemoration of this
criminal deed, which was the beginning of . . . social organization, of moral restrictions and of religion. (pp. 141–142)

After the sons had eliminated their father and, through
physical incorporation, satisfied their wish to identify with
him, their suppressed affection reappeared in the form of
remorse. Then, following the psychoanalytic principle of *deferred obedience* (conformity to the will of a deceased parent
whom one had resisted during his or her lifetime), the brothers

revoked the deed by forbidding the killing of the totem, the
substitute for their father; and they renounced its fruits by
resigning their claim to the women who had now been set
free. They thus created out of their filial sense of guilt the
two fundamental taboos of totemism, which for that very reason corresponded to the two repressed wishes of the Oedipus
complex. (p. 143)

Freud then went on to explain human culture in terms of
these mythical events:

Society was now based on complicity in the common crime;
religion was based on the sense of guilt and remorse attaching
to it; while morality was based partly on the exigencies of this
society [fraternal solidarity] and partly on the penance de-
manded by the sense of guilt [exogamy and attempts at
atonement]. (p. 146)

This highly condensed account of Freud's theory of the
origin of culture again illustrates the steps constituting the
approach of Psychoanalytic Anthropology: the choice of a
"model" from clinical practice (animal phobia and castration
anxiety); the selection of ethnographic data (totem meals, actually very rare; the "primal horde," actually nonexistent);
the analogy between individual dynamics (guilt leading to
"deferred obedience") and group process (the brothers' guilt
leading to exogamy). From these steps a conclusion is drawn,
in this case that "psychoanalysis requires us to assume that
totemism and exogamy were intimately connected and had a

simultaneous origin" (p. 146). Many more ideas are expressed in this essay, including the suggestion that "God is
nothing other than an exalted father" (p. 147), a discussion
of animal and human sacrifice (p. 151), and an analysis of
Christian communion as a descendant of the totem meal (p.
154). As in the essay on taboo, Freud draws together in this
hypothesis the most varied phenomena and provides a
dynamic and comprehensive explanation.

Nevertheless, the explanation of a universal (the incest
taboo) and a highly specialized social form (totemism) in
terms of hypothetical historical events is far from convincing. It has been subjected to devastating anthropological
criticism. How could such a historical event, even if it were
repeated in several groups, have such far-reaching effects?
Freud's ethnology was not bad for its day, but his generalizations about totemism are unacceptable. Still, despite its many
factual errors and logical fallacies, *Totem and Taboo* remains
an important and influential book. A. L. Kroeber (a great
anthropologist who was analyzed and who briefly practiced
psychoanalysis) suggests that we strip away the historical
claims and examine Freud's theory as "a generic, timeless
explanation of the psychology that underlies certain recur-
rent historical phenomena or institutions like totemism and
taboo" (Kroeber 1952:306; cf. Fox 1967:60–61).

Freud's insight that collective guilt is intimately related to
the origins of social organization was further developed in
his long essay *Civilization and Its Discontents* (1930). This work
is among his most pessimistic, but every anthropologist
should read at least the first chapter for the extended analogy between the stratification of Roman ruins and the structure of the mind, as well as the last two chapters for their
description of the *superego* as the internal representative of
external social authority.

In *Group Psychology and the Analysis of the Ego* (1921), Freud
turns his model around, so to speak, and asks what we can
learn about individual psychology from an examination of

crowd behavior and from institutions such as the church or the army. He expands the concept of identification, showing its role in group formation and morale, and offers several observations on the state of "being in love."

As we shall see, the whole thrust of Neo-Freudian psychology has been *away from* Freud's historical, biological, and often provincial sexual theories, and *toward* more ego-oriented and culturally sensitive interpretations. Anthropologists of the Culture and Personality school (Chapter Three) have generally felt more comfortable with the Neo-Freudian version than with the Orthodox one; but some of Freud's most penetrating insights are to be found in his most outrageous statements. These ideas have periodically been rediscovered by scholars approaching cultural phenomena from perspectives quite different from that of Freud (Brown 1959; Goffman 1963; Paul 1976).

PSYCHOANALYSIS AND CLOTHING

Perhaps a less exotic example will help clarify the psychoanalytic approach to culture. Unlike other animals, humans wear clothing, following the "dress code" of their particular society (Lurie 1976). Anthropological studies of clothing have usually been concerned with its history, manufacture, or practical functions, though some have studied its social symbolism or investigated changes in fashion as an example of general cultural processes (Kroeber 1952:358–372). But such studies rarely explain *why* particular garments are worn in one society rather than another. We turn to psychoanalysis in the hope that it may disclose the hidden meanings of clothing and the motives for its use: Of what human neurosis is clothing the symptom?

The best-known work on this subject is *The Psychology of Clothes* by the psychoanalyst J. C. Flügel (1950). Although much of the book is devoted to typologies of clothing and to

functional analysis, scattered through its pages are hints of
what a thoroughly dynamic treatment of the subject would
be like. Flügel points out that the motives of modesty and
display are fundamentally opposed to one another, and that
therefore our attitude toward clothing is necessarily ambivalent:

> Clothes . . . are essentially in the nature of a compromise;
> they are an ingenious device for the establishment of some
> degree of harmony between conflicting interests. In this re-
> spect [the use of clothes] resembles the process whereby a
> neurotic symptom is developed . . . due to the interplay of
> conflicting and largely unconscious impulses. (Flügel
> 1950:20–21)

Flügel maintains that the impulses of display and shame
"originally related not to the clothed but to the naked body."
Clothing that can conceal the body may also serve to en-
hance its beauty and call attention to it. Claims of greater
"comfort" or "hygiene" may actually be rationalizations of an
unconscious desire to display one's body, whereas an excessive interest in clothes may be interpreted as a displacement
of exhibitionistic tendencies. Exaggerated fear of the cold
and a tendency to "bundle up" may signify an unconscious
fear of losing maternal love (pp. 82–83).

Particular items of clothing have regular symbolic meanings, both in dreams and in the behavior of fetishists (individuals who derive sexual satisfaction in connection with
items of clothing or other objects). Shoes, ties, hats, and
trousers are male, or "phallic," symbols, whereas handbags,
jewels, girdles, and (sometimes) shoes are female symbols.
According to Flügel, "we can easily establish the existence of
a continuous transition, from blatant exhibition of the actual
genitals to the totally unconscious symbolism of them by
garments which resemble them but very little" (p. 27). The
padded and brightly colored "codpiece" of the English Re-
naissance is an intermediate example; long, pointed shoes are

another, less obvious one. Protective amulets may also have phallic connotations:

> The "evil eye" was supposed to harm its victims . . . by damaging their reproductive powers or reproductive organs [and it is] intimately connected with the castration complex. . . . most of the amulets used to ward off the evil eye appear to be symbols of the reproductive organs. (p. 74)

Transvestism (the wearing of clothing of the opposite sex) is considered an individual perversion in some societies, but in others it is an expected behavior on ritual occasions. The orthodox Freudian approach assumes that it is possible to explain these social customs by analyzing the motives of deviant individuals. Flügel suggests that the mechanism of identification is at work in both cases: Every lover identifies to some extent with the beloved, and in abnormal cases this may be achieved by dressing in clothing associated with the love object. The phallic symbolism of clothes is also important here. Otto Fenichel argues that male transvestites (who are often, but not necessarily, homosexual) dress as they do partly to *deny* the lack of the penis in women and partly to *identify with* an "imaginary penis-possessing woman" (quoted in Flügel, p. 120; see also Newton 1979).

The concept of identification is useful in understanding some social customs requiring transvestism (see Bateson 1958), but even Flügel recognizes that many such practices may result from any of several quite different motives:

> The direct transfer to one sex of some experience or characteristic of the other may be the end in view, as when in the couvade the magical transference of labour pains from the mother to the father is helped by some exchange of garments or when young male initiates are dressed as girls, or captured soldiers dressed as women. . . . Finally, the exchange of dress may only be a particular example of the general exchange of roles . . . that characterises special holidays. (p. 121)

What would Freud, Flügel, or Fenichel say about contemporary unisex styles and the adoption by many young people of "funky" clothing of uncertain age and origin? For many radical students, certain garments (for example, overalls or caps) consciously symbolize their identification with the working class, with blacks, or with farm laborers. For others, nostalgia or durability or both may be primary motives. Clothes may express more than one's conscious identification. The message of student styles of the late 1960s was brilliantly deciphered by journalist Garry Wills. Writing of the student demonstrators at the 1968 Democratic Convention in Chicago, he says,

> The keynote of the kids' clothing is softness. No edges. Even last year's military jackets have the padding torn out—droopy epaulettes, wilted fronts, frayed bottoms, every sag and hang eloquent: "I ain't a-marchin' anymore". . . . Their clothes are all of the muffling sort—blankets, capes, serapes, sheperd's coats, hoods, wooly sweaters, thermal underwear like tailored mattresses . . . Bell-bottom pants are mandatory for the girls, worn with light sweaters. No bras, of course. No edges. (Wills 1971:297–299)

These insights are highly compatible with psychoanalytic ideas, for Flügel was quite aware that certain kinds of restrictive clothing (for example, tight, stiff collars) may be "symbolic of duty or moral control" (1950:196). It is possible that loose clothes "of the muffling sort" symbolize both conscious rebellion against "the system" *and* an unconscious sense of loss of parental affection. (We shall return to this issue in connection with the "swaddling hypothesis" and Russian national character in Chapter Five.)

SUMMARY AND CRITIQUE

We have seen in this chapter how Freud and his disciples attempted to apply psychoanalysis to cultural topics. The basic analogy between neurotic symptoms and customs or institutions was developed in a number of different ways, some more enlightening than others. In the course of examining Freudian explanations for taboos, totems, and transvestism, I introduced several concepts that will be important in later chapters. These include Freud's dynamic model of mental life, in which conflict and ambivalence are to be expected; the defense mechanisms and their operation in daily life (for example, in forgetting) as well as in dreams or neuroses; and the Oedipus complex as a crucial stage in human psychosexual development.

Although I have presented these ideas with a minimum of critical commentary, the reader must realize that they were at first highly controversial. Some of them have passed into public knowledge and their origins may not be remembered. For example, the analysis of "dirty jokes" that Freud proposed in his book *Wit and Its Relation to the Unconscious* (1916) is now so generally accepted that George Orwell could summarize it without even referring to Freud:

> The reason . . . so large a proportion of jokes center around obscenity is simply that all societies, as the price of survival, have to insist on a fairly high standard of sexual morality. A dirty joke is not, of course, a serious attack upon morality, but it is a sort of mental rebellion, a momentary wish that things were otherwise. (Orwell 1954:121)

Other aspects of Freudian theory are still considered highly controversial or even disproved (Fisher and Greenberg 1977). Yet the things that make psychoanalysis a very powerful theory also make it virtually untestable. The recognition of instincts, which are by definition unconscious, and energy, which is by definition unmeasurable, present great challenges to objective investigation. Given the notion that anything may appear as its opposite in dreams or neurotic symbolism, the psychoanalyst can get out of any difficult position by claiming just such a transformation. In addition, the concept of resistance can easily be turned against a critic: If you do not accept the idea of the

Oedipus complex, it is because your own complex is as yet unresolved. This is a modern version of the *ad hominem* argument, but even harder to defend against since one cannot be conscious of the factors that produce resistance.

Freud and his early disciples assumed that "primitives" were a pretty homogeneous bunch. These writers shared many nineteenth-century ideas about "savage passions" and the "childlike" native. Thus, they never came to grips with the immense variability of human cultures, or with the tremendous diversity of psychological types in all societies. As we shall see, the developments in psychological anthropology that followed *did* account for this variability. Partly in reaction against earlier overgeneralizations, later anthropologists stressed cultural differences to the point where comparison and generalization became almost impossible.

Though Freud may have underestimated the differences among primitive societies, the main thrust of his work emphasized the "primitive urges" that survive in all of us. In his analyses of religious and political institutions, Freud showed the illusions and neurotic needs on which "civilized" accomplishments rest. And he demonstrated that "the kind of thinking which underlies mythology is still at work today in the minds of children and neurotics, of dreamers and artists" (Costigan 1965:301). Although this knowledge may make us uncomfortable (self-knowledge usually does), it is now an inescapable part of modern life and we must learn to live with it. (See Rieff 1961:361–392.)

Charles Darwin

THREE

Configurations
of Culture
and Personality

The field of psychological anthropology goes by other names in many colleges and universities. The most common of these is Culture and Personality. In this book, however, *Culture and Personality* is used to designate a particular school of thought within psychological anthropology (Hsu 1961:12–13). One reason for restricting our use of the term is that the word *personality* does not appear at all in the early work on primitive psychology; it occurs only rarely in Freud's own writing, though he did use the similar concept of character type. As we shall see, investigators in many recent studies avoid the term personality, or at least take a highly critical view of the concept, emphasizing instead direct and detailed observations of behavior in its natural settings (see Chapters Eight through Ten).

The Culture and Personality school comprises four major *approaches,* each of which will be treated in a separate chapter (Chapters Three through Six). These approaches are known, respectively, as configurationalist, basic/modal personality, national character, and cross-cultural (see Table 3-1). Each approach has its distinctive methods, concepts, and subject matter, but important continuities exist among them, both of ideas and of personnel. The last three approaches were also influenced in important ways by Psychoanalytic Anthropology. Let us begin our survey of the Culture and Personality school by discussing the concept of personality as it was understood by the school's founders.

Personality in this context refers to persistent characteristics of an individual inferred from a sample of his or her behavior. These characteristics may be thought of in three general ways: as *traits* (distinctive behavioral regularities); as *character* (interpersonal dispositions); or as *modes of organization* (ways in which an individual's experience and behavior are integrated). The trait approach tends to be used by those concerned with the measurement of differences among normal individuals, as in skill, intelligence, or aptitude testing. Assessments of character or of modes of organization are more in the province of clinical psychologists and other professionals who deal primarily with disturbed individuals. In either case, literally hundreds of testing instruments and interpretive methods are available for the characterization of individuals. (See Wolman 1973:775–857.)

Personality, like culture, is one of the concepts we use to understand human behavior. When someone behaves in what is (to us) an unusual or bizarre manner, we usually try to make it fit with whatever else we know about that person. If we attribute the behavior to a childhood trauma or to anxiety induced by stress, we are using a personality type of explanation. On the other hand, if we attribute the same behavior to familistic values or to the way Italian women are expected to act when ill, we are using a cultural type of explanation. Both types of explanation may be partly valid, but our decision to *accept* one or the other (or both) is a function of our own past experience and present needs. As Edward Sapir wrote in 1934,

Table 3-1 Major Schools and Approaches of Psychological
Anthropology

School	Approach and Dates	Leading Figures
Psychoanalytic Anthropology	Orthodox (1910–)	Freud, Róheim, Flügel, Ferenczi
	Neo-Freudian (1930–)	Fromm, Erikson, Bettelheim, Devereux
Culture and Personality	Configurationalist (1920–1940)	Benedict, Sapir, M. Mead, Hallowell
	Basic and Modal Personality (1935–1955)	Kardiner, Linton, DuBois, Wallace, Gladwin
	National Character (1940–)	Kluckhohn, Bateson, Gorer, Hsu, Caudill, Inkeles
	Cross-Cultural (1950–)	Whiting, Spiro, LeVine, Spindler, Edgerton, D'Andrade
Social Structure and Personality	Materialist (1848–)	Marx, Engels, Bukharin
	Positionalist (1890–)	Veblen, Weber, Merton
	Interactionist (1930–)	G. H. Mead, Goffman, Garfinkle
Cognitive Anthropology	Primitive Mentality (1870–)	Tylor, Lévy-Bruhl, Boas, Lévi-Strauss
	Developmental (1920–)	Piaget, Cole, Price-Williams, Witkin
	Ethnosemantic (1960–)	Conklin, Frake, Kay, Berlin

> Our natural interest in human behavior seems always to vacillate between what is imputed to the culture of the group as a whole and what is imputed to the psychic organization of the individual himself. . . . The study of culture as such . . . has a deep and unacknowledged root in the desire to lose oneself safely in the historically determined patterns of behavior. The motive for the study of personality . . . proceeds from the necessity which the ego feels to assert itself significantly. (Sapir 1949:194, 198; cf. Wagner 1975:81–82)

This quote is of special interest here because, although Sapir was an outstanding linguist and ethnologist, he had a deep distrust of cultural explanations. It has been suggested that he emphasized the role of the individual in cultural processes in order to "prove that culture doesn't matter" (M. Mead 1959:201, quoting a letter from Ruth Benedict).

The study of Culture and Personality involves much more than the subjective attribution of behavior to social or individual sources. The key to its early development can be found in the same essay of Sapir's that was quoted above. In it Sapir states that

> the more fully one tries to understand a culture, the more it seems to take on the characteristics of a personality organization. Patterns first present themselves according to a purely formalized and logically developed scheme. More careful explorations invariably reveal the fact that numerous threads of symbolism or implication connect parts of patterns with others of an entirely different formal aspect. . . . There is no reason why the culturalist should be afraid of the concept of personality conceived of as a distinctive configuration of experience which tends always to form a psychologically significant unit and which . . . creates finally that cultural microcosm of which official "culture" is little more than a . . . mechanically expanded copy. (Sapir 1949:201–203; italics added)

The three italicized passages in this quotation summarize the early approach of the Culture and Personality school. Let us examine closely the ideas they express:

1. A culture, fully understood, is like a personality. This is the basic simile on which the configurationalist approach is founded. The similarity with personality is not revealed in the usual ethnographic description of beliefs and practices within a culture: One can make the connections only by exploring beyond the superficial patterns of the "official culture." It is in its subtle, complex organization, integrated on many different levels, that a culture is said to be like a personality.

2. The patterns of a culture are connected by "symbolism and implication," that is, by both symbolic and logical linkages. One must be alert and sensitive to discover them; for example, "a word, a gesture, a genealogy, a type of religious belief may unexpectedly join hands in a common symbolism of status definition" (Sapir 1949:201). Again, one must get *behind* conventional ethnographic categories—the orderly but mechanical descriptions of "kinship," "technology," "religion," and so forth—to find these linkages.

3. Anthropologists need not shy away from studying individuals, provided that they understand personality as a configuration of experiences that tend to form psychologically significant (that is, meaningful) units. We can understand the growth, functioning, and integration of cultures only by realizing that the *human personality is a system that seeks and creates meaning*. It is because individuals are the ultimate locus of culture (the "cultural microcosms") that cultural integration can take place.

Sapir implicitly rejects a "trait psychology" and insists on viewing personality as an organized system. His choice of words clearly allies him with the school of Gestalt Psychology, which was well established by the 1920s. Terms such as "pattern," "organization," and above all "configuration" indicate his debt to this school, which consistently emphasized the importance of patterns and configurations as well as the organization of experience in a "field" of psychologically significant units.

The German word *Gestält* means literally "form" or "pattern." It was adopted about the year 1912 by three young psychologists (Max Wertheimer, Kurt Koffka, and Wolfgang Köhler) to designate their departure from the academic psychology of their time (especially the experimental approach of Wundt). In their early work, they emphasized the perception of colors, forms, and movement, maintaining that perceptual processes could be understood only when the thing perceived was viewed as an organized pattern (*Gestält*) rather than a collection of separate elements. For example, when we recognize a musical melody, we perceive a pattern of relationships rather than individual tones. This mode of perceiving can be demonstrated if we transpose the melody into a different key: All of the notes are changed, but the melody remains the same because the relationships among the notes are maintained. A melody is not present in its separate notes, for these same notes can be used to produce any number of other melodies. Thus, an *atomistic* approach, which breaks a melody down into its separate elements, destroys the meaning of the experience. The meaning is in the pattern.

A similar insight is fundamental to Sapir's contribution to anthropological linguistics. In his analyses of language he described the unconscious patterning of sound and grammatical categories and attempted to identify the dynamic processes of linguistic change (see Sapir 1921). David Aberle has argued that early Culture and Personality studies were strongly influenced by the linguistic theories of Boas and Sapir (Aberle 1960). It is thus important to grasp the Gestalt notion of configuration and to see how this concept was applied by Sapir's friend, Ruth Benedict, to the study of Culture and Personality.

CONFIGURATIONS OF CULTURE

Gestalt psychologists emphasize the fact that our perceptions are self-organizing; that is, we experience patterns according to certain principles (similarity, proximity, closure, and the like) that are rooted in the structure and functioning of our brains. They object to the atomistic theories of "associationism" and "behaviorism" on the same grounds: "Behavior no less than sensory experience shows us wholes that are not merely the sums of parts but have their own properties as wholes, and obsession with elements is never going to reveal the essential properties of the wholes" (Woodworth 1948:135). *Configuration* is another term for such whole patterns.

The concern for configurations in culture has a history similar to that of Gestalt psychology. In the first decades of the twentieth century, American anthropology had become highly atomistic and trait-oriented. Partly in reaction against speculative evolutionary theories, Boas and his students attempted a massive documentation of the basic elements of Amerindian cultures and their exact geographic distribution. (This research strategy is today often called *historical particularism*, for example, in Harris 1968, Chap. 9.) At its best, this approach produced much valuable data that made possible the delimitation of culture areas, historical reconstructions, and detailed studies of cultural transmission. At its worst, it yielded a mechanical listing of "culture traits" and an indication of their presence or absence in various social units. For example, a typical trait list would resemble Table 3-2, with a list of items down one side, and a set of social units ("tribes") across the top. A plus indicates that a given trait was present in the society, whereas a minus shows its absence; a blank or question mark indicates uncertainty.

The trait list served as a check on historical speculation, and in the hands of a master it could be made to yield interesting results. (For examples, see Sapir's famous essay on

Table 3-2 A Hypothetical Trait List Showing Presence (+) or Absence (−) of Material, Behavioral, and Ideological "Traits" in Four Societies

	Trait	Tribes			
		A	*B*	*C*	*D*
1	Ground-stone axes	+	+	−	+
2	Wood-plank houses	+	+	−	−
3	Woven-bark capes	−	+	−	+
18	Primary arrow release	−	+	−	−
19	Stone boiling	−	+	+	−
20	Fish drying	+	−	+	+
57	Exogamous matriclans	+	+	−	−
58	Totemic beliefs	+	+	+	+
59	Male puberty rites	−	+	−	+

"Time Perspectives," 1949:389–462, or any of Boas' essays on folklore or primitive art—1966:397–490; 535–592.) For all its appearance of precision, however, the trait list was far from being a dynamic model of cultural processes. It did not satisfy those who wished to understand the *reasons* for a distribution, or who questioned the meaning of "present" when applied to a complex mode of behavior. Note that the traits ranged from items of material culture (kinds of tools, shelters, clothing), through details of behavior (types of arrow release, techniques of cooking), to quite abstract types of social organization or religious belief (exogamous clans, totemism, puberty rituals). Each trait would be marked as present or absent in an entire society, often on the testimony of one or two elderly informants! The trait list implicitly *defined* a culture as equivalent to the sum of its parts, and it *assumed* a homogeneity of behavior that is contrary to common experience in any society.

Critiques of this approach have taken many directions, but we are concerned here with two main points:

1. *The meaning of a given trait will vary according to what other traits are present.* For example, in Table 3-2 we see that trait 58 is present in all four societies, but its significance will be modified by whether 57 or 59 is also present.

2. It follows that *a culture is greater than the sum of its parts.* A culture is a configuration in which elements interact with one another, producing meaningful patterns. The acceptance, rejection, or reinterpretation of a new trait depends on the preexisting patterns. Two societies with similar trait lists may nevertheless have cultures that are *organized* in quite different ways.

Let us examine how these criticisms affected the work of Ruth Benedict. Benedict began to study anthropology at Columbia University in 1921. This was "a period when Boas was still interested in diffusion and in having his students laboriously trace a trait . . . from culture to culture, showing the changes [in] the trait" (M. Mead 1959;11). Boas soon recognized Benedict's talent, and after only three semesters of study she completed her Ph.D. Her dissertation on "The Concept of the Guardian Spirit in North America," written under Boas' close supervision, was published in 1923. (A guardian spirit is a supernatural protector acquired by an individual—frequently in a dream or vision—who takes special interest in the person's welfare, often endowing him or her with spiritual powers.)

Benedict's study is based on a careful analysis of the *distribution* of guardian-spirit beliefs and their *association* with other traits. In good Boasian style, she concludes with the statement that "man builds up his culture out of disparate elements, combining and recombining them" (pp. 84–85). But despite this particularistic conclusion, Benedict's concerns already went beyond historical reconstruction "toward a more just psychological understanding of the data" (p. 7). While the "intricate fortunes of diffusion" might associate guardian spirits with one trait here and another there, elaborating now on one feature and then upon another, Benedict's main point was that in each society we are dealing with a unique type of *social patterning:*

> In one region [the guardian spirit] has associated itself with puberty ceremonials, in another with totemism, in a third with secret societies, in a fourth with inherited rank, in a fifth with black magic. Among the Blackfoot, it is their economic system . . . . Among the Kwakiutl, their social life and organization, their caste system . . . . It is in every case a matter of the social patterning—of that which cultural recognition has singled out and standardized. (p. 84)

Each individual trait may have a fortuitous distribution across the continent, but within a given society traits enter a *pattern* that selects, emphasizes, and combines elements. The pattern integrates the diverse elements provided by history, giving each a new significance, just as each individual integrates diverse life experiences into a coherent personality.

Benedict developed this basic insight over the next decade, as she struggled with what she called "the configurations book." Sapir contributed greatly to her thought, as a fellow poet, colleague, and critic, though I believe Aberle (1960) overestimates the influence of Sapir's linguistics per se on early Culture and Personality studies. The key ideas came from many sources, especially Gestalt psychology; and Margaret Mead also played an important role as student, colleague, and confidante. (See M. Mead 1972:138; also 1953a:136.)

While writing her major book, Benedict also published two important papers: "Psychological Types in the Cultures of the Southwest" (1928), and "Configurations of Culture in North America" (1932). Her ideas reached their fullest development in *Patterns of Culture*, published in 1934 (1946a). The impact of this book on anthropology and the general public was very great. For many laymen and future anthropologists it was a first introduction to the facts of cultural diversity and to the relativistic theories that were then central to the discipline. The book soon became a best-seller due to its clear and elegant style, its somewhat sensational contents, and its genuine contribution to the characterization of cultural wholes (see Redfield 1955, especially Chap. 5). Let us examine the structure of this landmark book in some detail.

Patterns of Culture begins with a chapter called "The Science of Custom," in which Benedict discusses cultures as learned solutions to the problems confronting every society. Culture is contrasted with genetic inheritance to point out the inadequacy of racial theories of social differences and to argue that there is no scientific basis for *racism* (compare Boas 1939). Her emphasis is on mankind's need to understand culture and the ways in which it affects our lives.

In the next chapter, "The Diversity of Cultures," Benedict discusses the unique pattern each society develops to cope with the human situation. In culture, as in language, *selection* is "the prime necessity." Each language makes use of only a few of the sounds our vocal chords can produce, and each culture elaborates certain aspects of human experience, ignoring others. Monetary values, technology, adolescence, and warfare are examples of phenomena on which some societies have erected "enormous cultural superstructures" but which have been virtually ignored in other societies. Puberty rites (for males, females, or both sexes) may be central to a society's ceremonial life, or the transition to adulthood may be casual and unmarked. Benedict then summarizes her own research on "guardian spirits," concluding that "the diversity of the possible combinations is endless, and adequate social orders can be built . . . upon a great variety of these foundations" (p. 40).

Cataloging the details of cultural diversity is not enough, since each living culture is more than "a list of unrelated facts."

> It tends also to be integrated. A culture, like an individual, is
> a more or less consistent pattern of thought and action.

> Within each culture there come into being characteristic pur-
> poses not necessarily shared by other types of societies. . . .
> Taken up by a well-integrated culture, the most ill-assorted
> acts become characteristic of its peculiar goals, often by the
> most unlikely metamorphoses. The form that these acts take
> we can understand only by understanding first *the emotional
> and intellectual mainsprings of that society.* (p. 42; italics added)

This patterning of behavior around a few central concerns is not, says Benedict, an "unimportant detail." Like
chemical compounds (and Gestalt configurations), cultural
wholes are greater than the sum of their parts. There is
nothing mystical about this cultural integration: It is the result of the operation of "unconscious canons of choice," such
as those that produce (over several centuries) great unified
art styles. Only when we abandon the fixation on isolated
traits in favor of whole cultures can we appreciate the importance of this patterning.

Explicitly citing Gestalt psychology, Benedict insists, "The
whole determines its parts, not only their relations but their
very nature" (p. 47). She then turns to several authors
(Wilhelm Dilthy and Oswald Spengler) who attempted to
characterize Western civilization in terms of extremely general patterns, but here she indicates that this task may be too
complex. "The whole problem of the formation of the individual's habit-patterns under the influence of traditional custom can be best understood at the present time through the
study of simpler peoples." Cultural configurations are also
significant in complex societies; however, "the material is too
intricate and too close to our eyes for us to cope with it suc-
cessfully" (pp. 50–51; but see Chapter Five, below).

In the next section of her book, Benedict considers at
length four societies: the Pueblo Indians of New Mexico,
whom she contrasts with the Plains Indians; the Dobu Islanders of Melanesia; and the Kwakiutl Indians of America's
Northwest Coast. The first description is a generalized por-
trait for, in addition to her own work at Zuñi Pueblo, she
draws on a number of other Pueblo studies; her "Plains In-

dian culture" is also a composite based on several tribes. The goal is to characterize the basic configuration of each culture—its "emotional and intellectual mainsprings"— exactly as a clinical psychologist might describe the personality structure of a patient. Benedict draws on all kinds of ethnographic materials. to formulate and document her configurations: economic practices, family structure, political authority, religion, warfare, folklore—all are grist for her mill. What follows here is a summary of Benedict's configurational types for the four societies:

1. *The "Apollonian" Pueblo Indians.* The central pattern of Pueblo culture (according to Benedict) is avoidance of extremes, and this characteristic requires that individuals be totally subordinated to the traditions of the group. The Apollonian ideal (this term is taken from Nietzsche) is adherence to "the middle way" and avoidance of all strong emotion: Evenness of behavior is prized, and violence, anger, jealousy, and any form of individual assertiveness are condemned as disruptive of good social relations. Cooperation and communal responsibility are taught from childhood. "Sanction for all acts comes from the formal structure, not from the individual" (p. 95). Communal forms are provided for all important activities: Elaborate group ceremonies insure fertility, cure illness, and guide the individual through various life crises. Ritual office confers limited authority, and "a man must avoid the appearance of leadership" (p. 91). The accumulation of personal wealth is deemphasized, and resources are channeled into ceremonial responsibilities from which the entire society benefits.

2. *The "Dionysian" Plains Indians.* The configuration of the Plains' culture is exactly the opposite of the Pueblo's. It follows the "path of excess" and glorifies the individual who can escape from the ordinary boundaries of the senses. The cultures integrated by this Dionysian pat-

tern (again, the term is from Nietzsche) greatly "valued all violent experience, all means by which human beings may break through the usual sensory routine" (p. 73). Dreams of power and guardian-spirit visions were actively sought by means that included fasting, drugs, and self-torture. Prestige accrued to those individuals who showed themselves fearless and violent, courting danger in warfare, glorying in their victories, and displaying wild abandon in their grief.

3. *The "Paranoid" Dobuans.* The Dobu Islanders live in an atmosphere of conflict and suspicion. Their institutions magnify these tendencies, setting husband against wife, neighbor against neighbor, and village against village. Like the *paranoid* character type who projects his own unacceptable desires onto others, the Dobuan pattern insists that one person's gain is necessarily another's loss. This pattern permeates marriage, gardening, economic exchange, and all other significant activities. A good yam harvest implies that one has magically lured the tubers from surrounding gardens into his own plot, so harvest size and magical formulas are guarded in the utmost secrecy. The Dobuan is "dour, prudish, and passionate, consumed with jealousy and suspicion and resentment," and it is assumed that a prosperous man "has thieved, killed children and his close associates by sorcery, cheated whenever he dared" (p. 155). In every aspect of social life, despite shows of friendship and cooperation, "the Dobuan believes that he has only treachery to expect" (p. 158). Constant watchfulness, powerful magic, and potent poisons are essential to survival in this culture, which views all existence as a "cut-throat struggle."

4. *The "Megalomaniac" Kwakiutl.* The Kwakiutl configuration centers on "their special ideas of property and of the manipulation of wealth" (p. 168), and incorporates many Dionysian religious practices that em-

phasize the "divine madness" of initiates. Family groups own hunting, gathering, and fishing territories, but individuals hold exclusive rights to certain material and nonmaterial items (totem poles, masks, songs, myths, names, and titles of nobility) that confer status and privileges on the owner. Prestigious items are usually inherited, but possession has to be "validated" by the distribution of wealth in the competitive feast known as the *potlatch*. The goal of these events is to shame one's rivals: "This will to superiority they exhibit . . . in the most uninhibited fashion. It [finds] expression in uncensored self-glorification and ridicule of all comers" (p. 175). Such a pattern would be called *megalomania* in an individual. Kwakiutl culture is integrated by this constant round of competitive gift-giving and/or destruction of property, for to avoid being shamed one has to repay (or destroy) a greater amount of wealth in a return *potlatch*. Triumph in such a contest increases a chief's claim to greatness—even if it means loss of all his possessions—and he arrogantly sings his own praises. This pattern permeates all Kwakiutl institutions: succession to office, marriage, religious ceremony, mourning, and warfare (pp. 186–205). (One could also acquire title to prestigious ceremonies by killing their owner!)

The lesson to be drawn from these case studies is that a dominant cultural configuration integrates many different activities: therefore, these activities can only be understood in relation to the total configuration. Not all societies have achieved neat configurations: "Like certain individuals, certain social orders do not subordinate activities to a ruling motivation [and] their tribal patterns of behaviour are uncoordinated and casual" (p. 206). Furthermore, Benedict insists, each configuration is an "empirical characterization" probably unique to a single culture. It would be a mistake to treat configurations as "types" and then attempt to fit other societies into the same categories. Even within the cases considered, "the aggressive, paranoid tendencies of Dobu and the Northwest Coast are associated with quite different traits in these two cultures" (p. 220). Our *own* culture centers on the desire "to amass private possessions and multiply occasions of display" (p. 226), but the American configuration is quite distinct from that of the Kwakiutl. (See the discussion of American national character in Chapter Five.)

In her final chapter, Benedict deals with essentially the same problem she treated in her paper "Anthropology and the Abnormal" (1934): What is the relation of the individual to the cultural pattern? Most people, she says, manage to adapt and conform (at least outwardly) to the configuration that dominates their society, but for many, the psychic cost is great. People whose individual temperaments are suited to the culture pattern of their time and place will be "at home" in their own society, pursuing its goals with genuine satisfaction. However,

> just as those are favored whose congenial responses are closest to that behaviour which characterizes their society, so those are disoriented whose congenial responses fall in that arc of behaviour which is not capitalized by their culture. These abnormals are those who are not supported by the institutions of their civilization. They are the exceptions who have not easily taken the traditional forms of their culture. (p. 238)

In other words, the individual who is frustrated and maladjusted in his or her own society—say, an aggressive, individualistic Pueblo Indian—might have been successful and content in another, for instance, on the Plains or in Dobu. "Normality" is relative to the dominant configuration of one's society; it is not an absolute quality of the personality, since "culture may value and make socially available even highly unstable human types" (p. 249). (See the excellent discussion of this point in Endleman 1967:580–598).

There is little doubt that this conclusion sprang from Benedict's own situation as a poet and "career woman," trapped in an unhappy marriage and finding little support for her ambitions in the institutions of her society. Her concern for the deviant, the person who in Sapir's phrase is "alienated from an impossible world," was shared by Margaret Mead. Benedict recognized that the "misfit" may develop a "greater objective interest" in his or her situation, for example, by becoming an anthropologist. She insisted in all her writings that an understanding of cultural patterning is liberating for the individual and essential in the modern world.

Benedict viewed *Patterns of Culture* as a "popular" book, one that was important because "people need to be told in words of two syllables what contrasting cultures mean" (letter to Reo Fortune, quoted in M. Mead 1959:321). There is no doubt that she selected and simplified her materials to suit this aim (some criticisms of this approach are cited in the Interlude). Underlying her popular message and personal motives is yet another level that, I believe, has been overlooked by most readers of the book: a Darwinian metaphor. Each cultural configuration functions as a kind of evolutionary *niche* within which well-adapted persons flourish, while the poorly adapted are constantly "selected against" by cultural pressures. Those whose characteristics are most opposed to the configuration (like the trusting and cooperative Dobuan who was considered a "simpleton" by his peers), and those who are unwilling or unable to conform, frequently become mentally ill and are isolated from their fellows.

Benedict comes very close to Freud's view of culture when she states that "Tradition is as neurotic as any patient; its overgrown fear of deviation from its fortuitous standards conforms to all the usual definitions of the psychopathic" (p. 252). Our own culture, for example, with its great emphasis on material success, necessarily creates "failures." She pleads for greater tolerance of individual diversity and suggests that future cultures may develop in this direction. Freud himself was more pessimistic:

A good part of the struggles of mankind centre round the single task of finding an expedient accommodation—one, that is, that will bring happiness—between this claim of the individual [to liberty] and the cultural claims of the group; and one of the problems that touches the fate of humanity is whether such an accommodation can be reached by means of some particular form of civilization or whether this conflict is irreconcilable. (1961:43)

We shall deal with some of Benedict's later work in connection with studies of "National Character." Let us now turn to the early writings of another founder of the Culture and Personality school, Benedict's friend and colleague, the late Margaret Mead. (Dr. Mead died while this book was being completed. Her absence will be felt by all anthropologists who are concerned with human experience.)

TO AND FROM THE SOUTH SEAS

Margaret Mead must be considered *the* major figure in the Culture and Personality school. Her long and productive career spanned all four approaches of the school. With Benedict and Sapir she was a cofounder of "configurationalism"; she then moved beyond them into first-hand studies of growth and development, cross-cultural socialization, sex roles and temperament, national character, and investigations of the relationship between personality and culture change. Like Ruth Benedict, Mead was concerned with the application of anthropological findings to contemporary American life, and a continuing theme of her work was the relations between the generations. We shall examine only her early work in this section, reserving her later contributions for other chapters. Her first three major books— *Coming of Age in Samoa* published in 1928 (1949), *Growing Up in New Guinea*, in 1930 (1953a), and *Sex and Temperament in Three Primitive Societies*, in 1935 (1963)—were all based on her fieldwork in the South Pacific. (Her more technical works on kinship and technology are not discussed here.)

Coming of Age in Samoa was the product of Mead's doctoral

research on a problem that was set for her by Franz Boas: She was to investigate "the way in which the personality reacts to culture" (M. Mead 1949: Foreword). Specifically, Mead was interested in sexual attitudes and the "crisis of adolescence" in a society with standards very different from our own. Samoa in the late 1920s had long been subject to Christian missionary activity, yet it had retained much of its traditional culture. Small villages subsisted on fishing and horticulture; there were titles of nobility and an elaborate ranking system; births and marriages were validated by property distributions similar to those of the Kwakiutl. However, the general *tone* of life and the expressive behavior of the Samoans was highly distinctive. Children were raised mainly by their older siblings, and adolescents had great personal freedom even though the culture permitted relatively few "choices" of occupations or goals.

In such a cultural setting, Mead asked, are the "conflicts and distress" characteristic of American adolescence inevitable? Or are these produced by aspects of our own culture that we take for granted, and that are thrown into relief by a comparison with the Samoan experience? To a large extent, she concluded, the crisis of adolescence is relative to the demands a culture places on young people during the transition to adulthood. The homogeneity of Samoan culture and its casual attitude toward early sexuality and responsibility make "growing up" relatively easy. As in the Pueblo culture, "excessive emotion, violent preferences, strong allegiances are disallowed. The Samoan preference is for a middle course, a moderate amount of feeling, a discreet expression of a reasonable and balanced attitude" (p. 89). Mead showed that the organization of families and villages encourages a greater *diffuseness* of relationships:

> Disagreements between parent and child are settled by the child's moving across the street, between a man and his village by the man's removal to the next village, between a husband and his wife's seducer by [the gift of] a few fine mats. . . .

Love and hate, jealousy and revenge, sorrow and bereave-
ment, are all matters of weeks. From the first months of life,
when the child is handed carelessly from one woman's hands
to another's, the lesson is learned of not caring for one person greatly, not setting high hopes on any one relationship.
(p. 132)

Two important characteristics of Margaret Mead's work
are evident in the above quotation: the fluency and persua-
siveness of her style (based on her intimate knowledge of an
exotic culture) and her emphasis on the early learning of
cultural patterns through nonverbal communication. Mead
does not attempt to sum up Samoan culture in a single
configuration, but she does write of "the lack of deep feeling
which the Samoans have conventionalized until it is the very
framework of all their attitudes toward life" (p. 133).

This *shallowness,* she feels, largely accounts for the painless
transition from childhood to adulthood. There are exceptions. In her treatment of "The Girl in Conflict" (Chap. 11),
we learn about the unhappy deviants who, through accidents
of birth or temperament, are prone to special kinds of suf-
fering: the shy and awkward girl whom the rank system has
cast in the role of household "princess," expected to enter-
tain and dance for her chiefly father's guests; or the beautiful but brash and assertive young woman whom no high-
ranking man will marry. For all its charm and grace, Samoan
culture is not a paradise, and the range of individual temperaments is always wider than the types selected as ideal.

In *Growing Up in New Guinea* Mead describes her second
trip to the South Pacific, in 1928, to study the Manus of the
Admiralty Islands. (See M. Mead 1972:190–205.) The emphasis in this book is on the development of personality:
"The manner in which human babies born into these
water-dwelling communities gradually absorb the traditions,
the prohibitions, the values of their elders and become in
turn the active perpetuators of Manus culture" (1953a:13).
The book offers a rich description of the traditional way of
life, with its emphasis on the accumulation of wealth through

trade and exchange. (Mead was to revisit this society twenty-five years later; she recounted the extensive changes that had taken place during her absence in *New Lives for Old*, 1956.)

Manus child-training patterns are highly distinctive. After the first year of life, the father plays a greater role in child-care than the mother, but both parents invariably "give in" to the child's demands for food or attention. There are a few basic taboos and skills, classified by the Manus as "understanding the house, the fire, the canoe, and the sea," but once the child has acquired these, he or she is left to play almost totally independent of adult control. A strong identification with the father is nevertheless established in the early years. Repetition and imitation play a large role in socialization, but the basic taboos—shame regarding the body and its functions, respect for the property of others, and fear of ghosts—are also communicated nonverbally.

Mead's treatment of the contrast between child and adult social life, and the ways in which this contrast affects personality development, is of great interest to psychological anthropologists. Manus children, says Mead, "live in a world of their own . . . based upon different premises from those of adult life" (p. 55). Exchange holds no interest for them:

> No attempt is made to give the children property and enlist their interest in the financial game. They are simply expected to respect the tabus and avoidances which flow from the economic arrangements, because failure to do so will anger the spirits and produce undesirable results. (p. 59)

All of this changes when marriage approaches. Gradually for girls, more suddenly for boys, the kinship and economic systems that have always surrounded them take on new meaning and begin to affect their behavior. Similarly, the spirits who guarded them (or perhaps made them ill) in childhood now become forces to be reckoned with. Manus children "reject the supernatural in favor of the natural" (p. 70), but Manus adults must engage in seances, divination, and magical rites of protection. Children's play is described as unorganized and unimaginative, and children's talk is practical and dull compared with adult conversations concerning "feasts and finances, spirits, magic, sin, and confessions" (p. 79). This situation has interesting implications for the issue of "primitive mentality," especially regarding "animistic" or "prelogical" thought. According to Mead,

> From this material it is possible to conclude that personalizing the universe is not inherent in child thought, but is a tendency bequeathed to him by his society. . . . Children are not naturally religious, given over to charms, fetishes, spells, and ritual. They are not natural story tellers, nor do they naturally build up imaginative edifices. . . Their mental development in these respects is determined not by some internal necessity, but by the form of the culture in which they are brought up. (pp. 83–84; cf. pp. 170–172; also M. Mead 1932)

On her third trip to the Pacific (1931–1933), Mead investigated several contrasting New Guinea societies with special attention to the social roles of men and women. One product of this research was *Sex and Temperament in Three Primitive Societies*, published in 1935 (1963). The message of this book can be condensed as follows: If we designate biological gender by the terms "male" and "female," we can speak of the ideal *temperaments* attributed to each sex as "masculine" and "feminine" respectively. The American pattern assumes that males will be strong, aggressive, and concerned with commercial and worldly achievements; females, by contrast, should be dependent, maternal, and concerned with domestic matters. American culture (at least until recently) takes this association between sex and temperament for granted and punishes those who display the "wrong" temperament with ridicule, ostracism, and names such as "tomboy" or "sissy."

Mead discovered that each of the three New Guinea societies she studied had conceptions of appropriate temperament for each sex, but that these did not accord with the

American pattern. The mountain-dwelling Arapesh saw little difference in the temperament of men and women; both were expected to behave in what we might consider a "feminine" manner—emotionally warm, nurturant, and peaceful. The Mundugumor of the Sepik River also saw little difference between male and female temperaments, but their ideal person (of either sex) was aloof and aggressive. Finally, the lake-living Tchambuli did recognize temperamental differences linked to gender, but these were quite the reverse of the American pattern: the ideal women were energetic, assertive traders, whereas Tchambuli men stayed home, occupying themselves with domestic tasks and engaging in gossip, personal decoration, and artistic endeavors! (The relations of temperament to sex in these societies are summarized in Table 3-3.)

What conclusions can we draw from this comparison? In each case, the conventional assignment of a standardized temperament to a given sex is partly arbitrary, though fitting the general configuration of the culture. The insistence that all members of a gender (or a society) display a single temperament is destructive and wasteful, causing misery to those who cannot (or will not) conform. It is far better, says Mead, to recognize the diversity of temperamental endowments present in every group, and to use it for positive social ends: "If we are to achieve a richer culture, rich in contrasting values, we must recognize the whole gamut of human potentialities, and so weave a less arbitrary social fabric, one in which each diverse human gift will find a fitting place" (1935:322). (For an appreciation of Mead's work, see the Summer 1975 issue of the journal *Ethos*.)

SUMMARY

We have seen how discontent with the historical and atomistic character of American anthropology led Sapir and Benedict to use the concept of personality in analyzing the

Table 3-3　The Relationship Between Sex (Male, Female) and Temperament (Masculine, Feminine) in Four Societies (Adapted from Mead 1935)

	Society			
Sex	*United States*	*Arapesh*	*Mundagumor*	*Tchambuli*
Male	Masculine	Feminine	Masculine	Feminine
Female	Feminine			Masculine

integration of culture. Douglass R. Price-Williams has commented on this development:

> When the concept of personality is linked with society, institutional forces are thought in some way to place a premium on certain personality characteristics so as to form a type which is special to that society. To be sure, various kinds of personalities may be arrayed around a set of social institutions, but . . . one trait or a clump of traits stands out, either because it is dominant or because it is the most frequent characteristic. (Price-Williams 1975:66)

Price-Williams also discusses the connection between configurational studies and contemporary developments of functionalism in ethnology. Just as functionalists such as Malinowski and Radcliffe-Brown emphasized the interdependence of customs and institutions within a single society, the configurationalists tried to match cultural elements with aspects of personality: "One might say that the aim was to interpret personality as being identical with an institutional feature, so that it could be fitted into the interdependent framework of society like any other social trait" (1975:71). Marvin Harris has made a similar point in his lengthy critique of the Culture and Personality school (1968:393–421). But in addition to this implicit functionalism, Benedict and Mead used a Darwinian model in which each configuration was viewed as selecting for personality types most in accord with its ideals.

Introducing the Culture and Personality school through the pioneering works of Sapir, Benedict, and Mead has given a somewhat uneven view of the development of psychological anthropology. Many other anthropologists who were attracted to psychological problems began at the same time to investigate and publish on a variety of topics. In addition to appearing in the standard anthropological journals, articles by anthropologists were published in such diverse places as the *Journal of Abnormal and Social Psychology*, the *American Journal of Psychiatry*, and *Character and Personality*. In 1937, the journal *Psychiatry* was founded under the direction of Harry Stack Sullivan; since then it has served as a major forum for the discussion of Culture and Personality issues.

Another important leader in early Culture and Personality studies was the ethnographer A. Irving Hallowell. While still a graduate student at the University of Pennsylvania, Hallowell began to study Freudian and Gestalt psychology, and he traveled regularly to Columbia to participate in seminars with Boas and Benedict. During the 1930s, he attempted to synthesize concepts from several psychologies with data from his work with Ojibwa Indians in order to demonstrate that the human environment is "culturally constituted." By this phrase he meant that human beings do not simply perceive what is "out there" in nature, but rather, that their perceptions are mediated by learned ways of perceiving and thinking, by "cognitive orientations that organize and confer meaning upon them [and that] are acquired in large measure from ... cultural symbol systems" (Spiro 1976:608). This is a point that many psychologists have just begun to appreciate (see Tart 1978).

Hallowell was a unique scholar with ideas far ahead of his time; he was also an influential teacher. Although never a Freudian (or follower of any "ism"), he made creative use of psychoanalytic concepts and was one of the first anthropologists to employ the Rorschach test in non-Western societies (see Chapter Four). (Mead had tried using it in Manus but with discouraging results. See Kaplan 1961: 302–304.)

Hallowell's major writings have been collected in two anthologies (Hallowell 1955; Fogelson 1976). Together these volumes cover an enormous variety of topics, from stress, anxiety, and aggression to psychological aspects of culture change and human evolution. Although he does not "fit" into any of the schools or approaches defined in this book, Hallowell contributed to most of them, and his works will be cited wherever appropriate. Like certain other scholars—A. Douglas Haring and Dorothy Lee among them—his major influence on the field will probably be effected through his students.

In the next chapter, we will examine the ways that psychoanalytic theory was blended with configurational interpretations to create new approaches to the study of Culture and Personality. These approaches, known as basic and modal personality, continued the configurationalists' concern with the integration of culture, adding to it a dynamic analysis of social institutions and a search for causal relationships between institutions and personality.

Sigmund Freud

FOUR

Basic and Modal Personality

Throughout the 1930s, Columbia University remained the center of activity for American Culture and Personality studies. At the University of Pennsylvania, Hallowell continued to develop his distinctive style of analysis, while at Yale, a number of social scientists under the leadership of Edward Sapir and John Dollard undertook studies that were to lead to the cross-cultural approach after World War II (see Chapter Six). In this chapter, we shall be mainly concerned with developments at Columbia, where, by the end of the decade, the configurational approach to culture and personality had been replaced by an approach based on the concepts of basic personality structure and of modal personality.

The leading figures in developing this new approach were the psychoanalyst Abram Kardiner and the anthropologists Ralph Linton and Cora DuBois. Kardiner was the catalyst around which this approach took form, but we shall begin by considering the skills and knowledge that Linton brought to the enterprise.

Ralph Linton came from the University of Wisconsin in

Drawing by David Levine. Reprinted with permission from *The New York Review of Books.* Copyright © 1975 NYREV Inc.

1937 to replace Boas as chairman of the Department of Anthropology at Columbia. Linton had extensive field experience as an archeologist and as an ethnographer in the Mar-
quesas Islands (Polynesia), in Madagascar, and among the
Comanche Indians. He had also been involved in studies of
acculturation, but aside from one chapter in his influential
textbook *The Study of Man* (1930), there was little in his work
to indicate an interest in psychology. The circumstances of
his appointment caused extreme coolness in his relationship
with Benedict (since she had hoped to succeed Boas as
chairman) and the two never worked together closely.

Linton was soon deeply involved in a series of Culture and
Personality seminars in which he and other anthropologists
"presented" the cultures with which they were most familiar,
after which Kardiner and other psychologists "interpreted"
the data to reveal their dynamic significance (Linton and
Wagley 1971). Kardiner's seminars had begun in 1935 at the
New York Psychoanalytic Institute; after 1940 they were
moved to Columbia and became part of the anthropology
curriculum. By 1939, when he and Linton published *The Individual and His Society*, the basic methods and concepts of
this approach had been worked out, especially the concept of
basic personality structure (BPS). According to Linton, this concept

> suggests a type of integration, within a culture, based upon
> the common experiences of a society's members and the per-
> sonality characteristics which these experiences might be ex-
> pected to engender. This sort of integration differs sharply
> from that which the functionalist anthropologists have made
> a focal point in their researches and from that posited by
> Benedict in her well known *Patterns of Culture*. (Kardiner and
> Linton 1939:viii)

BASIC PERSONALITY STRUCTURE

Linton calls the functionalist approach to institutional integration "superficial" and describes it as yielding an image of

culture like "a mass of gears all turning and grinding against each other," but lacking any focus. Benedict's configurational approach has greater potential, says Linton, but it runs into difficulties in cultures that "are not dominated by an *idée fixe*." The concept of BPS, on the other hand, "places the focal point of culture integration in the *common denominator of the personalities* of the individuals who participate in the culture" (pp. viii–ix; italics added). He further suggests that BPS may help us understand phenomena of culture change, such as acceptance or rejection of culture traits, or their "reinterpretation" (the imposition of new meanings by the borrowing society).

The BPS approach thus extends the configurationalist assumption that culture and personality are integrated in similar ways; Linton and Kardiner wish to understand the *causal* relationship between the two. Culture is integrated, they say, because all the members of a society share certain early experiences that produce a specifiable basic personality structure, and because this BPS in turn creates and maintains other aspects of the culture. This assumption leads to a division of culture into two parts: *primary institutions,* which produce a "common denominator" of basic personality, and *secondary institutions,* which are produced by the BPS. This causal chain is diagramed in Figure 4-1.

The other key concepts used in this approach are *adaptation* and *projection.* Kardiner does not usually attempt to account for the origins of the primary institutions: He assumes that they are largely the result of a society's historical adaptation to its environment. That is, he regards subsistence technology, social organization (household and community), and child-training disciplines as "givens" for a particular society. Individuals born into a society with a certain set of primary institutions are thus "obliged to adapt to them one way or another." "The particular constellations caused by the necessity of the individual to adapt to these institutions become a part of his effective functional tools of adaptation, and eventually a part of his sense of reality" (Kardiner and Linton 1939:248–249).

Environment →	*Primary institutions* →	*Basic personality* →	*Secondary institutions*
	including subsistence type, household form, and child training	including shared anxieties, defenses, and neuroses	including religion, mythology, and folklore

Figure 4-1 A causal chain linking primary institutions (viewed as adaptations to the environment) to basic personality structure (individual adaptations to the primary institutions), which in turn develops and maintains secondary institutions (due to the projection of shared conflicts). (Based on Kardiner 1939; 1945.)

Kardiner places great stress on the "ego functions" of reality testing and adaptation to objective frustrations; however, he insists that the "secondary institutions can . . . be understood only from the effects of the primary ones on the human mind" (p. 249). These effects include unconscious conflicts and anxieties produced by early experience. Secondary institutions such as "taboo systems, religion, ritual, folktales, and techniques of thinking" (p. 471) are to be analyzed (as in *Totem and Taboo*) as symptoms of intrapsychic conflict given their form by projection and other defense mechanisms. In his later work, Kardiner referred to the secondary institutions as the "projective system." Let us examine some examples of this type of analysis.

In a series of brief "preliminary studies," Kardiner discussed data on the culture of the Trobriand Islanders, the Zuni Pueblo, the Kwakiutl, the Chuckchee, and the Eskimo. Since he, like Linton, criticized Ruth Benedict's characterizations as vague and inaccurate (pp. 84–85), it is interesting to see how Kardiner approaches the Zuni and Kwakiutl materials: "The whole point of Zuni culture is . . . the formation of a powerful in-group with great increase in security for the individual" (p. 116). Kardiner emphasizes the cooperative and peaceful nature of Zuni social life, which rests on a strong sense of shame as well as "mutual advantages" of the complex social organization. He relates these to a strong dependency on and fear of desertion by the mother, and to the relative insignificance of sibling rivalry. Elaborate taboos affecting a Zuni who kills an enemy are interpreted (following Freud, though unacknowledged) as revealing strong ambivalence concerning aggression (see "The Origins of Psychoanalytic Anthropology" in Chapter Two).

Kwakiutl customs are said to "permit ample opportunity for expressing aggression in unsublimated or displaced forms," but "their religious practices show deeply repressed anxieties and methods of draining these [including] typical Oedipus myths and rituals" (p. 117). Intense rivalries and desires to humiliate others are common, and Kardiner attributes these factors to the frustrations imposed by the strict ranking system. He interprets the Cannibal Society initiation as an acting out of Oedipal fantasies and sibling rivalries. Kardiner relies on the principle that "certain basic disciplines . . . will create a definite type of personality which will lead to the formation of institutions according to the needs and perceptions of the personality" (p. 120). On this assertion rests the entire basic personality structure approach. (See Abel and Métraux 1974:113–115; also Whiting and Child 1953:3–7.)

The remainder of *The Individual and His Society* deals with three cultures that Linton had studied at first hand. Although his field research had been directed to different ends, Linton's phenomenal memory provided rich data for Kardiner's dynamic analyses. For example, Linton presents (in forty pages) a description of the Tanala and Betsileo—two related societies of Madagascar—following which Kardiner analyzes (in sixty pages) the psychological "constellations" that connect primary with secondary institutions in those societies. According to Kardiner, the key to the basic Tanala personality is the principle that obedience brings safety and security. Early child discipline and the structure of the family (powerful father, polygyny, and primogeniture) insure that "the pattern of love or security in return for obedience is the most prominent pattern of adaptation for

the greatest number of people in the culture." A younger
son in particular "must suppress hatred toward father and
oldest brother, be diligent, ingratiate himself with his
superiors real and supernatural, anticipate offence with
prophylactic sacrifice, or atone afterward" (p. 361).

In a chart outlining the relation between primary and secondary institutions in Tanala culture, Kardiner indicates that
the repressed hatred, submission, and ingratiation of
(younger) sons are elements of the BPS that result in fear of
ancestral ghosts who are believed to cause illness when dis-
pleased by the sins of their descendents. Similarly, the severe
and early anal training of Tanala children is related to
"obedience" in the BPS; this, in turn, results in a cultural
emphasis on cleanliness and on "compulsive acts" as part of
all cures for illness. Finally, the primary institution of *sibling
inequality* (primogeniture) produces sibling hatred in the
BPS: When repressed, this aggression results in the secondary institutions of blood brotherhood and male homosexuality; when expressed, the aggression takes the form of special social roles—the *ombiasy* (shaman), or the warrior who
directs his hostility against the out-group (1939:326).
Women are less subject to these dynamics, although conflict
between a chief and his secondary wives in polygynous
households does lead to the occasional practice of sorcery.

Even more interesting than Kardiner's characterization of
Tanala BPS is the contrast with Betsileo culture and personality. Like the Tanala, the Betsileo were originally small-scale
horticulturalists living in isolated, equalitarian, and highly
endogamous communities. With the shift from dry to the
more productive irrigated rice cultivation, however, Betsileo
culture changed markedly in its "social organization, and
hence created important changes in the basic adaptation of
every individual" (p. 329). Changes in the primary institutions included use of new techniques of labor (especially related to water supply); diversification of village structure (including slaves); increases in exogamous marriages; an increase in the importance of personal property with a de-

crease in the significance of family ties; and the development of new levels of organization "from joint family to tribal organization to kingdom" (pp. 329–330).

Such changes are exactly what cultural-evolutionary theorists would expect under conditions of population growth and adoption of a more intensive form of food production. However, Kardiner is primarily interested in the consequences of these changes for *individual adaptation* and, ultimately, for the secondary institutions of the society. For example, under the irrigated rice system, the power of the father was diminished and the authority of the "king" became both great and arbitrary. New conflicts and new types of loyalties developed, while accumulation of property became "the most important element in the security system of the individual" (p. 331). The technique of ingratiation no longer worked:

> New needs as well as new anxieties were added to the individual's problem of adjustment. New needs were created in that the individual required different qualities to get along in this new society, and new anxieties in that he was susceptible to new dangers, dangers of poverty and degradation. (p. 331)

Child training in Betsileo society came to emphasize deference to authority, and individual insecurity increased. Obedience no longer insured security. There was also an increase in homosexuality, spirit possession, ritual, and sorcery. The king and the sorcerers replaced the father and ancestral ghosts as agents of social control.

These examples illustrate the explanatory model used in the basic personality approach. Changes in subsistence technology and social structure (primary institutions) produce changes in ritual and belief (secondary institutions), but the "functional integration" of these institutions is *mediated* by psychological processes. "The new [secondary] institutions can be derived from the anxiety defenses made necessary by the alteration in basic personality structure" (p. 346).

It is essential to note that the only *individuals* who appear in this analysis are several of Kardiner's clinical patients. They are introduced (anonymously) to illustrate the "dynamics of projection" or the "psychology of ingratiation." There simply are *no data* on Tanala or Betsileo individuals! What Kardiner has done (ingeniously) is to link one part of a cultural description with other parts by means of an invented BPS for which there is no independent evidence. Used in this way, the BPS has the logical status of a *hypothetical construct*—an entity or process having interpretive value even though it is not directly observed (see MacCorquodale and Meehl 1948). The reader must decide just how valid a given BPS is in relation to a body of data. However, when the data have been preselected by the analyst, the danger of confounding fact with interpretation is very great (see Interlude, below).

Like Freud, Kardiner uses individual neuroses as models, but he emphasizes ego structure as well as instinctual processes, so the BPS is an adaptation both to reality and to intrapsychic conflicts. Kardiner is highly critical of those psychoanalytic anthropologists (Róheim, Reik, Fromm, Erikson) who rely heavily on Freud's instinct theory, but he also denounces "those without psychodynamic training who employ psychological concepts in cultural studies" for their errors concerning the nature of adaptation (Kardiner and Preble 1963:222). In one of his last statements on this topic, Kardiner insists that

> the functioning of a society depends on the social arrangement necessary to insure co-operation in dealing with the environment, on the impact of this arrangement on the integrative processes of the human unit, and on the institutions created by the members of society in response to the adaptive problems associated with a particular process of individual integration. The human unit is the variable that makes a functional analysis of cultural institutions possible. (Kardiner and Preble 1963:221)

Kardiner was fully aware of the need for independent evidence concerning the "human unit" to validate and to enrich his construct of basic personality. An opportunity for this kind of validation came in the person of Cora DuBois, a Berkeley-trained anthropologist who participated in Kardiner's seminars in 1936–1937. Working from descriptions of culture was, she felt, "a good exercise," but it provided no opportunity to *verify* one's inferences. The key question was this: "Were individuals predominantly what we might suppose them to be from the institutions under which they lived, the childhood conditioning they received, the values they shared, the goals for which they strove?" Her conclusion was that "only field work could test the procedure" (1961:viii).

DuBois undertook fieldwork in the Dutch East Indies during 1938–1939. The book that resulted from this experiment, in 1944, is *The People of Alor* (1961; see also Kardiner et al., 1945:101–258). Although written in the days before confessional complaints came into style, the book makes it clear that this was a difficult field situation. DuBois had first to learn Dutch, then Malay, and finally an unwritten native language, which she named Abui. She lived for eighteen months in a small mountain village on the island of Alor among hostile people (formerly headhunters) who found her strange, clumsy, and somewhat frightening. She worked hard and learned well.

THE MODAL PERSONALITY APPROACH

The People of Alor is a collaborative effort. As in the seminars, DuBois presents ethnographic data (stressing childhood experience) and life histories (autobiographies of eight Alorese, four men and four women); Kardiner provides chapter-by-chapter commentary on child development and an analysis of adult character. The final part of the book contains the results of psychological tests that DuBois administered in the field: the Porteus maze test, word associations, children's drawings, and the Rorschach test (discussed in the following section).

In *The People of Alor,* DuBois uses the logic developed in earlier basic personality studies: She links primary institutions such as gardening techniques and household form to maternal neglect of young children; this relationship produces a typical personality structure that lacks the capacity to engage in sustained human relationships. In turn, the weak superego, instability, and distrust characteristic of Alorese personality find outlets in the secondary institutions: ritual competition for status and wealth, mythology, and (formerly) warfare.

Nevertheless, the Alor study differs from earlier BPS work in several important respects. First, the data were gathered by an experienced ethnographer who had also been trained in psychological methods and who knew what was important to the approach. Thus, DuBois' material on Alorese early childhood is much richer and more systematic than Linton's recollections about Marquesan childhood or the brief notes on this topic in many ethnographies.

Second, ample data are presented on selected individuals, in both autobiographical accounts (including dreams) and test *protocols* (response records). Thus, the inferred basic personality can be checked against concrete cases. The value of this evidence was enhanced by the independent analyses performed by Emil Oberholzer (a psychiatrist) of the thirty-eight Rorschach responses. DuBois compared these analyses with Kardiner's character analyses based on cultural and biographical materials. In addition, Stanley Porteus analyzed the results of his maze test, making brief comments on the intelligence and personalities of the subjects. The children's drawings are reproduced and both word associations and Rorschach protocols are included so that the reader can compare them with the suggested interpretations.

These important improvements over earlier works have been incorporated into many subsequent Culture and Personality studies. The close accord between these relatively independent analyses led Kardiner to claim that the Alorese material had validated his basic personality approach. Nevertheless, in addition to receiving high praise, *The People of Alor* has been intensively criticized, partly *because* the inclusion of data on individuals permits alternative interpretations. For example, Rorschach tests can be scored and evaluated in many different ways (see Rickers-Ovsiankina 1977). The eight biographies displayed such diversity of character types that many readers questioned whether any significant "common denominator" existed. Others wondered how a handful of biographies (including some of admitted deviants) and several dozen test protocols could accurately represent the 70,000 culturally and linguistically diverse people of Alor.

Kardiner parried many of these criticisms by insisting that, though some details may be wrong, "there can be little doubt about the main trend." He argued that BPS is a result of primary institutions and, in Alor, the "combination of influences acting from birth to adulthood *must* create a deeply insecure and isolated individual" (Kardiner et al. 1945:169; italics added). DuBois, perhaps because she knew these people at first hand, was more reluctant to accept this global interpretation. Without explicitly rejecting the notion of BPS, she put forward an idea that many psychological anthropologists have found more acceptable than Kardiner's formulation—the concept of *modal personality (MP)*. The term *mode* refers to a statistical concept that can be simply expressed as "most frequent." Therefore, when we speak of the modal personality of a group, we are referring to the most frequent type encountered in our sample. The modal type need not be the "average" person. Indeed, it may not even be in the majority; it is simply the most frequent.

For DuBois, modal personality is primarily a *descriptive* concept, "an abstraction and a generalization" comparable to a racial type (1961:4). MP also has a *dynamic* aspect: It helps us to understand processes of stability and change. Suddenly sounding a great deal like Sapir, DuBois states that "only when we have some comprehension of the link between institutions which the individuals bearing those institutions may make on an emotional level, shall we begin to grasp the repercussions involved in social alterations" (1961:5).

In her preface to the paperback edition of *The People of Alor*, DuBois considerably modified the claims made (mainly by Kardiner) in the original (1944) edition. She admits that their analysis "may have oversimplified the congruities and largely ignored incongruities and discrepancies" between institutions and personality (1961:viii). The use of projective tests, even in "homogeneous" groups, is now expected to give "multimodal rather than unimodal results," and there is a "high probability that only a small percentage of people in a society belong to these modal groups" (p. xx).

In my opinion, modal personality has two important advantages over basic personality as a way of conceptualizing relations between culture and personality:

1. The MP approach does not assume that all or even most of the members of a society share the same personality structure. The degree of sharing becomes an empirical problem rather than an assertion based on purely cultural data.

2. In MP studies, biographical and test data on individuals are invariably collected (and usually published). In theory, such data could be collected by researchers using the BPS approach. However, since test data always show a wide range of variation, they are much more compatible with an MP approach, which gives careful attention to techniques of sampling and of statistical analysis.

These advantages later attracted a number of young scholars to the MP approach, but before we can consider their contributions, we must examine the methods of testing and scoring in some detail.

PROJECTIVE TESTS: RORSCHACH AND THEMATIC APPERCEPTION

Since the remaining studies to be considered in this chapter make use of projective tests, this is a good point at which to pause and consider the nature of these tests. Projective methods for the study of personality include a great variety of "devices that enable the subject to project himself into a planned situation." When using such methods, we are primarily interested in what a person "indirectly tells us about himself through his manner of confronting the task" (Murphy 1947:669). For example, a *sentence-completion test* can be viewed as a projective method because it presents an open-ended situation in which a person may express his or her thoughts, needs, and anxieties. A sentence such as

When I have to take an examination, I feel ———.

may tap both conscious and unconscious attitudes and feelings. In addition, the speed or hesitancy of response, or the refusal to respond at all, may be as significant as the word or phrase supplied. Using these factors, the analyst can get behind individual or cultural defenses to understand thoughts and motives of which the subject is not aware.

Projective methods are used both to *characterize* the personality structure of normal individuals and to *diagnose* psychological problems. Probably the best known of these methods is the Rorschach, or "inkblot," test, developed early in the century by the Swiss psychiatrist Herman Rorschach. The traditional test consists of ten white cards, each with an irregular but symmetrical inkblot. These cards are presented to subjects in a standard order, and the subjects are asked to report what they see in each card. Half the blots show differences in black-gray shading and half include color. Besides the total number of responses, three aspects of the responses are used in scoring the Rorschach test:

1. *Locations.* Whether the response is to the whole blot (W), to large or to small details (D,d), or to the white spaces (S).

2. *Determinants.* Use of form (F), color (C), and/or perception of movement (M), including various combinations of these.

3. *Content.* Perception of animal, human, or botanical forms with or without movement, and whether these

responses are common, original, or bizarre relative to the population on which the test has been standardized.

The test is scored and the ratios of certain types of responses are calculated. The scoring is then interpreted. Several alternative methods of interpretation exist, but Gardner Murphy gives a good summary of the traditional method:

> In general, the use of form represents objectivity, a disciplined recognition of fact. The affective (i.e., emotional) life of the individual is revealed primarily through color; the person with an outgoing emotional disposition piles up a considerable color score. To use both form and color indicates integration of objective and emotional tendencies. To give numerous form-color responses (form being the primary determinant, and color the secondary) indicates control, but control with some appreciation of affective realities; to give numerous color-form responses, color being dominant, is likely to mean loss of control through dominating affect. A person with a rich inner life typically has a high human movement score. A richly intuitive, subtle, responsive person, the very gifted or artistic, typically gives many responses of both color and human movement; the pedant gives neither. (Murphy 1947:674–675)

By scoring the test in other ways, and by looking for responses and ratios that are often indicative of psychological problems, it is possible for an investigator to obtain a quick estimate of a subject's overall adjustment level. Experienced diagnosticians can tell a good deal from this test, but they make use of the entire pattern of responses, and do not rely on any "single indicator" of pathology.

Great caution must be exercised in using the Rorschach cross-culturally. When Oberholzer did his analysis of the thirty-eight Alorese protocols, he warned that errors of interpretation were likely because of the small sample (less than a hundred) and the fact that the test had been standardized on a European population: What would be a bizarre detail for a Swiss adult might be fairly common in Alor. Nevertheless, he thought it significant, for example, that Alorese males produced many responses to small and unusual details (24.4 percent) and that they showed a high ratio of color to movement responses (27 percent as against less than 1 percent). "The more there exists a predominance of the C over the M, the less there exist self-control and balance of mind" (Oberholzer in DuBois 1961:590–591). However, in the absence of local norms, interpretation and (above all) comparisons between populations must be evaluated critically (Henry and Spiro 1953; Kaplan 1961; Spain 1972).

During the 1940s and early 1950s, the Rorschach test was a favorite tool of psychological anthropologists (Hallowell 1955:32–74). They hoped that it would be especially useful with nonliterate peoples. It is currently in disfavor, partly for the reasons just mentioned and partly because attempts to validate its findings on Euro-American clinical subjects have often been disappointing. New types of inkblots, techniques of scoring, and ways of integrating findings with other types of tests continue to be proposed by clinicians; some of these may turn out to have cross-cultural relevance (see Edgerton 1970; LeVine 1973:175–184).

The other projective method used most frequently in anthropological studies is the Thematic Apperception Test (TAT). Developed during the 1930s by Henry Murray at Harvard, this test consists of a set of cards each showing an ambiguous picture of one or more human figures. Ten of the cards are for men only, ten for women only, and ten for both sexes. The subject is asked to tell a story about each card as it is presented. There is no time limit and the stories are recorded verbatim. Subjects tend to identify with one of the figures (usually of their own age and sex) and tell their stories from the point of view of this character; in doing so, they reveal their own self-concepts. The number of responses and the subjects' general emotional tone during the test are also noted.

Protocols are usually scored in relation to Murray's theory of human needs (for example, the need for aggression, affiliation, dominance, nurturance, autonomy, and the famous "need for achievement"). Many subjects find the TAT less threatening than clinical interviews or the Rorschach: The pictures are familiar and "anyone can tell a story." With the TAT, a subject may "betray his deep wishes without consciously focusing on them" (Murphy 1947:672). When used cross-culturally, TATs have usually been modified to make the figures and situations more familiar to subjects, and alternative methods of scoring have been developed; however, these alterations affect the kinds of comparisons that can be made. TAT-like scoring procedures have also been used to interpret literature, folklore, and reports of dreams, often with interesting results (see Colby 1966).

APPLICATIONS OF PROJECTIVE TESTS

Throughout the 1940s, Hallowell had demonstrated the potential of the cross-cultural use of Rorschachs in a series of papers that dealt not only with pathology but also with intelligence, emotional structure, and the psychological consequence of acculturation (Hallowell 1955:125–150; 345–357). In the late 1940s, one of his doctoral students, Anthony F. C. Wallace, undertook an ambitious study of an Iroquoian Indian community near Buffalo, New York. The full title of Wallace's study, published in 1952, is *The Modal Personality Structure of the Tuscarora Indians as Revealed by the Rorschach Test*. Wallace went on to become one of the most significant figures in psychological anthropology. I shall give an extended account of the Tuscarora study, for I believe it represents an important advance in the MP approach.

Wallace states the problem to be investigated as follows: *"What is the type of psychological structure most characteristic of the adult Tuscarora Indians of this community, insofar as it can be inferred from the obtained Rorschach sample?"* (1952:1; italics in original). The sample consists of seventy adult Rorschach protocols, and to these data Wallace applies an intentionally mechanical type of analysis. He takes the statistical definition of "mode" seriously, and attempts to establish the modal class for Tuscarora personality through explicit and replicable operations.

The sample was similar in age and sex distribution to the adult population of the Tuscarora reservation: It consisted of thirty-six males and thirty-four females whose ages ranged from sixteen to more than seventy years. Wallace reports that looking at the inkblots became "a minor fad, in certain circles" (p. 41), and only two or three of the persons approached refused to take the test. Although a larger sample would have been desirable, seventy out of 352 adults is certainly adequate. Though there might be some biases, Wallace felt that the sample was "a fair representation of Tuscarora society" (p. 42).

Wallace's goal was to describe the "distribution of individual personality traits or types which distinguishes a population" without making any prior assumptions about how these traits relate to culture (p. 50). Furthermore, he was not concerned with isolated traits as such, but with the pattern of association among them.

In their earlier Rorschach studies, Hallowell and Oberholzer had calculated *average* scores for each of the main factors of the test (locations, determinants, content, and ratios); they then interpreted the average profile of their entire sample as if it were the Rorschach of a single, typical individual. This approach assumes that a common denominator can be discovered by averaging all cases. Wallace, however, used the *mode* for each of twenty-one factors to establish a *modal class of individuals*. This class included only those individuals whose scores were within one standard deviation of the modal score. (See Hay 1976 for a discussion of these methods.)

Wallace found that twenty-six of the seventy individual records fell within his modal class; another sixteen records (called *submodal*) clustered around the modal class, differing in only a few factors or ratios. He then calculated an average profile for the twenty-six members of the modal class only. Working with Hallowell, he interpreted this profile as if it were the record of a single individual. What kind of person is this? According to Wallace,

> one might describe the Tuscarora modal personality type as displaying: (1) on a basic but presumably largely unconscious level, a strong urge to be allowed to become passive and dependent; (2) a fear of rejection and punishment by the environment and by the self for these demands; (3) a compensatory drive to be hyperindependent, aggressive, self-sufficient; (4) an ultimate incapacity to feel, to adapt, to evaluate the environment realistically, and a concomitant dependence upon categories, stereotypes, and deductive logic. (p. 75)

Although this characterization of Tuscarora MP structure is the core of his monograph, Wallace also presents a concise description of Tuscarora culture, past and present. He discusses sex differences in personality and the relationship of Tuscarora MP to culture. He then presents an intriguing comparison of his findings with a series of Ojibwa Indian Rorschach protocols, which had been gathered and scored by Hallowell. The comparison showed a core of personality traits common to both peoples, but the method also revealed several important differences in modal personality—differences that are "congruent with the obvious cultural differences between Tuscarora and Ojibwa" (p. 107).

One of the most interesting observations in this monograph is tucked away in a footnote. Describing a Tuscarora woman with a highly deviant Rorschach record, Wallace comments that although one might think Tuscarora culture would be "uncongenial" to her, this woman "functions well" as a widely respected and well-liked clan mother. He suggests that Ruth Benedict may have overemphasized the dependency of personality on culture: "It would seem that people with widely differing personalities can within certain limits use the same culture—for different purposes, perhaps—and thereby play successful and rewarding roles"

(p. 82n). This brief note anticipates Wallace's later position on the "organization of diversity" (1970:23–24). This concept focuses attention on the way in which diverse personalities are organized into functioning, changing social groups. It will be discussed further in the Interlude and in Chapter Eight.

The other major work to be considered here is *Truk: Man in Paradise* by Thomas Gladwin, an ethnographer, and Seymour B. Sarason, a psychiatrist (1953). Truk is a cluster of small islands in that part of the South Pacific known as Micronesia. This area came under U.S. control following World War II and was the subject of intensive study by the federally funded Coordinated Investigation of Micronesian Anthropology (CIMA). Gladwin gathered ethnographic, life-history, and projective-test data during a seven-month period, supplementing his material with studies by other CIMA professionals; Sarason was in charge of test interpretation.

I shall try to give a brief account of the culture, the kinds of data collected, and the conclusions reached in this massive, 650-page book. The subtitle, "Man in Paradise," refers to the natural beauty and equable climate of the islands as well as the assured food supply and rather casual attitudes towards sexuality (especially for unmarried adolescents). As Gladwin writes,

> the natural environment of Truk is remarkable in the degree
> to which man can find in it fulfillment of his needs with a
> minimum outlay of effort and hazard. This [is] important . . .
> for here is a case in which it is clear that any anxieties which
> the Trukese may feel acutely are, in the last analysis, of their
> own making. (Gladwin and Sarason 1953:33–34)

The underlying question of this study is: Can human beings be happy, even in "paradise"? The first quarter of the book is devoted to the essentials of Trukese culture—the setting, the technological system, the social structure, and the life cycle from birth to death. The remainder deals with

Trukese modal personality. For a sample of twelve men and eleven women of various ages and degrees of local "popularity," we are given detailed life histories, Rorschach protocols, and responses to a modified TAT, together with Sarason's interpretations of the test data. Working without knowledge of Gladwin's cultural description, Sarason interpreted the TATs in terms of *themes* characterizing men, women, and the group as a whole. These themes include

1. Conflict between men and women, particularly regarding sexuality and female "assertiveness."

2. Inconsistency of parent-child relationships, with a lack of opportunity to identify with stable parent figures.

3. Anxieties concerning adequacy of food supply apparently deriving from early frustrations.

4. Separation anxiety involving fear of loss and isolation, present throughout life and related to food anxieties.

5. "Laziness," in the sense of a strong preference for an easy, passive life. (Sarason comments on the great number of stories in which people are relaxing, playing, eating, strolling, or bathing.)

6. Suppression of hostile feelings such that "the Trukese have difficulty in giving overt and direct expression to their hostility" (p. 238).

Gladwin felt that the TAT analysis had validly portrayed many aspects of Trukese social life. Commenting on the last theme, he notes, "This of course coincides with our observation of the high incidence of gossip and fear of sorcery, the latter being a classic mechanism of anonymous aggression" (p. 241). It appears that "man in paradise" is *not* entirely happy. Inconsistency in child training tends to produce an individual who "has great difficulty in formulating a mode of behavior which . . . will be effective in dealing with his social environment," and who becomes a conformist intent on avoiding conflicts and difficult choices (p. 457). Paradoxically, in a society in which food supply and male dominance are assured, people show deep-seated food anxieties, and the men display a variety of anxieties in relation to women (p. 458).

Gladwin and Sarason acknowledge their methodological debt to *The People of Alor,* but state that they tried to improve on DuBois and Kardiner's approach by using more representative samples and by using projective tests "as a primary datum in the definition of personality rather than as a coroborative device" (p. 459). They also suggest that projective tests can be of value to anthropologists as a means of guiding their attention to areas or problems they may have overlooked or failed to emphasize sufficiently. The Rorschach and TAT yield different kinds of data, and the authors feel that, wherever possible, *both* tests should be utilized (p. 455; cf. Spain 1972).

SUMMARY

We have seen in this chapter how the basic personality approach developed out of the configurationalist approach by the infusion of psychoanalytic concepts and the construction of a causal model of explanation. Further, the modal personality approach employed the systematic collection of individual data and was based on the assumption that the proper object of investigation was the most frequent personality type rather than a basic structure shared by all members of a society. We noted that the MP approach was refined further in the work of Wallace and of Gladwin and Sarason: the former using inductive statistical procedures to define the modal class, the others a combination of different tests integrated with observational data. In the next chapter, we turn to the approaches developed during the 1940s for the study of national character, after which, in the Interlude, I shall critique the entire range of studies so far considered.

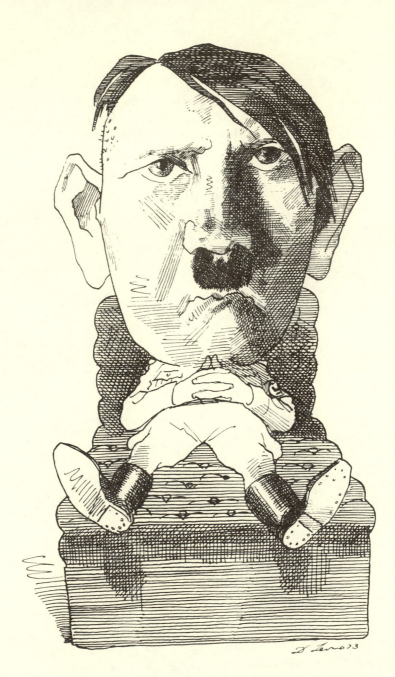

Adolph Hitler

FIVE

National Character Studies

In the last two chapters, I outlined the development of several approaches to culture and personality. No doubt identifying differences among these approaches is easier than recognizing similarities. However, these viewpoints do share the assumption that a one-to-one correspondence exists between a type of personality structure (ideal, basic, or modal) and a culture (or society). Despite explicit disclaimers and occasional references to deviant individuals and groups, the entire Culture and Personality school assumes that each society can be characterized in terms of a typical personality and that these characterizations can be compared. The logical outcome of applying Culture and Personality methods to larger and larger social units is the study of *national character*.

"Everyone knows" that the English are "reserved," the French "excitable," the Spanish "proud," the Germans "industrious," and so forth. The tradition of nonscientific and literary characterizations of nations dates back at least to Theophrastus (372–287 B.C.) and continues via Tacitus, Thucydides, and de Tocqueville to recent best-selling authors (for example, Luigi Barzini, *The Italians,* or Hedrick Smith, *The Russians*). In short, there is a widespread popular assumption that citizens of different nations have certain distinctive psychological characteristics in common. This opinion is held with varying degrees of certainty and explicitness. Like most stereotypes, popularly agreed upon national characters are difficult to verify or refute, since such constructions usually contain contradictory elements (for example, the "reserved" English are also thought to be highly "eccentric"); also, they can account (after the fact) for virtually any kind of behavior, and are therefore scientifically useless.

Still, stereotypes do perform important social functions: They are often used to justify modes of behavior (slavery, discrimination, exploitation) that are advantageous to those holding the stereotypes. Thus it is not surprising that, in the United States, scientific studies of national character were first undertaken in connection with World War II. It was thought that understanding the psychology of our enemies and their leaders could be helpful in planning wartime operations and postwar policy. Similarly, it would be useful to know the psychological characteristics of our allies— especially if they might someday become our enemies! For that matter, knowledge of American national character could help the war effort by indicating ways to increase morale and effectiveness under stress.

As early as 1939, Margaret Mead, together with Gregory Bateson, Eliot Chapple, and Lawrence K. Frank, worked with the Committee for National Morale "to consider ways in which the sciences of anthropology and psychology . . . could be applied to the problems of morale building in wartime." After America entered the war, Ruth Benedict, Clyde Kluckhohn, and other anthropologists moved to Washington to take part in research and planning: "By 1943 there were a large number of anthropologists in various government agencies in Washington . . . interested in the problems of studying national character and in developing techniques for research on cultures at a distance" (M. Mead 1974:57–58).

The notion of studying cultures *at a distance* was one of the more interesting developments of this period. Making a virtue of a necessity (since the enemy was naturally unwilling to be studied at first hand), Mead and others devised methods for analyzing literature, films, newspapers, travelers' accounts, and government propaganda. These studies combined the logic of configurationalist and BPS approaches. When possible, recent immigrants, refugees, and war prisoners were intensively interviewed and tested. They did not constitute a representative sample of their countrymen, but Mead argued (1953) that *any* member of a society could contribute to the study of national character provided that his or her position in the society was specified (see Chapter Eight).

THE YELLOW PERIL

America's most "exotic" enemy in World War II was, of course, Japan. The behavior of Japan's government and its soldiers was puzzling to Americans in many ways. For example, even allowing for American racism and propaganda, the Japanese did seem "fanatical" in their devotion to the Emperor and their willingness to endure hardships or undertake suicidal missions. Paradoxically, Japanese soldiers who were captured seemed to be willing immediately to "change sides" and work enthusiastically for their captors! It took some time for anthropologists to analyze this apparent shift in loyalty and then to convince the U.S. Army of its genuineness. As Clyde Kluckhohn explained, a Japanese war prisoner conceived of himself as *socially dead*. He regarded his relations with his family, his friends, and his country as finished. But since he was physically alive, he wished to affiliate himself with a new society:

> To the astonishment of their American captors, many Japanese prisoners wished to join the American Army. . . . They willingly wrote propaganda for us, spoke over loud speakers urging their own troops to surrender, gave detailed

information. . . . To anthropologists who had steeped themselves in Japanese literature it was clear that Japanese morality was a situational one. As long as one was in situation A,
one publicly observed the rules of the game with a fervor that
impressed Americans as "fanaticism." Yet the minute one was
in situation B, the rules for situation A no longer applied.
(Kluckhohn 1957:137)

We are dealing here with an aspect of culture (situational
versus absolute ethics). However, we may inquire about the
kind of personality adapted to a situational ethic, with its reliance upon external authority and "shame," as opposed to a
personality with internalized (absolute) standards and a
strong, guilt-producing superego. (See Piers and Singer
1953.)

Japanese concepts of the self and of responsibility were
one focus of Ruth Benedict's wartime studies. Although she
continued to resist psychoanalytic formulations, Benedict increasingly made use of materials on child training. She "developed her own style of approach . . . in which published
materials were integrated with interview data," and she devised methods for "extracting cultural regularities from a
very miscellaneous assortment of literary sources—history,
travel accounts, plays, and novels—and from a variety of
sources on current wartime behavior" (M. Mead 1974:59).

Following the war, Benedict spent a year in California
compiling research on Japan (much of which was still
classified). *The Chrysanthemum and the Sword* (1946b), as its
title indicates, focuses on the contradiction in Japanese
character between restrained aestheticism (seen in art and
ceremony) and fanatical militarism (typified by the ideal of
the samurai warrior). Benedict felt that one key to this complex character lay in the distinctive Japanese notions of social
responsibility and obligation. From their earliest experiences
and well into adult life, Japanese are drawn into a web of
social relations in which their personal desires must be subordinated to family and group demands. The childhood
emphasis on "shame" develops into the pervasive adult con-

cern for "face," and individuals must be constantly aware of their social positions to avoid disgracing themselves and their families. Serious disgrace can only be wiped away by an honorable death in battle or by suicide.

Benedict considered *The Chrysanthemum and the Sword* her most important book and, despite thirty years of criticism from American and Japanese scholars alike, it stands as a landmark in national character studies (see Stoetzel 1955). The necessity for working at a distance led to some errors and overgeneralizations, but many of Benedict's conclusions have been validated by more objective methods. For example, she pointed out that Japanese moral categories cut across American concepts in ways that can be most confusing: *Giri* is a term usually translated as "repayment" for a social obligation but it refers to both what we call "gratitude" and "revenge."

> A good man feels as strongly about insults as he does about the benefits he has received. Either way it is virtuous to repay. He does not separate the two, as we do, and call one aggression and one non-aggression because so long as one is maintaining giri and clearing one's name of slurs, one is not guilty of aggression. One is evening scores. (Benedict 1946b:146)

Does this statement describe national culture or national character? For Benedict, the distinction was never that important: She wished to demonstrate the *isomorphism* (formal identity) of cultural patterns with personality structure. In this case, the cultural value on repayment of obligations corresponds to the Japanese notion of a "good man," and cuts across the Western distinction between gratitude and revenge. Often she found a correspondence with patterns of child training, but Benedict's main interest was in the kind of adults that a cultural system produced. In the case of Japan, she emphasized the centrality of *obligation* to adult character, pointing out that middle-aged Japanese have less personal freedom than either young children or elderly persons. This is exactly the opposite of the American pattern, in which children and older persons have little freedom relative to persons in what we consider the "prime of life." The real value of Benedict's work lies in her intuitive grasp of such general patterns. (See Befu 1971, Chap. 6.)

Benedict also detected an isomorphism between the structure of the Japanese family and the political organization of the state. In both, "the officials who head the hierarchy do not typically exercise the actual authority" (1946b:301). However, as Alex Inkeles has noted, these generalizations assume a homogeneity within large populations that has yet to be demonstrated:

> The basic difficulty with this approach, one pervasive in the culture and personality literature, is its failure to take adequate account of the differentiation within large national populations. It emphasizes the central tendency, the existence of which it presumes but does not prove, and neglects the range of variation within and around the typical. (Inkeles 1961:173)

ON THE WESTERN FRONT

This same criticism applies to such famous studies of German national character as Erich Fromm's *Escape from Freedom* (1941). Fromm was concerned with why the German people had submitted to Hitler's dictatorial rule. He tried to explain the appeal of the Nazi movement in terms of the prevalence in Germany of the *authoritarian personality*. A person of this character type is exceptionally obedient and subservient to superiors but behaves in an overbearing and scornful manner toward social inferiors—especially those under the individual's control. Fromm felt that persons with this character react with anxiety to democratic institutions and thus show a strong tendency to "escape from freedom" into authoritarian systems in which they are more comfortable. These ideas helped many Americans to understand the

European enemy, and "authoritarianism" became a key variable in social psychology for several decades (Adorno et al. 1950; cf. Bettelheim 1971:260–292).

Other approaches focused on Hitler himself. Walter C. Langer was called on by the OSS (an American intelligence agency) to produce a study of Hitler's personality. His secret report has recently been published; it contains fascinating material on the Führer's private life, neuroses, and style of leadership (Langer 1973). For example, although most Germans refer to their country as the "Fatherland," Hitler almost always called it the "Motherland." From this and other evidence about his early life, Langer concluded that Hitler transferred his Oedipal feelings for his mother onto the German nation while projecting his hostility toward his father onto the old and declining Austrian Empire. Thus, when Hitler writes of his longing to go to Germany, "where since my early youth I have been drawn by secret wishes and secret love," and when he contrasts his intense love for Germany with his "bitter hatred against the Austrian state," Langer infers that the alliance between Austria and Germany represented his parents' marriage:

> Unconsciously, he is not dealing with nations composed of millions of individuals but is trying to solve his personal conflicts and rectify the injustices of his childhood. [Thus, when World War I broke out, Austrian-born Hitler joined the German army.] To him it did not mean simply a war . . . but an opportunity of fighting for his symbolic mother, of proving his manhood and of being accepted by her. (Langer 1973:159–160)

Erik Erikson, whose work will be discussed at length in Chapter Seven, also analyzed German national character. He was interested in Hitler's appeal to German youth. In particular, Erikson looked at the *image* that Hitler tried to project through his autobiography and other propaganda, and at the kind of *identity* he offered to the angry, frustrated adolescents of prewar Germany. (On the background of this study, see Evans 1967:65.)

Erikson's analysis is highly suggestive. He points out the mythical elements in "The Legend of Hitler's Childhood" (1963:326–358). These include the "striking use of parental and familial images" (for example, the father is shown as a harsh, autocratic man who has betrayed his own youthful idealism, and the son—Hitler—rebels against him in order to shape his own destiny). To German youth, Hitler's image became that of "a glorified older brother, who took over prerogatives of the fathers without overidentifying with them." His appeal was that of the "gang leader who kept the boys together by demanding their admiration, by creating terror, and by shrewdly involving them in crimes from which there was no way back" (p. 337; on the theme of "shared guilt" see Freud 1950:143–150).

Like Langer, Erikson notes the "abundance of superhuman mother figures" in Hitler's imagery (p. 339), but he also stresses the *new identity* that was offered to adolescents by fanatical German nationalism and racism. Hitler used anti-Semitic stereotypes as a projection of a *negative identity* against which the German "master race" could view itself as good, pure, and strong. Unfortunately for the rest of Europe, Hitler's personal pathology corresponded to the unconscious conflicts of an entire generation, giving him an uncanny power over them. Millions of Germans responded to Hitler's megalomaniac visions: "Let everything go to pieces, we shall march on. For today Germany is ours; tomorrow, the whole world" (p. 343).

THE SLAVIC SOUL

For reasons that are easy to divine, Russian national character became the focus of research in the immediate postwar years. In this connection, the British anthropologist Geoffrey Gorer developed the famous (or infamous) "swaddling hypothesis." Margaret Mead also had a role in the formulation and popularization of this hypothesis, while Erikson adapted it for his own purposes in the article "The Legend of Maxim Gorky's Youth" (1963:359–402), a parallel to his study of Hitler's childhood.

The swaddling hypothesis is a good deal more subtle than it appears at first. Gorer pointed out that Russian infants were traditionally tightly swaddled during the early months of life. The rationale for this practice was that swaddling enabled infants to grow straight and strong, and that, without swaddling, children might "hurt themselves." Children were released from the wrappings for short periods each day, during which time they were cleaned off and actively played with.

Gorer imaginatively related this alternation between long periods of externally imposed immobility and short periods of intense social interaction and muscular activity to certain aspects of Russian character and politics. Many Russians are said to experience intense mood swings between long periods of introspective depression and short bursts of frantic social activity; also, Russian political behavior seems to consist of long periods of willing submission to a strong external authority punctuated by brief periods of intense revolutionary activity.

It would be a mistake to view this hypothesis as a causal argument, for it is actually a configurationalist statement of isomorphisms. Gorer does *not* claim that the practice of swaddling children causes Russians to have autocratic political institutions (Tsarism, Stalinism), nor that it produces a manic-depressive basic personality in all Russian adults. Rather, he is content to note the formal similarity among various cultural patterns, and to suggest that prolonged, tight swaddling is *one of the means* by which Russians communicate to their children that a strong external authority is necessary.

What does it mean to say that "the Russians swaddle their children"? In this form, the statement is equivalent to a + on a culture trait list (see Chapter Three): Russians "have" the trait of swaddling. Gorer, of course, is interested in this practice as part of a larger pattern, but the impression remains that swaddling is an objective "social fact" rather than an inference from highly variable human behavior. Several kinds of variability must be considered in dealing with such statements (see Bock 1974:54). These may be applied to swaddling as follows:

1. *Spatial variability*. How large a group is denoted by "the Russians"? After all, Russia is the largest nation in the world, its borders encompassing great industrial cities, peasant villages, numerous ethnic groups, and even some tribes of nomadic pastoralists. Gorer, and his collaborator John Rickman entitled their book *The People of Great Russia* (1948). "Great Russia" refers to the geographic district within which only the Russian language is spoken. This territory too is enormous, and general statements about its population call for careful and extensive sampling.

2. *Temporal variability*. This term refers both to the *period* of time for which the statement is true and to the *duration* of the swaddling. Swaddling is probably a very ancient custom, but when was it first used? Is it still practiced in postrevolutionary Russia? If not, when was it abandoned, and why? The length of time during which babies were swaddled may also have varied considerably, from a few weeks to more than a year. Different durations might have very different effects on children, and might be consistently related to other types of variability (spatial or intracultural).

3. *Intracultural variability*. Within the specified area (Great Russia) and time period (say, 1850–1920) other types of variation may have existed. Rural-urban differences may be significant, since rural peoples frequently cling to a custom long after it has been modified or abandoned in cities. Social classes also differ with regard to child training, and duration of swaddling may have varied considerably among individual

families. Obviously, establishing the range of variation and the mode for this one practice would require considerable effort and expense. Even if swaddling were found to be rapidly disappearing in Russia, Gorer could maintain that the "message" concerning the need for strong authority is transmitted in many different ways. (Gorer and Rickman 1962:198)

It is also essential to state the kind of *sample* on which a given statement about child rearing is based. Fortunately, we have some fairly detailed data on this topic from the Russian Research Center at Harvard (Kluckhohn 1962:210–243). In a sample of 172 Great Russian defectors, the research staff found only three persons who denied any knowledge of swaddling. It was clear that swaddling was an emotion-laden topic, since the "majority of the subjects manifested some tension or uncomfortableness in this part of the interview" (p. 238). Several of the informants had heard of the Gorer hypothesis and they rejected it with some force! Nevertheless, most of the subjects agreed that swaddling had been practiced in all sectors of Russian society before the revolution, and that it had become less prevalent in the last few generations.

Swaddling is found more frequently in rural than urban areas. Except for a few who defended the practice, almost all of Kluckhohn's informants considered it "old-fashioned" and "not cultured." Reasons given for swaddling included protecting the baby against self-injury and giving strength to the bones. It was also claimed that the swaddled child sleeps longer and more quietly, particularly in nurseries with several infants, and that swaddling makes children easier to handle. (People who rejected the practice spoke of it as unhealthy and a "torture.") The interviews revealed a wide range of reported durations: "The modal figure for the duration of swaddling was three to five months, but a number of informants extended the period to a year and one to a year and a half . . . . Some stated that hands and/or feet were

left free 'after the child could sit up' or 'after eight months'"
(p. 239).

There is, of course, much more to the study of Russian
national character than the swaddling hypothesis. Clinical interviews and psychological testing of large samples showed
the Great Russian modal personality to be "warmly human,
tremendously dependent upon secure social affiliations,
labile [emotionally unstable], nonrational, strong but undis-
ciplined, and needing to submit to authority." However, the
Communist Party sets forth a very different ideal, demanding "stern, ascetic, vigilant, incorruptible, and obedient personalities who will not be deflected from the aims of the
Party and the State by family or personal ties and affections"
(pp. 214–215). According to Kluckhohn, this conflict sets the
stage for a "national character drama" in which a small
ideological elite attempts to remake an entire people to suit
an image that is quite contrary to its traditional personality
type. The conflict is summarized in Table 5-1.

Inkeles has suggested that socialization is always future-
oriented, that is, that parents raise their children in ways that
anticipate the situations that the children will have to face.
Though it is difficult to understand how this process operates, some evidence indicates that at least people at the
"managerial" levels of Russian society are training their children in line with the new Soviet ideal (Inkeles 1967).

Deliberate attempts at socialist character building are also
found in the Russian school system, which emphasizes collective responsibility over individualism. In his excellent book
Two Worlds of Childhood, Urie Bronfenbrenner contrasts the
Russian and American educational systems with special reference to their effects on values and personality structure.
Although the Russian system emphasizes cooperation and
conformity, Bronfenbrenner notes that in the late 1960s
Soviet "upbringing" (*vospitanie*) was showing many signs of
increasing flexibility: "In particular, both within and outside
the family, there is a shift away from features which foster
dependency and conformity, toward new configurations

Table 5-1 Themes in the Russian "National Character Drama" (Adapted from Kluckhohn 1962:241–242)

Traditional Russian Personality	Ideal Soviet Personality Type
"Oral-expressive"	"Anal-compulsive"
Warm, expansive	Formal, controlled, orderly
Trusting, responsive	Distrustful, "conspiratorial"
Identification with primary group—personal loyalty	Loyalty directed upward to superiors—impersonal
Emphasis on "dependent passivity"	Emphasis on "instrumental activity"

more conducive to the emergence of individuality and independence" (1973:94). Bronfenbrenner concludes that

> if the Russians have gone too far in subjecting the child and his peer group to conformity to a single set of values imposed by the adult society, perhaps we [Americans] have reached the point of diminishing returns in allowing excessive autonomy and in failing to utilize the constructive potential of the peer group in developing social responsibility and consideration for others. (p. 170)

THE LONELY CROWD

Americans are inordinately fond of being told what a great (or miserable) people they are, and have made best sellers out of many works on their national character, from Alexis de Tocqueville's *Democracy in America* (1830) to Philip Wylie's *Generation of Vipers* (1946). Here we shall examine a few examples that come out of the Culture and Personality tradition.

Aside from Margaret Mead's World War II morale-booster, *And Keep Your Powder Dry* (1942), the earliest study of American national character is Geoffrey Gorer's *The American People*, published in 1948 and revised in 1964. As a wartime liaison officer between American and British officials, Gorer became convinced that most misunderstandings between the two groups were due to the false assumption that they shared a cultural identity, when England and America had in fact evolved "most strongly contrasting national characters" (Gorer 1964:12). He claims that a distinctive character is found in "a significant number" of Americans, and that these modal characteristics and patterns of behavior have been "influential in molding the institutions in which the whole society lives" (p. 17).

Gorer's book is filled with fascinating insights based on his travel, reading, and interviews with Americans from all walks of life. For example, he maintains that American society is based on a *rejection* of the European ancestry and traditions of its largely immigrant population:

> The individual rejection of the European father as a model and a moral authority, which every second-generation American had to perform, was given significance and emphasis by its similarity to the rejection of England by which America became an independent nation. (p. 27)

Gorer sees this rejection as analogous to Freud's myth of the primal parricide "which establishes the legal equality of the brothers, based on common renunciation of the father's authority and privileges" (p. 29). The themes of *equality* and of *resistance to authority* in American life thus have a deep psychological basis. This insight explains why all persons in positions of power must present themselves as "conspicuously plain citizens, with the interests and mannerisms of their fellows" (p. 40; see also Wills 1971:140–145, on Richard Nixon).

Since respect and awe are highly painful emotions for most Americans, debunking leaders and institutions is a favorite pastime. These attitudes also permeate family life, where "the father is not a model on which the son is expected to mold himself," but rather someone to be surpassed (p. 46). American children, especially males, are "constantly urged toward independence and activity and initiative" (p. 86), while the admiration of other people "becomes essential to the American sense of self-esteem" (p. 108).

Gorer finds in the comic strips, especially *Blondie,* an exaggerated but accurate portrayal of American family life. Dagwood, the untidy, incompetent, greedy, lazy, and easygoing father, is "kind, dutiful, diligent, well-meaning within his limits; but he has so completely given up any claim to authority that the family would constantly risk disintegration and disaster, if it were not for Blondie" (p. 49). The American child, who during the 1930s and early 1940s was fed on a strict time schedule, often grows up with an irrational fear of hunger. This is the unconscious motive for the "great erotic fetishist value given to women's breasts." Gorer believes the addiction of American men to drinking milk probably has "symbolic significance" (pp. 77–78).

Gorer also comments on American attitudes toward love, friendship, youth, machinery, and material acquisitions, skillfully pointing out patterns of behavior that Americans take for granted but that are clearly related to the dominant values of "Americanism." Although his evidence is fragmentary and anecdotal, many statements ring true even thirty years after the first publication of the book. He anticipates the Male Liberation movement in his remark that "the lives of most American men are bounded, and their interests drastically curtailed, by [the] constant necessity to prove to their fellows, and to themselves, that they are not sissies, not homosexuals" (p. 129).

One of the most influential books of the 1950s was *The Lonely Crowd* by David Riesman (written with Nathan Glazer and Reuel Denney and published in 1950). Subtitled "A Study of the Changing American Character," it documents a shift in the modal personality of Americans, using extensive interviews together with sociological surveys and analyses of books and films. Riesman uses three general "modes of conformity" to describe character types:

1. *Tradition-directed.* Most persons in premodern
societies who look to cultural tradition when making
decisions, on the premise that "one must do what the
ancestors did."

2. *Inner-directed.* Persons primarily in developing
societies who listen to their own "inner voice" for guidance, and whose internalized "moral gyroscope" enables them to act effectively in times of rapid change.

3. *Other-directed.* A character type found increasingly in
affluent societies, mainly among the "organization men
in gray flannel suits," but also the consuming public
whose tastes and decisions are determined by what they
think others value.

Much of *The Lonely Crowd* is devoted to describing the
other-directed personality and documenting its rise to dominance in the United States. Inner-directed people are shown
to be out of place in modern bureaucratic-corporate society;
their "moral gyroscopes" have given way to the "psychological radar" of the other-directed, who are constantly scanning
their social environment for cues to the correct ("in") behavior, attitude, or purchase.
Riesman does not glorify either of these character types.
Inner-directed individuals may have been necessary during
the rapid industrial growth of the nineteenth and early
twentieth century, but they were often unfeeling and unre-
sponsive to the needs of others, driving themselves and their
dependents ferociously to achieve distant goals. Other-
directed people, however, seem to be without *any* guiding
principles, easy prey to the advertisers and "image-makers"
of contemporary America, substituting peer approval for
substantive achievement. The inner-directed person conforms as readily as the other-directed person, although the
voices he listens to are "more distant, of an older generation,
their cues internalized in his childhood" (Riesman 1961:31).
Furthermore, "each of us possesses the capacity for each of

the three modes of conformity," and individuals may change from one mode to another during their lifetimes (p. 30).

It must be noted that the three modes of conformity have no real cultural content. Since any mode may be found in any individual in any society, only the degree of dependence on a mode or the frequency of its occurrence vary among groups and over time. Riesman associates each mode of conformity with a particular phase of socioeconomic development; he states in reference to Benedict's *Patterns of Culture* that all of the tribes, "as long as they are in the phase of high population growth potential, would be more or less dependent on tradition-direction" (p. 231). The unique configurations that Ruth Benedict described vanish at this level of analysis.

Riesman asked students who had read Benedict's book which of the societies they felt was most similar to America. (See pp. 69–71, above, and formulate your own answer before reading further.) He was somewhat surprised to discover that

> the great majority see Americans as Kwakiutls. They emphasize American business rivalry, sex and status jealousy, and power drive. They see Americans as individualists, primarily interested in the display of wealth and station.
>
> A minority of students . . . say that America is more like Dobu. They emphasize the sharp practice of American business life, point to great jealousy and bitterness in family relations, and [in politics. However, no students argue] that there are significant resemblances between the culture of the . . . Pueblos and American culture—many wish that there were. (p. 227)

Riesman's own view is quite contrary to that of the students. He feels that the tone of Pueblo life, with its insistence on equality, cooperation, and emotional restraint, is most like "the American peer-group, with its insulting 'You think you're big.'" One of the striking patterns in the interviews with young Americans was that so many considered their *best* trait to be their ability to "get along well with everybody."

The most frequently mentioned *worst* trait was "temper," though it usually turned out that the interviewee did not really have much of a temper! Riesman reports his impression that "temper is considered the worst trait in the society of the glad hand. It is felt as an internal menace to one's cooperative attitudes" (p. 232). (For a different view of the American configuration as compared to the societies studied by Benedict, see Kardiner 1939:115.)

Riesman is, at heart, an apologist for individualism. His solution to the negative aspects of other-directedness is the development of an *autonomous* character structure that would remain sensitive to others and capable of conformity, but that would also be "free to choose whether to conform or not" (p. 242). Is this really possible? On what basis would the autonomous individual make the choice? In what spheres of life? Do the many cultural "alternatives" that our complex culture offers really make "more room for autonomy" (p. 257), or are these alternatives simply the icing on the cake of conformity, like mass-produced consumer items personalized with "your very own initials"?

In a later book, Riesman clearly sounds the individualist's creed: "No ideology, however noble, can justify the sacrifice of an individual to the needs of the group" (1954:27). But Philip Slater has pointed out that this creed is contrary to a basic principle:

> Riesman overlooks the fact that the individual is sacrificed either way. If he never sacrificed to the group the group will collapse and the individual with it. Part of the individual is, after all, committed to the group. Part of him wants what "the group" wants, part does not. No matter what is done some aspect of the individual . . . will be sacrificed.
>
> An individual, like a group, is a motley collection of ambivalent feelings, contradictory needs and values, and antithetical ideas. He is not, and cannot be, a monolithic totality, and the modern effort to bring this myth to life is not only delusional and ridiculous, but also acutely destructive, both to the individual and to his society. (Slater 1970:27)

This quotation is from Slater's seminal book *The Pursuit of Loneliness*—in my opinion one of the most significant recent studies of American culture and character (see also Lifton 1970 and Wills 1971). Written at the height of the Viet Nam War, it is a passionate indictment of the old "scarcity-oriented technological culture," and a call for revolutionary change to a "true counterculture" based on social consciousness and recognition of interdependence. Insightful, humorous, and more realistic than most books on the counterculture, it ranges critically over every aspect of American society, pointing out our enormous ambivalences (for instance, our desire for privacy versus the craving for community). Slater insists that "nothing will change until individualism is assigned a subordinate place in the American value system—for individualism lies at the core of the old culture, and a prepotent individualism is not a viable foundation for any society in a nuclear age" (p. 118).

A different approach to American national character can be found in the work of Francis L. K. Hsu. Born in China, educated there and in England, and for many years a professor in the United States, Hsu has a distinctive view of American culture. His analyses tend to be more critical than those of American-born scholars. He writes of the deep value conflicts in the United States, especially between the official ideology of equality and the actual practice of racial and ethnic discrimination. He also says that "our understanding of American values is today no better than it was several decades ago. Periodically we note the conflicts and inconsistencies among the different elements, but we leave them exactly where we started"(Hsu 1961:212).

Hsu argues that in examining the positive connections among these contradictory values we find that they are actually manifestations of one core value, "*self-reliance,* the most persistent psychological expression of which is the fear of dependence" (p. 217). Self-reliance is similar to individualism but it also implies "the individual's militant insistence on economic, social, and political equality" (p. 217). From this core value Hsu derives both the *resentment of status and authority* noted by Gorer and the *fear of dependence* discussed by Slater. Hsu does not maintain that all Americans are self-reliant, but he does argue that self-reliance is an ideal taught in the home and the school, and that "an individual who is not self-reliant is an object of hostility and called a misfit" (p. 219). In America it is an insult to call someone "dependent," even though each of us is necessarily dependent on others

> intellectually and technologically as well as socially and emotionally. Individuals may have differing degrees of needs for their fellow human beings, but no one can truly say that he needs no one. It seems that the basic American value orientation of self-reliance, by its denial of the importance of other human beings in one's life, creates contradictions and therefore serious problems, the most ubiquitous of which is insecurity. (p. 219)

These inherent contradictions include the fact that successful competition in America today requires the "individualist" to conform to the norms of many organizations and peer groups. "In other words, in order to live up to their core value orientation of self-reliance, Americans as a whole have to do much of its opposite" (pp. 219–220)! Unlike Riesman, Hsu sees contemporary Americans as highly individualistic, but forced to use "other-directed" means to achieve self-reliance. Hsu believes that several other contradictions are causally related rather than accidental. These include the connection of

a) Christian love with religious bigotry.
b) Emphasis on science, progress, and humanitarianism with parochialism, group-superiority themes and racism.
c) Puritan ethics with increasing laxity in sex mores.
d) Democratic ideals of equality and freedom with totalitarian tendencies and witch hunting. (p. 220)

Many anthropologists would agree with Hsu's statement that, in those societies where self-reliance is not a core value, and where obedience to authority and dependence relations are encouraged, individuals "tend to have much less need for competition, status seeking, conformity, and, hence, racial and religious prejudices" (p. 224; see Dumont 1970).

AND ELSEWHERE

Among the other interesting studies of national character is *Themes in French Culture* by Rhoda Métraux and Margaret Mead (1954). The authors stress the role of *orality* in French behavior as well as the importance to the French of intellectual and emotional *control*. They are also concerned with general patterns of the national culture. For example, Métraux and Mead discuss at length the concept of *le foyer*—an "untranslatable" term that connotes the warmth, comfort, and family relationships of the idealized French bourgeois household.

Salvador de Madariaga, in his classic *Englishmen, Frenchmen and Spaniards* (1928), also analyzed "key terms" as a way of comprehending cultural differences. Madariaga contrasts the French emphasis on *thought* with the Spanish stress on *emotion* and the English emphasis on *action*. He suggests that "fair play" is a key term in English culture. An alternative view of English personality is found in Gorer's *Exploring English Character* (1955), which should be read in conjunction with Gorer's *The American People* (1964).

G. Morris Carstairs' *The Twice Born* (1957) is a study of high-caste Hindus in Rajasthan, India. The book is based primarily on psychiatric interviews. Carstairs emphasizes the passive-dependent element of the Hindu personalities, relating it to religious ideology and strong pressures for obedience in early socialization and later family experience. Carstairs presents a good deal of life-history material, and cautions the reader that his conclusions should not be generalized beyond the caste or region for which they are valid. Others have suggested that strong tendencies toward dependency and conformity, and a lack of "initiative" (self-reliance?) are in fact common to much of India's population. Louis Dumont (1970) has even stated that hierarchy and inequality are so fundamental to the social structure of India that humans there should be designated as *Homo hierarchicus* in contrast to the individualistic, achievement-oriented *Homo aequalis* of Western civilization. Erik Erikson (1969) takes up this theme in his psychobiography of Gandhi (to be discussed in Chapter Seven).

Gregory Bateson and Margaret Mead authored an innovative book, *Balinese Character* (1943), in which they used hundreds of still photographs to document Balinese behavior patterns and modes of interaction (including the extraordinary development of postural balance and of trance). They produced a series of films on Balinese childhood, as well as a film in which family life in Bali was compared with that in France, Japan, and Canada. As usual, Mead emphasized the nonverbal learning of values and interaction patterns in her commentary (*Four Families*, National Film Board of Canada).

In a seminal essay written in 1949, Bateson wrote about Balinese culture and character. He claims that, in Bali, rather than being directed to a goal, activity is "valued for itself" (1972:117). Balinese enjoy doing things in large crowds—fortunately so, since the island has the highest population density of any area on earth. Conformity to complex cultural ideals is "aesthetically valued," so that deviants are considered stupid or clumsy rather than immoral. In general, Balinese children learn to avoid any kind of "cumulative interaction" that might build to a climax, and daily life is structured in ways that prevent "competitive interaction." For these reasons, Bateson refers to the society as existing (ideally) in a "steady state" (p. 125).

SUMMARY

We have surveyed the history of the national character approach. Although such studies were made less frequently in psychological anthropology during the 1960s, they have by no means come to an end; they are presently in vogue in political science (see Needler 1971:75–81). My emphasis in this chapter has been on the "findings" of the studies rather than their methods, because the method used was primarily the application of the basic and modal personality techniques to national states. In the Interlude, which follows, I assess the early Culture and Personality approaches, after which I will turn to the cross-cultural correlational approach, the final flowering of the school.

INTERLUDE

The Crisis in Culture and Personality

The year 1950 was an important turning point in the history of psychological anthropology. At about this time, the Culture and Personality school came under serious attack from several different quarters. These criticisms clearly revealed some of the underlying assumptions of the school, and suggested that these assumptions were invalid or at least unproved. As a result, Culture and Personality studies went into a brief decline. Many of the founders of the school were now dead (Sapir, Benedict, and—by 1952—Linton). Some studies of modal personality and national character continued to be produced, but the interests of American anthropologists were changing (see Spindler 1978:3). (The major exception to these statements was the cross-cultural approach, to be discussed in Chapter Six.)

All of the approaches considered in Chapters Three, Four, and Five have both strengths and defects. I have tried to present each of them in terms of its own logic, emphasizing positive accomplishments. Now, however, it is time to consider the errors and weaknesses of the Culture and Personality school and to ask what can be done to correct them.

Five *basic assumptions* are common to all these approaches. Let us consider each of these in turn.

The continuity assumption. This assumption is the notion that early childhood experiences (for instance, nursing, weaning, swaddling, and toilet training) *determine* adult personality. The continuity assumption is relied on to some extent in all Culture and Personality studies, and especially in those influenced by psychoanalysis. Infantile trauma is assumed to produce fixations, anxieties, and neuroses that form the basis of cultural character and institutions.

This assumption was effectively challenged by Harold Orlansky in the important paper "Infant Care and Personality" (1949). Orlansky pointed out that very little evidence really existed to support the assumption that a given pattern of child training necessarily produces a given adult personality. Indeed, different researchers have attributed contradictory effects to identical childhood experiences! Some kinds of early learning are probably important to later behavior, but we have yet to sort out just what is learned in infancy, or to give correct weight to postchildhood experiences.

The proper way to establish continuity between infancy and adulthood is through *longitudinal studies* that follow sets of individuals throughout their lives, starting, if possible, with their prenatal environments. Some such work has been undertaken at Berkeley, Stanford, and the Fels Research Institute, but longitudinal studies are difficult and expensive. For the present we must accept Orlansky's caution that the continuity assumption is still unproved. (See Lomax et al. 1978.)

The uniformity assumption. Virtually all writers on Culture and Personality assume that each society can be characterized in terms of a single (dominant, basic, or modal) personality type. Despite disclaimers in introductory chapters, the idea that a one-to-one correspondence exists between a culture and a personality is persistent. Even in modal personality studies where the diversity of individuals in the sample is apparent, one is usually left with the impression that the "most frequent" type adequately explains the dynamics of the culture.

Yet, as Lindesmith and Strauss pointed out in their "Critique of Culture and Personality Writings" (1950), most anthropological characterizations of typical personalities are "imprecise and oversimplified," tending to ignore variability and to explain away negative evidence. Furthermore, it is disturbing that "the number of questions that are raised concerning any characterization tends to increase with the number of investigators familiar with the society" (Lindesmith and Strauss 1950:589). (A veritable "scandal" erupted in the late 1940s concerning what the Pueblo Indians are "really like." See Bennett 1946.)

Anthony F. C. Wallace reformulated this critique a decade later in his book *Culture and Personality* (1961). He argued that traditional Culture and Personality studies had been primarily concerned with the "replication of uniformity," that is, the process by which each society allegedly produced a new generation of individuals who would perpetuate a static culture and conform to an ideal personality type. Such studies, he suggested, must give way to a greater concern with the "organization of diversity." This concept refers to the way in which "various individuals organize themselves culturally into orderly, expanding, changing societies" (Wallace 1970:23). Just as the individual may use cultural norms for his or her own purposes, all cultures need a variety of personalities—leaders and followers, artists and shamans, warriors and nurses—if they are to survive. Wallace called for an inductive study of the distribution of personality characteristics within different societies. Similarly, after comparing Rorschach protocols from several cultures, Bert Kaplan (1954) suggested that psychological variation is probably greater *within* any society than it is *between* different societies. In view of these criticisms, we must conclude that the uniformity assumption is false.

The causal assumption. As was noted in Chapter Four, a concept such as "basic personality structure" (or "dominant configuration") has the logical status of a hypothetical construct. It is no more *observable* than, say, Freud's "primal horde" or Oedipus complex. Its value (if any) rests in its plausibility: The construct indicates how a variety of observations might make sense *if* the hypothesized basic personality structure were actually shared by the members of a society.

Unfortunately, it is an easy step from formulating such a construct to reifying it into a causal entity. Thus, the anxieties and fantasies that are inferred from cultural institutions are often transformed into the *causes* of certain (secondary) institutions. But when a culture is described by the same persons who formulate the basic personality, fact and interpretation tend to be mixed together. "Psychic entities" that were inferred from overt behavior may later be used to explain that same behavior:

> Whenever it is postulated that a given people have a given trait such as "aggressiveness," "passivity," "withdrawnness," "impulsiveness," as part of their "basic personality structure," it is easy to take the unwarranted step of regarding specific behavior as a manifestation or effect of the given trait. Conclusions of this type are buttressed not so much by evidential proof as by the piling up of illustrations which are unlikely to convince anyone who is not already sold on the underlying ideology. (Lindesmith and Strauss 1950:592)

This whole procedure is circular and scientifically unacceptable. In most cases, the causal assumption is unjustified.

The projective assumption. The emphasis of most Culture and Personality studies on early, indirect learning and on unconscious motives leads to a heavy reliance on projective tests as a means of validating inferences from cultural materials. (Examples include *The People of Alor, Truk: Man in Paradise,* and many national character studies.) The assumption is that projective tests developed and standardized in one society can be used elsewhere with only minor modifications in content, scoring, or interpretation.

Lindesmith and Strauss objected that the use of projective tests in non-Western societies suggests "an illusory precision," especially if the usual statistical safeguards are not employed. In any case, test results "are not self-explanatory, but must . . . be interpreted like other data," and interpretation of the Rorschach is "a matter of controversy" even within Western cultures (Lindesmith and Strauss 1950:593).

Several authors reviewed the use of projective tests in anthropology during the 1950s (for example, Henry and Spiro 1953). The most pessimistic of these was Bert Kaplan, who wrote:

> I have looked for the positive values in these tests and found them very scant. I have looked at the difficulties in their use and found them to be enormous, and have concluded that as these tests are being used and interpreted at present, only a modicum of validity and value can be obtained from them. (Kaplan 1961:252)

Although projective tests have a place within modern psychological anthropology (LeVine 1973:173–202), as a general principle the projective assumption is invalid.

The objectivity assumption. This term refers to the implicit claim that anthropologists can take an objective view of alien peoples and, either directly or "at a distance," describe their psychological characteristics as well as their cultural patterns. Yet, as Lindesmith and Strauss suggested, "Western biases must inevitably find expression in the inferences made about the psychological characteristics of a given people" (1950:593). National character studies initiated during wartime are particularly vulnerable to criticism; in retrospect, characterizations of Germans and Japanese appear to have been biased by the historical situation, as were later Cold War descriptions of Russian character and mentality.

It is hoped that anthropologists were never quite as biased as the psychiatrist J. C. Carothers, who once wrote:

> The native African in his culture is remarkably like the lobotomized Western European and in some ways like the

traditional psychopath in his inability to see individual acts as part of a whole situation, in his frenzied anxiety and in the relative lack of mental ills. (quoted in Hsu 1961:49)

But anthropologists are *not* free of prejudice and racism just by virtue of their profession. When Francis L. K. Hsu (1973) pointed out the intellectual effects of prejudice in American anthropology, his article was met by an embarrassed silence. Until psychological anthropologists can demonstrate greater independence from political and emotional prejudice, the objectivity assumption will remain highly questionable.

Perhaps the most general criticism came from within the Culture and Personality school itself. Melford E. Spiro (a student of Hallowell's) published a long article in *Psychiatry* called "Culture and Personality: The Natural History of a False Dichotomy" (1951). In it he argued that the school had failed to clarify its two central concepts, and that most Culture and Personality work was necessarily *circular,* because "the development of personality and the acquisition of culture are one and the same process" (p. 31). Instead of seeking causal relationships between personality and culture, we should try to overcome the "false dichotomy" that separates them into mutually exclusive categories.

We are quite close here to the configurationalist notion of isomorphism, but Spiro is pointing in a somewhat different direction. He insists that *social interaction* is the process uniting individual with cultural phenomena. The existence of a "cultural heritage" is a necessary prerequisite for the emergence of a new human personality, but as a result of interaction with parents and other enculturated persons, "the culture of any individual is incorporated within his personality" (p. 43). One may analytically separate culture from personality (as did Spiro in his later works), and study patterns of interaction apart from the subjective meanings that individuals develop as a consequence of their interactions. But if we regard culture and personality as aspects of the same learning process, simplistic causal models do not make sense.

Table I-1 Basic Conceptions of Culture-Personality Relations
(After LeVine 1973:59)

Position	Formula	Approaches and Leading Figures
Psychological reductionism	$P \rightarrow C$	Orthodox psychoanalysis (Freud, Róheim); social motivation (McClelland)
Personality *is* culture	$P = C$	Configurationalism (Benedict, Mead, Gorer)
Anticulture and personality	$C \rightarrow P$	Cultural determinism (White); materialism (Marx); symbolic interactionism (Goffman)
Personality mediation	$C_1 \rightarrow P \rightarrow C_2$	Basic personality (Kardiner); modal personality (DuBois); cross-cultural correlations (Whiting and Child)
Interaction ("two systems")	$P \longleftrightarrow C$	Psychocultural adaptation (Spiro, Edgerton); congruence (Inkeles); Neo-Freudian (Erikson, Fromm)

QUO VADIS?

The ways in which different approaches have characterized the relationship between culture and personality are summarized in Table I-1. For this table, I have borrowed a notation developed by Robert LeVine in his excellent (but highly technical) book *Culture, Behavior, and Personality* (1973). Culture (C) may be viewed as caused by psychological states, motives, or complexes (P→C); or the two may be considered virtually identical (P = C). In some approaches, personality is considered to be completely determined by cultural or social-structural conditions (C→P). In others, personality is viewed as *mediating* between different parts of a culture, integrating its customs and institutions (C_1→P→C_2). Finally, in one view, personality systems *interact* with sociocultural systems, and relative stability is attained only when psychological needs and social demands are "congruent" (P⟷C).

As we shall see, most of the approaches developed during the next twenty-five years can still be classified in one of these five categories. But after 1950, it was clear that changes had to be made if psychological anthropology was to continue as a scientific discipline. New methods for the systematic observation of interaction and for cross-cultural comparisons were already being developed. After a brief lull, increasing awareness of the importance of biological, ecological, situational, and linguistic determinants of behavior combined to give renewed vigor to the field. Today, psychological anthropology is alive and well, but the basic assumptions of the Culture and Personality school are no longer unquestioned.

Erik Erikson

SIX

Cross-Cultural
Correlations

As we have seen, the Culture and Personality school had reached a crisis by 1950. Its fundamental assumptions, methods, and findings were under attack from several directions. Meanwhile, at Yale University, an alternative approach had been developing. Although progress was interrupted by World War II, this new perspective was to become one of the two dominant approaches in psychological anthropology during the 1950s, and it is still influential today. The *cross-cultural correlational approach* was a product of interaction between psychologists and anthropologists at the Yale Institute of Human Relations, principally Clark Hull, John Dollard, G. P. Murdock, and John Whiting.

THE YALE SYNTHESIS

In retrospect, Yale University seems the only place in the country where this particular synthesis of ideas and skills could have occurred. As you may recall, in 1931 Edward

Sapir had come to Yale, where he began a series of seminars to study the impact of culture on personality (1932–1933). The Institute of Human Relations was established in part to continue the research Sapir had stimulated. The leading psychologist at Yale was then Clark L. Hull, whose systematic theory of learning had enormous influence in American psychology (Hull 1943). John Dollard was instrumental in applying the behavior theories of Hull to human social learning. In *Frustration and Aggression* (Dollard et al. 1939) and *Social Learning and Imitation* (Miller and Dollard 1941), he showed how Hull's laboratory analysis of *habit* could be extended to complex human behavior.

Dollard was also a psychotherapist, and he wished to integrate Freudian insights into general learning theory. This goal was achieved in *Personality and Psychotherapy* (Dollard and Miller 1950), an elaborate translation of Freudian concepts and mechanisms into the vocabulary of Hull's learning theory. In this book, Dollard's clinical experience was combined with the careful experimental approach of Neil Miller to give scientific respectability to Freudian concepts.

Another key figure in the "Yale synthesis" was George Peter Murdock, an anthropologist with extensive background in sociology and an encyclopedic knowledge of world ethnography. Murdock carried out research on North America, the Pacific, and Africa, and probably knew more facts about more different societies than any other single person. His approach to many anthropological problems rested on worldwide comparisons of technological and social systems. It was Murdock who, at Yale, established the Human Relations Area Files (HRAF), a research device that makes available data on hundreds of societies, indexed and cross-listed under dozens of specific topics. (Originally bulky and stored only at Yale and a few other places, the files have since been duplicated on microfilm and are available in most major university libraries.) Together with Clellan S. Ford, Murdock developed analytical methods for testing hypotheses about functional relationships using cross-cultural data from the HRAF. Murdock's *Social Structure* was the first major study to use these methods to investigate kinship, residence, and sexual relationships.

During the late 1930s, John W. M. Whiting was a graduate student at Yale, where he was strongly influenced by Dollard and Murdock. Whiting became convinced that anthropology lacked an adequate theory of how culture was learned and that anthropologists had failed to gather the kinds of data on which a theory of socialization could be tested. His field research (1936–1937) among the Kwoma, a tribe in Australian New Guinea, aimed at providing some of the necessary data.

In preparation for his fieldwork, Whiting underwent a brief psychoanalysis, but he did not actually study formal learning theory until he had completed his dissertation. After studying with Hull, Miller, and Otto H. Mowrer, he reanalyzed his Kwoma data; the resulting book, *Becoming a Kwoma* (1941), is in two parts. In the first chapters, Kwoma culture is described as it affects individuals from infancy to adulthood. In the second part, the various "techniques of teaching" Whiting observed in the Kwoma village are examined and discussed in terms of the drives, cues, and rewards identified in Hullian theory (as modified by Dollard and Miller). A final chapter, dealing with the "inculcation of supernatural beliefs," asks how Kwoma children come to share certain "unrealistic" notions about spirits, sorcery, and taboos and why these beliefs are not "extinguished" by later experience.

The data in Part One of Whiting's book are rich in individual examples, but the theoretical interpretations in Part Two, while often interesting, have a *post hoc* quality. For example, here is one of the explanations of avoidance learning:

> During childhood a Kwoma boy learns to avoid the house tamberan while ceremonies are being held. The drive in this case is anxiety (he is warned that he would die if he did so); the response is avoiding the house tamberan; the cues are the sound of the gong rhythms, the statements of others that a

ceremony is being held, the sight of his father, *uncles,* and older *brothers* [classificatory] decorating themselves; the reward is escape from anxiety. (Whiting 1941:176)

Whiting published his book on the Kwoma in the hope "that this pioneering attempt will suggest methods of gaining a better understanding of the process of socialization" (p. xix). When he returned to Yale following World War II, he tried to apply Murdock's cross-cultural methods to the study of socialization. This approach seemed to offer a solution to the crisis in Culture and Personality studies. If cross-cultural data could be used to test hypotheses about the relationship between child training and adult personality, it might be possible to validate the continuity assumption (see Interlude) and to decide between equally plausible theories of causation. Working with the psychologist Irvin L. Child, Whiting set out to formulate hypotheses in learning-theory terms that would be testable using data from the HRAF. In 1953, Whiting and Child's book *Child Training and Personality* appeared, setting forth a new paradigm for research. Let us examine this landmark work in some detail.

Early in the book, Whiting and Child acknowledge the crisis in Culture and Personality. They state that configurational and national character studies are often interesting attempts at "coherent interpretations" of single societies, but that such studies are inherently unable to validate their hypotheses (assumptions). For instance, although Margaret Mead's study of Samoa presents evidence that emotional disturbances are not a necessary accompaniment to adolescence, her eclectic methods are not suited to testing more specific ideas. Kardiner believed that his BPS approach constituted a test of Freudian hypotheses, but Whiting and Child suggest that "publications like his seem rather to *use* hypotheses, of whose validity the author has little doubt, as conceptual devices in the interpretation of specific case materials" (Whiting and Child 1953:7; italics added).

The authors then state their own ideas of what constitutes "an adequate test of a scientific hypothesis" (p. 8). The hypothesis must be in the form of a statement relating two events, one an "antecedent," the other a "consequent." These events must be isolated from other conditions, and observations must be made to determine if, in a suitable sample of independent cases, the consequent consistently follows (or accompanies) the antecedent. Evidence for the connection should be *objective* in the sense that other investigators following the same procedures will arrive at the same results.

The ideal way of testing scientific hypotheses is the *experimental method.* It allows the investigator to control the "other conditions," and repeatedly to verify the consequents of a given set of antecedents. Ethnologists are seldom able to use a truly experimental approach, so they compromise by using other, less well-controlled methods. Among these is the *correlational method,* used in anthropology since the time of Sir Edward Tylor (1889), and developed by Murdock, but not previously applied to culture and personality. According to Whiting and Child,

> In the correlational testing method the supposed antecedent condition is looked for as it occurs or fails to occur in the natural course of events in a number of cases. Instances are collected of its presence and its absence, or of its presence in various degrees. The supposed consequent condition is also looked for in each of these cases and determined to be present or absent, or present in a given degree. It is then possible to determine whether there is a consistent relation between the two, and thus whether the hypothesis is confirmed or negated. Statistical techniques may be applied [and the] evidence of connection may be based entirely on objective procedures which are repeatable. (p. 10)

CORRELATIONS AND CUSTOMS

Put another way, the correlational method requires a kind of "trait list" (see Chapter Three) showing which of the events are present (+) or absent (−) in a suitable sample of societies (Table 6-1). A trait list such as that in Table 6-1 can easily be

Table 6-1   Trait List for Two Customs in Ten Societies

Customs	*Societies*									
	1	*2*	*3*	*4*	*5*	*6*	*7*	*8*	*9*	*10*
A	+	+	−	+	−	−	+	−	+	−
B	+	−	−	+	+	−	−	−	+	−

transformed into a figure called a *two-by-two correlation display*, showing the association between customs A and B (Figure 6-1). When we enter each society into the appropriate cell of the figure, as in Figure 6-2, we find that customs A and B "go together" in three societies, and that in the remaining cases A is found twice without B, and B occurs once without A. Both customs are absent in four cases. This sample is too small to have any significance, but a slight positive association is exhibited between the two traits; A and B "go together" in enough cases that one might wish to investigate their association in a larger sample. Let us imagine that we have a sample of one hundred societies and have gathered valid information on the presence or absence of traits A and B in each. A and B could be material items (pottery containers or iron tools), social institutions (patrilineal descent groups, divine kings), or quite specific "customs" (puberty rites for girls, belief in ancestral ghosts, and the like). The possible kinds of two-by-two tables, whatever the trait selected, are shown in Figures 6-3 through 6-6.

What do each of these tables indicate about the relation between A and B? Figure 6-3 is an ideal demonstration of a purely *chance association;* that is, whether trait A is present or absent seems to have no effect on the presence or absence of trait B, and vice versa. The correlation is *zero*, and even slight departures from this equal distribution of cases among the four cells would make no difference. Since each combination of traits is equally likely, the *null hypothesis* (that there is merely a chance association between A and B) is strongly

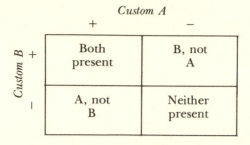

Figure 6-1 The format of a "two-by-two" correlation display.

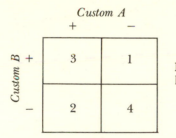

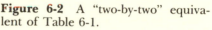

Figure 6-2 A "two-by-two" equivalent of Table 6-1.

supported. (Any textbook in elementary statistics will explain these ideas more fully.)

Figure 6-4 is an ideal example of a very strong association between A and B: Whenever one is present, so is the other, and whenever one is absent, so is the other. This is called a *perfect positive correlation* (+1.00), and is usually found only in cases where A and B are actually aspects of the same trait complex (for example, harpoon heads and shafts) or where they are both effects of some third factor. Even if a few societies were recorded in the +A, −B and −A, +B cells, the large number of cases in the "Both" and "Neither" cells would produce a statistically significant positive correlation. This kind of result both rejects the null hypothesis ("just chance") and lends support to hypotheses that predict the association.

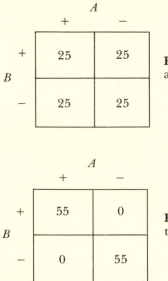

Figure 6-3 Zero correlation (chance association).

Figure 6-4 Perfect positive correlation.

Figure 6-5, with most of the cases in the +A, −B and −A, +B cells, shows a *strong negative correlation* (about −0.85). A and B are almost mutually exclusive of one another. With only eight exceptions, whenever A is present, B is absent, and vice versa. Such negative correlations can be as important as the positive ones; they enable us to reject the null hypothesis, and they lend support to hypotheses that predict this kind of negative relationship.

Figure 6-6 shows a more typical result of a correlational study. The majority of the cases (66 out of 100) are in the "Both" or "Neither" cells, indicating a positive correlation; however, more than a third fall into the other cells. Here we need a criterion to tell us whether, for a sample of this size (N = 100), there is a significant departure from the null hypothesis of no association. The methods used to evaluate such cases need not concern us here. It is important to remember that a correlation, no matter how significant, shows

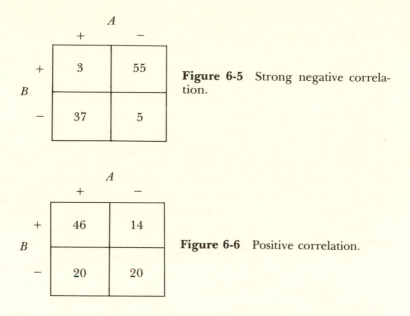

Figure 6-5 Strong negative correlation.

Figure 6-6 Positive correlation.

only the association between traits, and does not in itself prove anything about a *causal relationship*. Even a perfect positive correlation, such as that shown in Figure 6-4, does not indicate whether A caused B, B caused A, or some third factor caused both. A good theory would provide hypotheses that reliably distinguished antecedent from consequent events and predicted associations, both positive and negative.

In *Child Training and Personality*, the authors' hypotheses derive from Freudian theory, restated in behavioral terms. The "traits" that Whiting and Child wish to correlate are customs of two kinds: child-training practices (C_1) and beliefs concerning the causes of illness (C_2). In this approach, child and adult personalities are hypothetical constructs that mediate between two parts of a culture, represented in the formula:

$$C_1 \longrightarrow \text{Child} \longrightarrow \text{Adult} \longrightarrow C_2$$
$$\text{personality} \quad \text{personality}$$

It should be obvious that this is a version of Kardiner's basic personality approach (Chapter Four), in which child-training practices and other primary institutions are related to belief systems and other secondary institutions via basic personality dynamics. Like Kardiner, Whiting and Child present no data on individual children or adults; rather, they examine two kinds of cultural data as reported in ethnographies. From the association between customs in a sample of societies, they infer support for their hypotheses regarding the mediating personality type. As with BPS, the logic of this approach assumes that similar childhood experiences will produce similar unconscious fixations and conflicts in a population (the continuity assumption; see Interlude). These neurotic tendencies should be clearly expressed in the society's beliefs about illness because, in the absence of scientific medicine, folk beliefs are largely projections of shared anxieties.

Whiting and Child divide child-training customs into five universal *systems of behavior:* "oral, anal, sexual, dependence, and aggression—on the assumption that these systems would occur and be subject to socialization in all societies" (p. 54). Children are assumed to derive *initial satisfaction* and/or to develop *socialization anxiety* in each of these behavior systems depending on how (and for how long) their society indulges and/or restricts particular types of behavior. For example, "high oral indulgence" occurs when infants are constantly near their mothers and are nursed whenever hungry or unhappy. Early and/or severe weaning customs are assumed to produce a high degree of "oral socialization anxiety" (especially after a period of initial indulgence). High oral anxiety is hypothesized to produce adult beliefs that illness results from oral behavior: "It must have been something you ate or said or someone else said." (The belief that a magical spell causes illness is also considered an "oral explanation.")

Customs that might create oral socialization anxiety in childhood are expected to correlate with oral explanations of illness in the adult culture. A similar explanation has also been offered for the presence of food taboos in a society (Ayres 1967). Traumatic toilet training (anal), modesty discipline (sexual), or severe socialization with regard to dependency or aggression are each assumed to produce characteristic forms of anxiety that should be projected in distinctive explanations of illness. Extreme concern with cleanliness, masturbation, disobedience, or anger as causes of disease are indicative of anal, sexual, dependence, or aggression anxiety, respectively.

Whiting and Child base their contention that socialization practices are connected with specific types of anxiety on a combination of Freudian and behavioral theory. Positive correlations between a given type of anxiety-producing socialization custom and the same type of explanation for illness would support the hypotheses. In their sample of thirty-nine societies, one association is positive and highly significant: Oral socialization anxiety (inferred from age and severity of weaning) is strongly correlated with oral explanations of illness (see Figure 6-7).

This is the most impressive finding in the entire book. Other associations are much weaker, ranging down to a *zero correlation,* shown in Figure 6-8, between sexual socialization anxiety and sexual explanations of illness (beliefs that disease is due to improper sexual behavior or contact with "sexual excretions" including menstrual blood).

A crucial question still must be asked: What do the numbers in these tables actually mean? Who *decided* whether the Arapesh or the Chagga had customs that would produce anal socialization anxiety, or if the Siriono had "sexual explanations" of illness? Following procedures developed in social and clinical psychology, Whiting and Child used *independent judges* to evaluate the ethnographic evidence. They chose this method to insure that judges would not know what hypotheses were being tested, and also because the volume of materials to be considered (from the HRAF and other sources) was enormous. Five persons (professionals and graduate students) made literally thousands of judg-

Oral anxiety	*Oral explanations* Present	Absent
High	17	3
Low	6	13

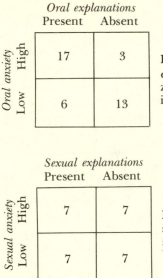

Figure 6-7 Correlation between oral explanations of illness and oral socialization anxiety. N = 39. (After Whiting and Child 1953:156.)

Sexual anxiety	*Sexual explanations* Present	Absent
High	7	7
Low	7	7

Figure 6-8 Zero correlation between sexual explanations of illness and socialization anxiety. N = 28. (After Whiting and Child 1953:159.)

ments, rating each society on dozens of customs, ranking relative amounts of indulgence or severity of restrictions, and evaluating their own confidence in the judgments. Agreement among the five judges was reasonably good, for Whiting and Child provided explicit criteria and eliminated cases for which good data were unavailable or for which the judges lacked confidence in their ratings. Thus, in Figure 6-7, the number 17 in the "Both Present" cell indicates the number of societies for which the judges agreed that oral explanations of illness *and* customs likely to produce oral anxiety were both present. In the book, exact ratings are usually presented for each society, but no consideration is given to spatial, temporal, or intracultural variability (see pp. 116–117, above).

Child Training and Personality contains much more material than I have indicated. Sophisticated discussions of methodology, including statistical techniques, appear, along with excellent chapters on positive and negative fixation, the "Origins of Guilt" (beliefs about the patient's responsibility for his or her own illness), and "Origins of the Fear of Others" (various "unrealistic" beliefs in ghosts and spirits). (For his earliest discussion of the latter issue, see Whiting 1941:Chap. 8; also Spiro and D'Andrade 1958 for a cross-cultural study of the relationship between child-training customs and adult beliefs in friendly versus hostile spirits.)

GALTON'S PROBLEM

One annoying problem (acknowledged by the authors) is that some correlations might be due to historical connections among societies in the sample rather than to the hypothesized relationship between child training and adult culture. As Francis Galton recognized nearly a hundred years ago, correlations lose their significance if the cases are not *independent* of one another. For example, two of the twenty-three societies rated as having oral explanations of illness are the Navajo and the Chiricahua Apache. Since these two societies are known to be closely related historically (speaking similar languages and having quite similar cultures), should they be counted as two cases or as one? Some anthropologists (Melvin Ember, for example) feel that this is a false problem, because social conditions must be right for a custom to be adopted or retained. Still, lengthy controversy has ensued over "Galton's problem," and several techniques are now used to select samples that contain a minimum of historically related cases (see, for example, Naroll and Cohen 1970, Chap. 47). A brief example may sensitize the student to the dimensions of this problem.

In 1962, R. W. Shirley and A. K. Romney published a brief cross-cultural study, "Love Magic and Socialization Anxiety." They followed the correlational method, using Whiting and Child's 1953 ratings of sexual socialization anxiety. Shirley and Romney's hypothesis is as follows: If the child-training practices of a society produce individuals with a high level of sexual anxiety, adults might then be expected to use love magic as a means of reducing their sexual anxiety. This is a plausible idea, for it has long been recognized that one function of magic is to reduce anxiety and give people confidence in risky undertakings (Malinowski 1955).

Shirley and Romney never define what they mean by "love magic," but presumably the term covers the use of verbal spells and magical substances to gain the affection of persons of the opposite sex. The authors found a significant, positive correlation between high ratings on sexual socialization anxiety and the presence of such customs. Unfortunately, a strong *geographic bias* exists in their sample, which casts doubt upon their conclusions. This bias can be seen in Figure 6-9, where presence or absence of love magic (as the authors judged it) is shown to be correlated with major culture areas.

In the sample of 39 societies, 26 were judged to have love magic while 13 were not. Of the 26 with love magic, 22 are located in North or South America, Africa, or Melanesia (an area of the Pacific including New Guinea and nearby islands); of the 13 societies without love magic, only 3 are located in these geographic areas (Bock 1967:213). What is the significance of this distribution? While it is still plausible that societies with high sexual anxiety make use of love magic to reduce that anxiety, the geographic bias in this sample cannot be ignored. The correlation between love magic and geographic area is actually *higher* than that between love magic and child-training practices! (See Driver 1966.)

Another question remains: Why do people in different societies raise their children so differently? This question troubled many people using the cross-cultural approach. After his move to Harvard, where he established the Laboratory of Human Development in the mid-1950s, Whiting began to extend his investigations into the determinants of child-training patterns. He sought an explanation for these "primary institutions" in the environmental adaptations of

	Love magic Present	Love magic Absent
Americas, Africa, or Melanesia	22	3
Other geographic areas	4	10

Location

Figure 6-9 Correlation between "love magic" and geographic areas. N = 39. (Data from Shirley and Romney 1962.)

different societies (cf. Kardiner 1945). This work eventually led to a much more comprehensive theory, in which the "test case" was the widespread custom of male initiation rites.

MALE INITIATION RITES

Many (but not all) primitive societies carry out puberty rituals for young boys. Whiting and his coworkers wanted to understand why some societies have these customs while others do not, and why the rites range from brief, simple ceremonies to long, elaborate rituals involving isolation, taboos, painful hazing, and genital operations such as circumcision. Most native explanations of the rituals refer to the need to "make boys into men," and many involve symbolism of death and rebirth. What are the psychological motives for carrying out such "bizarre" and bloody rites?

Applying the logic that he and Child had developed in *Child Training and Personality,* Whiting reasoned that certain customs of childhood might produce in young boys such a strong identification with their mothers that traumatic rituals would be psychologically necessary to "make men of them." If the same childhood customs generate hostility between father and son, the fathers might act out their sadistic re-

venge through circumcision—a symbolic castration in good
Oedipal fashion! Antecedent customs that might produce
these consequences were

1. Exclusive mother–child sleeping arrangements, in
which the mother and nursing infant share the same
bed for an extended period of time.

2. Lengthy postpartum sex taboos, which forbid the
father of a young child to have intercourse with the
mother for a period of one year or longer.

These two customs were associated in many societies; Whiting hypothesized that they would create both a strong maternal identification in the boy and the likelihood of hostility
between father and son. Correlational analysis indicated
that, especially in societies where both customs were present
and of long duration, the performance of elaborate and painful initiation rites at puberty was highly likely (Whiting, Kluckhohn, and Anthony 1958). Thus, the authors explained the
rites "psychogenically"—showing that these rituals helped
to resolve an Oedipus complex that had been made especially severe by specific child-training practices. (Compare
Stephens 1962; Cohen 1964.)

Why do some societies have such sleeping arrangements
and postpartum taboos to begin with? Here, Whiting in-
voked the notion of environmental adaptation. He was able
to show that these customs were most prevalent in tropical
areas where infants' diets would be deficient in essential pro-
teins unless they were allowed to nurse for several years
(Whiting 1964). The causal chain was thus extended back to
environmental conditions. The full argument took the following form: In environments where long nursing is necessary to prevent protein deficiency, children will tend to sleep
with their mothers and a long postpartum sex taboo will develop to guard against premature pregnancy. In such
societies, boys develop strong emotional relations (identification) with their mothers, which could lead to an incestuous
attachment to the mother and a hostile rivalry with the

father unless steps were taken to prevent these results. Puberty rites involving painful hazing, isolation from women, trials of manliness, and genital operations appear to be "effective means" for preventing conflict and incest.

This argument did not go unchallenged. Frank W. Young (1965) responded that Whiting had overlooked the ways in which puberty rites function to dramatize male solidarity. J.-F. Saucier demonstrated that long postpartum taboos correlated with a variety of technological traits and social customs, suggesting that this onerous taboo can be maintained only in specific types of communities (Saucier 1972:263). (For a lively if somewhat rambling discussion of recent views, see Brain 1977.)

More important than the solution to the initiation-rite problem, I feel, is the image of man and culture implied by the correlational approach. Ruth Benedict's conception of cultures as integrated wholes analogous to individual personalities was surely overstated, resulting in highly simplified characterizations. On the other hand, the opposite danger of cultural atomism accompanies the correlational approach. The old trait list has returned, with cultures represented by a series of pluses and minuses, or ratings on a ten-point scale. The names of the societies in correlational studies are frequently omitted from tables, and their geographic locations ignored. Hypotheses and uncertain ratings from one study tend to turn up as established facts in later studies, and correlations are often erroneously interpreted as proof of causation. And, as in basic personality structure studies, no data are presented on individuals.

I am not arguing against determinism, but I do oppose simplistic notions of causation. Correlations are always open to alternative explanations. Ingenious ways may be found to explain cases that do not fit the original hypothesis, and a strong temptation also exists to adjust one's hypothesis after the data are in to give an impression of accuracy (Bock 1967:217). Moreover, reducing a society to a single set of ratings leads to neglect of intracultural variability, and this is

one form of the uniformity assumption. When the investigators themselves perform the ratings, the objectivity of the
correlational method is called into question.

Despite these caveats, the correlational method can be a
powerful tool for generating hypotheses. In the hands of
knowledgeable and responsible investigators such as Whiting
or John M. Roberts, it can lead to fascinating findings. As the
HRAF was expanded to cover more than three hundred
societies, larger and better samples could be drawn (see
Murdock 1957). More suitable statistical techniques were developed and replications of a few important studies were
attempted. Large samples do not solve all problems, however, for the *quality* of ethnographic data on many issues is
highly variable. One solution to this dilemma would be to
study only a few societies, but intensively and at first hand
(see Chapter Nine on the Six Cultures project). Alterna-
tively, one might work with existing data from a few particularly well-documented cases. An example of this approach is
Robin Fox's cross-cultural study of *sibling incest*.

BROTHERLY LOVE

Incest taboos have long interested anthropologists and psychologists. Among the theories suggested to account for the
widespread prohibition on intercourse between brother and
sister are those of Edward Westermarck and Sigmund
Freud. Westermarck, a sociologist and anthropologist, believed that the experience of being raised together produced
natural aversion to sexual contact between brother and sister.
He thought that the taboos were an expression of this aversion. Thus his theory can be summed up in the formula:

Childhood nearness ⟶ Natural aversion ⟶ Taboos

Freud, as you may recall, traces all taboos to unconscious
emotional ambivalence (Chapter Two). Pointing out that one

does not need taboos (or laws) against actions that people do not want to perform, he insists that family members are the earliest objects of erotic desire. The reason that incest is regarded with such "horror" and punished so severely is that all members of a society have had to *repress* these forbidden wishes. Thus, his theory can be summarized as

Strong unconscious desire ———→ Severe taboos

How can we decide between these two theories? Freud's point about not needing taboos against undesired behavior is certainly valid. Yet many people say, without any trace of conflict, that they are simply "uninterested" in their sisters, or brothers, as erotic objects. Furthermore, while some societies show extreme punitive reactions to the act (or even the suggestion) of sibling incest, other societies show little concern with this offense: People deny in a matter-of-fact way that it occurs very often, and offenders may be punished only with mild ridicule. Indeed, in several societies (ancient Egypt, Hawaii), brother–sister *marriage* was the approved form, at least for the upper class.

In an exemplary small-sample cross-cultural study, Robin Fox (1962) suggested that the theories of Westermarck and Freud are not really incompatible. Together they provide a framework for understanding cultural variation in the intensity of incest taboos. Different types of childhood experience could lead to quite different psychological reactions. The "Westermarck effect" is found in societies where siblings are raised in close physical contact: The "natural aversion" is *learned* as a result of the necessary frustration produced by unconsummated sexual experience between young siblings. Placing the two theories together, we are led to ask what kind of childhood experience might give rise to strong incestuous desires predicted by Freud?

Westermarck: Nearness→Learned aversion→(Mild) Taboos

Freud: ???   → Strong desire→Severe taboos

If childhood *nearness* produces a learned aversion to incest, Fox reasons, perhaps childhood *separation* gives rise to strong desires. Cultures that keep brother and sister apart do not permit the natural aversion to develop and thus defeat their own purposes. Especially when alternative erotic objects are absent, Fox reasoned, early separation of siblings could lead to an emotional ambivalence that produces both a "horror of incest" and severe, punitive taboos.

The seven societies that Fox selected for comparison include four cases of a nearly pure "Westermarck effect," two examples of the Freudian dynamic, and one intermediate case. The most interesting is the Israeli kibbutz' described by Spiro (1958). Here children are raised in coeducational communal nurseries with much physical contact and no prohibitions on sex play. Yet at puberty, members of these peer groups (which include siblings) show no sexual interest in one another. They impose a kind of incest taboo *upon themselves* and seek mates outside the community. A typical comment is that "you can't love someone you sat on the potty with." Arthur Wolf (1970) reported similar findings from his research on extended families in Taiwan.

At the other extreme is a traditional Apache society, where brothers and sisters, although raised together in isolated households, were forbidden to have physical or even verbal contact from about the age of six. Here we find an extreme "horror of incest" with strong taboos and severe punishment: Offenders were considered to be witches and were sometimes burned alive. This case seems to combine a maximum of temptation with a minimum of alternatives, leading to a strong "Freudian effect." A similar situation is found in the Trobriand Islands, where, Malinowski reported, the sister is "the centre of all that is forbidden." The African Tallensi and Pondo are more examples of the Westermarck effect, as are the Mountain Arapesh. An intermediate example occurs on the island of Tikopia, where intimacy between adult siblings leads to temptation (shown in dreams) and occasional acting out. (Offenders, if caught, are expected to commit suicide.)

The advantage of a small-sample approach is that each case can be considered in some detail and the context of various customs specified. Seven cases are too few to be evaluated by statistical tests, but Fox's article is more convincing than many studies using a hundred or more cases. He concludes that the *"intensity of heterosexual attraction between co-socialized children after puberty is inversely proportionate to the intensity of heterosexual activity between them before puberty"* (Fox 1962:147). There is nothing to stop us from testing this hypothesis on a large sample or from seeking individual clinical data that might confirm or refute it.

Fox adds some intriguing speculations to his findings. For example, if the concept of "learned aversion" is accurate, it may explain why father–daughter incest is empirically much more frequent than mother–son incest. In most societies, fathers have much less physical contact with young children than do mothers. Thus, learned aversion is more likely to develop between mother and son than father and daughter. Since the amount of interaction between brother and sister is highly variable, we would expect to find sibling reactions to incest ranging from "unthinkable" to "strong desire" (Fox 1962:148).

Finally, an interesting series of studies relate aspects of early childhood experience and nutrition to physiological and motor development. Animal experiments have shown that rats who are exposed to stress early in life (rough handling or electric shocks) grow to be longer and heavier than unstressed rats. Few people would advocate deliberately shocking human babies to see if they grow taller, but the cross-cultural method makes it possible to test such a hypothesis, and—surprisingly—the results are positive:

> In societies in which infants experience immediate postnatal separation from the mother or are tattooed, scarified, or bathed daily in scalding water, adult height is greater. The average height of adult males in the infant-stressed societies exceeds that in societies without these customs by more than two inches. The association between stress and height was statistically independent of other factors that might be

thought to influence stature, including race, climate, mode of subsistence, and estimated diet. (Munroe and Munroe 1975:34)

SUMMARY

Despite all its faults, the cross-cultural method will probably continue to be used in psychological anthropology because it enables us to test hypotheses that contain both cultural and psychological variables. Experimenters should insist, however, that their samples (large or small) contain only cases for which high-quality, comparable data are available. Whether the goal of such studies is to understand causal relationships or simply to identify areas for further research, it is important to avoid biased samples and unanalyzed assumptions.

Most cross-cultural research uses data from existing ethnographic monographs but, as we shall see in Chapter Nine, it is also possible to gather quantitative data by first-hand investigations of a number of selected societies. The next chapter, though, deals with some important developments in Psychoanalytic Anthropology since the death of Freud, and asks whether these ideas can help in overcoming the crisis in Culture and Personality research.

Bruno Bettelheim

SEVEN

The Return
of the Repressed

In Freudian parlance, "the return of the repressed" refers to the tendency for repressed psychic materials to crop up later in the life of an individual (or a society). Oedipal strivings forced into unconsciousness during the latency period may reappear later, influencing the individual to choose a mate who in some respects resembles the forbidden parent. Repressed hostile impulses toward a parent or sibling frequently return to trouble the individual in the form of guilt feelings, "delayed obedience," or difficulties with authority. In a parallel manner, it has been argued that problems that a society refuses to face consciously will inevitably return to trouble it, for example, the "specter haunting Europe" (communism) or the "American dilemma" (racism).

As the title for this chapter, the phrase refers to the return of certain problems that were "repressed" by the Culture and Personality school. Various writers modified the orthodox Freudian framework by selecting and redefining concepts. Frequently, they substituted vague "cultural factors" for the intrapsychic conflicts of psychoanalysis, ignor-

---

Drawing by David Levine. Reprinted with permission from *The New York Review of Books*. Copyright © 1974 NYREV Inc.

ing ambivalence and equating "internalization" with socialization (Wrong 1961). Many of these Neo-Freudians (and
here I include such people as Fromm, Dollard, and Whiting)
made important contributions to psychological anthropology; however, to the extent that they watered down Freud's
tough-minded positions on human sexuality, aggression, and
religion, the problems were destined to reappear. This contributed to the crisis in Culture and Personality studies discussed in the Interlude.

INSTINCT AND CULTURE

The orthodox Freudian view, in which culture is analogous
to a neurosis, had been kept alive by, among others, the
Hungarian anthropologist and psychoanalyst Géza Róheim.
In his brief monograph "The Origin and Function of Culture," Róheim undertook to analyze *all culture* as a manifestation of the sexual instincts. Róheim argued for the "fundamental identity of neurosis and civilization," recalling
Freud's comparisons of philosophy to paranoia, art to hys-
teria, and religious ritual to compulsion neuroses. From this
point of view, it appears that "we only grow up in order to
remain children," that is, to achieve in the real world the
fantasies of childhood, though usually in substitute forms
(Róheim 1943:31).
     Socialization is necessary because of the human's long in-
fancy, and this process involves an adaptation to reality.
However, Róheim maintains, the dominant adult ideas
(configurations) of a society are themselves the products of
the infancy situation: Not just the "secondary institutions,"
but such practical activities as trade, agriculture, and pas-
toralism can be traced to their unconscious roots (1943:40–
72). A person's choice of occupation always has a dynamic
motive, and the main "professions" of modern society can be
viewed as sublimations of infantile impulses. Thus, "a scien-
tist is a voyeur prying into the secrets of Mother Nature, a

painter continues to play with his feces—a writer of fiction never renounces his day-dreams, and so forth" (p. 72).

In the final chapter of "The Origin and Function of Culture," Róheim expands on the concept of sublimation, which, he says, is fundamental to the formation of culture. If sublimation is the "normal" way of dealing with anxiety, it is nevertheless a compromise with and substitute for direct wish-fulfillment. Sublimation is always a compromise that gives the individual some security against the loss of a loved person, since "to be alone is the great danger" (p. 85). Ultimately, says Róheim,

> civilization originates in delayed infancy and its function is security. It is a huge network of more or less successful attempts to protect mankind against the danger of object loss, the colossal efforts made by a baby who is afraid of being left alone in the dark. (p. 100)

Róheim conducted fieldwork in Australia, Melanesia, Africa, and North America, and analyzed the dynamics of particular cultures in such works as *The Riddle of the Sphinx,* first published in 1934. He anticipated Kardiner by suggesting that, in many cases, "the character of a people and their social organization can be derived from their infantile trauma or explained as a defense reaction to an infantile experience" (Róheim 1974:149–150). Róheim was also one of the first anthropologists to make systematic use of data on primate behavior in understanding human customs. Outrageous as many of his interpretations first appear, his work contains a number of brilliant insights that are only now being appreciated by anthropologists. He had a knack for grasping the symbolic significance of words and actions. Freud himself acknowledged that Róheim had "extended" and corrected some of the ideas in *Totem and Taboo,* demonstrating the interplay between the biologically universal and the culturally specific elements of human development.

Róheim laid the foundation for "an anthropology that sees cultural institutions as a series of defenses against unconscious drives" (1974:xvii). It would be a mistake to stress the negative aspect of this vision, for he also understood the positive satisfactions provided by culture, and he explored the relationship between the stages of sexual development and cultural evolution. Róheim died in 1953, leaving the task of elaborating these ideas to others, in particular Bruno Bettelheim and Erik Erikson. (For further discussion of Róheim's contribution, see Calogeras 1971.)

SYMBOLIC WOUNDS

Bruno Bettelheim was trained in Vienna as an art historian and, later, as a child psychoanalyst. In his early work with severely disturbed children, he accepted the orthodox Freudian view that neurotic symptoms are caused by intrapsychic conflicts and that they represent unsuccessful solutions to problems rooted in early childhood. However, a dramatic personal experience led him to modify this view and to take greater account of the role of situational factors in the causation and treatment of mental illness.

In 1938, Bettelheim was suddenly arrested and imprisoned in the Nazi concentration camps at Dachau and Buchenwald. During his imprisonment, he used his psychoanalytic training to understand what was happening to him and the other prisoners. Released in 1939, he came to the United States and, in 1943, published an article in which he set forth his understanding of these experiences. "Individual and Mass Behavior in Extreme Situations" dealt with the impact of the camps on different kinds of people and with the long-term effects of imprisonment.

Bettelheim argued that the Nazis systematically set out to destroy the prisoners' will to resist by using forms of punishment that placed the prisoner in a dependent, infantile relationship to the guards. The traumatic experiences of arrest and of torture during transportation to the camps usually produced a reaction of *denial* in the new prisoner: "This can't be happening to me." Those who survived the first few days adapted to the camp situation as best they could, trying to keep their egos intact. Different groups of prisoners (criminal, political, nonpolitical middle-class, and upper-class) reacted in quite different ways, drawing on their earlier experience to support their self-esteem, but all were gradually worn down and forced into increasing dependency (see Bettelheim 1971:108–231).

Eventually, those who had been in the camps more than three years developed a distinctive set of attitudes. They no longer showed concern with people or events outside the camp. Everything that happened had become "real" to them and many were afraid of returning to the outer world. Most striking was the tendency of the "old prisoners" to mimic the behavior and appearance of the camp guards—punishing other prisoners severely, dressing in pieces of Gestapo uniforms, and even adopting the values of the guards. Bettelheim interpreted this behavior as an example of the Freudian defense mechanism known as *identification with the aggressor.* Just as most boys resolve their Oedipus complex in part by identifying with the "castrating" father, so these prisoners, who had regressed into a state of infantile dependency, tended to identify with their powerful captors. Bettelheim cautions that this was only part of the story because these same old prisoners who sometimes identified with the Gestapo at other times defied it, demonstrating great courage in helping their fellow prisoners.

The crucial point for Bettelheim was the recognition of how rapidly drastic changes in personality could be produced by such "extreme situations." Much of his later work involved attempts to integrate this realization with traditional psychoanalytic theory and therapy. For example, Bettelheim designed an institution, the Orthogenic School of the University of Chicago, that could provide a "therapeutic milieu" for autistic and schizophrenic children twenty-four hours a day (see *A Home for the Heart,* 1974). Together with other psychoanalysts such as Anna Freud, Heinz Hartmann, and

Erik Erikson, he came to stress the positive, integrative functions of the ego, rather than seeing it as a passive victim of
unconscious processes. Even the mute, autistic child is defending a self, though one that has, tragically, become an
empty fortress: "The self is stunted, most unevenly developed, but still seems to function in some minimal way to protect them from further harm" (Bettelheim 1967:92).

   In the early 1950s, an event occurred at the Orthogenic
School that renewed Bettelheim's interest in anthropology.
Three disturbed adolescents (two girls and a boy) spontane-
ously banded together and created a kind of initiation ritual
that clearly expressed their intense ambivalence about growing up. These children both desired and feared the changes
that were taking place in their bodies and their lives. The
ritual, which was supposed to insure wealth and fame, centered on the girls' experience of menstruation and involved
their attempt to impose monthly bleeding on the boy. The
children were prevented from carrying out the ritual, but
the event stimulated Bettelheim to write *Symbolic Wounds,* a
study of primitive initiation ceremonies.

   First published in 1954 (revised in 1962), this book argues
that the unconscious motivation and many "bizarre" details
of initiation rites can be understood as expressions of male
envy of female anatomy and reproductive functions. In this
context, the traditional Freudian emphasis on female envy
of the male organs ("penis envy") was reversed, but Bettelheim documents case after case in which the rituals symbolically assert that men are able to bear children. For both
boys and girls, "the human being's envy of the other sex
leads to the desire to acquire similar organs, and to gain
power and control over the genitals of the other sex"
(1962:146).

   Symbolic Wounds was written during the period when Whiting and Child were completing *Child Training and Personality*
(1953). It is instructive to compare Bettelheim's clinical use
of cross-cultural material with the others' hypothesis-testing,
correlational approach, even though Whiting's own studies

of male initiation rites, described in Chapter Six, came somewhat later. Bettelheim uses anthropological materials as Freud did in *Totem and Taboo*. He adopts the psychoanalytic assumption that children, neurotics, and primitives clearly display many processes that are hidden (repressed) in normal, civilized adults (1962:49); however, he proclaims that he is not concerned with "primitive man (a concept I have no use for) but with the primitive in all men" (1962:11). Like Freud, he too makes imaginative use of the best anthropological sources available to him, and his interpretations are guided by analogies with his clinical experience.

Bettelheim emphasizes the positive ego functions served by initiation rituals: They aid young people to master their ambivalence toward the opposite sex and toward becoming adults. (Compare Endleman 1967:309–322.) By means of the ritual, initiates achieve new levels of psychic integration:

> Like the spontaneous actions of the children we observed, initiation ceremonies may be meant to foster personal and social integration in a difficult transitional period of life. They should then be understood as efforts of the young, or of society, to resolve the great antitheses between child and adult and between male and female; in short, between childish desires and the role ascribed to each sex according to biology and the mores of society. Whether or not they succeed is another question. (Bettelheim 1962:55)

Several other works of Bruno Bettelheim are relevant to anthropology. In particular, *Children of the Dream* (1969) is a study of communal child rearing in the Israeli kibbutz. It grew out of Bettelheim's dissatisfaction with Melford Spiro's study (1958) and concludes, essentially, that a good institution is better than a bad family. In *The Uses of Enchantment* (1976), Bettelheim has analyzed a series of popular fairy tales and suggested that, like initiation rites, fairy tales perform important positive functions. They offer children support, insight, and reassurance in a context of fantasy, and many children find this safer than more "realistic" literature:

In the traditional fairy tale, the hero is rewarded and the evil person meets his well-deserved fate, thus satisfying the child's deep need for justice to prevail. How else can a child hope that justice will be done to him, who so often feels unfairly treated? And how else can he convince himself that he must act correctly, when he is so sorely tempted to give in to the asocial proddings of his desires? (1976:144)

Adults who want to tidy up the traditional tales—making them less violent or overtly sexual—may be depriving children of the most useful parts.

INSIGHT AND IDENTITY

The year 1950 is a landmark in anthropology not only for the reasons discussed in the Interlude, but also because it marks the first publication of Erik H. Erikson's *Childhood and Society* (revised edition, 1963). Like Bettelheim, Erikson began in the arts, was trained as a child analyst, and came to the United States to avoid Nazi persecution. His interest in anthropology was stimulated by his association with H. S. Mekeel and Alfred Kroeber, both of whom took him into the field in the late 1940s. Erikson's research on disturbed children, normal students, and famous persons led him to study the individual's sense of *identity*. He came to understand both normal and pathological processes in terms of the individual's progression through the life cycle, always modified by the historical context.

Childhood and Society is a complex book containing a great variety of materials. In the first chapter, two contrasting case histories are described, one of a young boy and the other of a Marine veteran. Both patients present bizarre neurotic symptoms. Erikson shows that these cases can be fully understood only if we take into account the interplay among organic, psychic, and sociocultural factors. He stresses the continuing attempts of each patient's ego to cope with its situation, even though it may be periodically overwhelmed by irrational forces of the id or superego. He views society as supporting certain ways of coping, discouraging others, and as building some conflicts into major cultural institutions.

In the second chapter, Erikson suggests an important expansion of Freud's theory of psychosexual stages of development. The oral-anal-genital sequence is retained, but these are labeled *zones,* and each zone is associated with characteristic *modes* of behavior (incorporative, retentive, intrusive, and so forth). Thus Erikson subdivides the psychosexual stages, presenting his scheme in a two-dimensional diagram that he calls an *epigenetic chart* (see Figure 7-1). Normal development, in this scheme, is not linear but "stepwise," proceeding from the lower left zone-mode ("oral-receptive") to the upper right (though some gender differences do occur in the later stages).

The newborn infant starts as a passive receiver of nourishment and stimulation, primarily through its mouth. If its oral-receptive needs are met—in a culturally patterned way—the newborn develops *basic trust* in itself and its social world. Building on this foundation of trust, the child becomes a more active partner in social interaction. By about six months of age, he or she enters the "oral-incorporative" substage, in which biting is the characteristic activity. By actively taking and holding onto objects (including other people), the child can further build its trust and confidence. However, if the pain of teething is aggravated by too early weaning or separation from the mother, this trust can be undermined, resulting in a deep-seated rage or infantile depression. In Erikson's scheme, a child may become *fixated* at a given zone and/or mode; thus, the wish to remain a passive receiver or an active "taker" may be established very early in life, and these modes may be generalized to zones other than the oral.

Erikson associates the anal zone with retentive and eliminative modes—hanging on and letting go—and he includes in these stages the child's development of muscular control that makes possible a sense of *autonomy.* Toilet train-

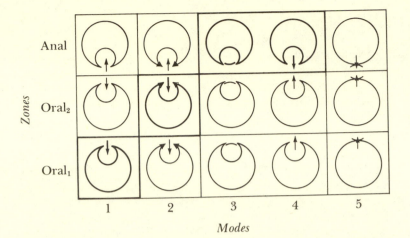

Figure 7-1 Part of Erik Erikson's "epigenetic chart," showing normal progression through the oral and anal zones as these intersect with the receptive, incorporative, retentive, and eliminative modes (modes 1–4; mode 5 is the intrusive mode). (From *Childhood and Society*, 2d ed., rev., by Erik H. Erikson, adapted with permission of W. W. Norton & Company, Inc., and The Hogarth Press, Ltd. Copyright 1950, © 1963 by W. W. Norton & Company, Inc.)

ing is only one example of the interplay between social restrictions and a toddler's need to act on his world, but it is a crucial one, since the child who does not (or cannot) learn to control his bowels may suffer shame and doubt of a pervasive kind (compare Bettelheim 1967:33–39). Again, fixation can take place in zone and/or mode, so that enduring "anal" character traits may be established at this time. For Erikson no simple formula connects severe toilet training with miserliness or sorcery. What is at stake is the *ego strength* necessary for making mature choices, including the ability to cooperate with others:

> If outer control by too rigid or too early training insists on robbing the child of his attempt gradually to control his bowels and other ambivalent functions by his free choice and will, he will . . . be forced to seek satisfaction and control either by regression or by false progression. In other words, he will return to an earlier, oral control—i.e., by sucking his thumb

and becoming whiny and demanding; or he will become hostile and intrusive, using his feces as ammunition and pretending an autonomy, an ability to do without anybody to lean on, which he has by no means really gained. (Erikson 1963:82–83)

Stepwise progression (at least for males) leads to the "genital-intrusive" stage, usually toward the end of the third year of life. By this time, mastery of locomotion has also taken place and the child begins to show real *initiative* in his dealings with others. His learning is "intrusive" in the sense that "it leads away from him into ever new facts and activities; and he becomes acutely aware of differences between the sexes" (p. 86). The boy's infantile genitality is destined to be repressed as part of the resolution of the Oedipus complex; but at this stage, depending on how the conflicts are handled in the family and larger society, initiative can either be encouraged or stifled by guilt. (The ultimate achievement of mature, adult genitality also requires the development of a capacity for *intimacy* and a concern for *generativity*—the procreation of and care for a new generation.)

One can best appreciate the subtlety and eloquence of Erikson's formulations by reading them in the original. However, we can examine here how he used these concepts of psychological development to understand cultural differences. In two concise essays in *Childhood and Society,* one on the Sioux Indians of South Dakota and the other on the Yurok of northern California, Erikson brings out the connections between patterns of childhood experience and adult character as expressed in cultural institutions. He makes use of his developmental scheme to understand how each society provokes and then exploits particular childhood conflicts to produce adults who will be motivated by needs that sustain the culture. (In this effort his goals are quite similar to those of the basic personality approach, but Kardiner's influence, if there was any, is not acknowledged.)

The Sioux were the best-known mounted warriors and bison hunters of the Great Plains—they were nomadic, generous, brave, and proud of their freedom. Erikson shows that their self-confidence and initiative were grounded in childhood experience (pp. 133–147). He also discusses the conflict between traditional Sioux character and the conditions of life imposed on them by military defeat, economic dependency, and restriction to the reservation. (Some of their psychological reactions are like those found in "old prisoners" in concentration camps and may be due to a similar identification with the aggressor.)

By contrast, the Yurok were sedentary river-dwellers who lived in a highly circumscribed universe, fishing for salmon and trading for goods or shell money. "The acquisition and retention of possessions is and was what the Yurok thinks about, talks about, and prays for. Every person, every relationship, and every act can be exactly valued and becomes the object of pride or ceaseless bickering" (p. 167). Where the Sioux value strength and assertiveness, the Yurok are concerned with "purity," and they engage in compulsive rituals and avoidances to insure success in fishing, hunting, and trade: "Only once a year, during the salmon run, are these avoidances set aside. At that time, following complicated ceremonies, a strong dam is built which obstructs the ascent of the salmon and permits the Yurok to catch a rich winter supply" (p. 168).

Erikson relates these ceremonials and the Yurok concerns with purity and accumulation of wealth to early conflicts regarding the retentive mode (though not necessarily the anal zone). The annual closing off of the river is a dramatization of the tendency to "hold on" to people, property, and feces. The corresponding Sioux ceremony was the annual Sun Dance, which enhanced the prosperity of the entire tribe through individual sacrifice and self-torture. Erikson offers a dynamic interpretation of this last feature by suggesting that the infantile rage of the "biting stage" is turned by the Sioux child against himself, and acted out in these masochistic rites (pp. 148–149).

In these two essays, Erikson's approach is quite similar to a traditional Culture and Personality approach, but he insists that he is dealing with the "mutual assimilation of somatic, mental, and social patterns which amplify one another and make the cultural design for living economical and effective" (p. 156), rather than with "simple causality." The relationship between historical pattern and individual identity is complex and circular: If culture creates neurosis by exploiting infantile needs, it also gives *meaning* to the compulsions it has created (p. 185). And there is no way for human beings to forge a valid identity outside of a particular historical situation.

PSYCHOHISTORY AND THE INTERPRETATION OF MYTH

The concept of ego identity continued to gain importance in Erikson's work as he turned to the study of exceptional persons in the context of their times. Freud wrote an early essay, "Leonardo da Vinci and a Memory of His Childhood," and his final book was *Moses and Monotheism*. But Erikson is the real founder of the enterprise known as *psychohistory*. His studies of Luther, Gandhi, Jefferson, and Hitler are landmark works whose relevance to psychological anthropology is still to be evaluated and made explicit.

Young Man Luther (1958) and *Gandhi's Truth* (1969) focus on revolutionary figures who changed their respective worlds. In Erikson's framework, they were able to do this because (for a variety of reasons) they felt the contradictions of their times more keenly than others, and because (again, for many reasons) each achieved a new and more comprehensive identity, which enabled him to lead an entire nation into a new era.

Not many anthropologists have followed Erikson's lead, although those who study comparative socialization, life cycles, or innovative leadership could certainly profit from his insights. Most of Erikson's followers are psychotherapists who are strongly concerned with social issues. Outstanding among these are Robert Coles and Robert Jay Lifton. Coles, who wrote a biography of Erikson (1970), has systematically applied Erikson's ideas to a number of neglected groups within American society. In a series of books called *Children of Crisis,* he has studied the children of Southern blacks, of migrant workers, of sharecroppers, and other young people. At the other end of the life cycle, *The Old Ones of New Mexico* (1973) is a brief, sensitive study (with superb photographs by Alex Harris) of aged couples living in the small Spanish-American villages of northern New Mexico. Coles manages to reveal the great dignity of these people despite their poverty, and he probes the social and psychological sources of their strength.

Lifton has written on women in America (before this topic was popular), on "thought reform" and the Cultural Revolution in China, and on the survivors of Hiroshima. He is also the author of numerous articles on psychohistory, many of which are collected in *History and Human Survival* (1970). Like Coles, Lifton is a superb interviewer with a deep commitment to studying contemporary social problems. Like Erikson, he is able to enter into very different cultural traditions. Lifton writes that

> what is unique to Erikson's approach (particularly in *Young Man Luther*) is his ability to maintain an individually oriented depth-psychological perspective while simultaneously immersing himself and his subject in the ideological currents of the period under study. (Lifton 1970:296)

This kind of work requires extraordinary qualities of scholarship and insight. With contributors such as Erikson, Coles, and Lifton, psychohistory could become "a means of bringing psychoanalysis and history together in a way that does justice to the richness of human experience" (Lifton 1970:296).

The interpretation of myth and legend is another area in which psychoanalysis has continued to be influential. Anthropologists and other scholars have used Freudian concepts to analyze folk tales from both familiar and exotic cultures (for example, Jacobs 1959; Bettelheim 1976). One of the most interesting of these analyses is Alan Dundes' study of the "earth-diver" myth (1962). In this widespread North American creation myth, a small animal dives deep into the primeval sea to bring up some dirt, which then rapidly expands to become the earth. Often in these tales a number of other animals try unsuccessfully before the earth-diver rises to the surface, nearly dead from his effort, with a bit of mud beneath his claw. (Compare Genesis 8:7–11.)

Dundes' interpretation of this tale seems bizarre at first, but it does account for many details. He argues that, like many children today, early people held a vague theory of "cloacal birth," that is, the notion that babies and feces come out of the same body opening. (See Erikson 1950:21–34 for a case study of a young boy who refused to defecate because he believed himself pregnant.) If we add to this notion the recognition that males frequently envy female reproductive powers (Bettelheim 1962), we can begin to understand the motives that lie behind this myth: Earth-diver's achievement is the symbolic excretion of the world by a male.

Freud's colleague, Sandor Ferenczi, had noted the intense interest that children have in the waste products of the body—nasal mucus, feces, dead skin—but he thought that most adults repress or sublimate this interest. As Dundes writes,

> the common detail of the successful diver's return with a little dirt under his fingernail is entirely in accord with Ferenczi's analysis. The fecal nature of the particle is also suggested by its magical expansion. One could imagine that as one defecates one is thereby creating an ever-increasing amount of earth. (Dundes 1962:1041)

In short, this analysis views the earth-diver myth as a creation of the male who simultaneously sublimates his interest

in feces and fantasies great reproductive powers by identification with the hero. Psychological studies like this one
supplement but do not replace analyses of the geographic
distribution and formal structure of myths (compare with
the discussion of clothing at the end of Chapter Two).

PSYCHOSOCIAL ADAPTATION

The most recent attempts to synthesize psychoanalytic and
anthropological theory are found in the works of Melford E.
Spiro and Robert A. LeVine. These scholars have been
trained in both disciplines, have had extensive clinical experience, and have carried out ethnological fieldwork. Each
has tried to develop a conceptual framework in which psychological and cultural variables will play a part in explaining human behavior. Both of their syntheses emphasize the
adaptation of individuals to their social environments, by intrapsychic or societal means, while noting the interaction between these alternative modes of adaptation.

In a widely discussed article, Spiro argues that many stable
societies provide institutionalized modes of adaptation for
people who suffer from *typical* forms of emotional conflict.
For example, although Burmese men with "idiosyncratic"
conflicts may, under prolonged tension, become psychotic,
those who suffer from typically Burmese conflicts (including
features such as extreme defensiveness, withdrawal from
emotional situations, fear of women, and strong self-
preoccupation) have available a culturally valued alternative
to ordinary life. Such men can enter a Buddhist monastery
and, in this setting, "resolve their conflicts with a minimum
of distortion" (Spiro 1965:109). Religious institutions in
many societies provide similar alternatives, enabling individuals to reduce their tensions and to achieve an adequate level
of social and cultural functioning. Following Hallowell (and,
more distantly, Benedict), Spiro claims that

as a culturally constituted defense, the monastic institution re-solves the inner conflicts of Burmese males, by allowing them to gratify their drives and reduce their anxieties in a disguised—and therefore socially acceptable—manner, one which precludes psychotic distortion, on the one hand, and criminal "acting-out" on the other. Hence, the monk is pro-tected from mental illness and/or social punishment; society is protected from the disruptive consequences of antisocial be-havior; and the key institution of Burmese culture—Buddhist monasticism—is provided with a most powerful motivational basis. (Spiro 1965:109; cf. Endleman 1967:497–526)

LeVine's more ambitious synthesis also hinges on the con-cept of adaptation, which he defines as "the shaping of the organism's response potentials toward fit with environmental conditions" (1973:5). Drawing heavily on the work of Spiro and of John Whiting, LeVine argues for a Darwinian view of personality processes, in which variations in "personality phenotypes" are subject to selection by the environment, and the likelihood of survival of the best-adapted types is thereby increased (1973:113). Farther on, he presents a "cost-benefit analysis" of research on psychosocial adaptation.

LeVine's emphasis on populations and their variability is useful, as is his discussion of alternative strategies for per-sonality study. However, his mixing of metaphors and of frameworks is troublesome. "Personality phenotype," "re-sponse potentials," and "cost-benefit analysis" are uneasy bedfellows. *Culture, Behavior, and Personality* is less a new synthesis than an eclectic attempt to salvage the Culture and Personality approach. One passage shows how little progress we have made since 1934, when Sapir had his early insights, or since 1951, when Spiro identified the "false dichotomy" between culture and personality. LeVine writes:

If internal motive and environmental demand lead to the same response, as they do in the case of adaptive fit, *observed responses can be attributed either to psychological disposition or im-mediate environmental pressure* according to the theoretical in-

clination of the investigator. (LeVine 1973:286–287; italics
added)

True enough! But LeVine implies that *if only our diagnostic
methods were better* we could make the attribution (to personality or to culture) with certainty. Yet this kind of implicit
dualism is exactly what prevents a fuller understanding of
the relationship between person and institution (see Watts
1969; Sisk 1970; Bateson 1972; Chein 1972). In the chapters
that follow, we shall discuss some of the attempts that have
been made to overcome this dilemma.

SUMMARY

What is the present relationship of psychoanalysis to anthropology? Psychoanalysts are still concerned with social
and cultural problems, but many contemporary anthropologists are uninterested in (or unaware of) their contributions. Attacks, both reasoned and impassioned, have
been made on psychoanalytic therapy and theory; critics
claim that the former is ineffective and the latter implau-
sible. Such claims are part of a general reaction against
psychoanalysis, which many social scientists now criticize as
reactionary and privatistic or as radical and dangerous, depending on the critic's political orientation.

Clearly, psychoanalysis is a total world view that one
adopts out of a kind of conversion experience rather than as
a cool, detached, rational decision. But the view of humans
as cool, detached, rational creatures is precisely what psychoanalysis has undermined in this century. We are just realizing the extent to which *all* our actions are overdetermined.
All human knowledge is "personal knowledge" for, as
Michael Polanyi says, "Our believing is conditioned at its
source by our belonging" (Polanyi 1964:322). Humans cannot escape from history, even if they view it as a nightmare
from which they struggle to awaken.

Psychoanalysis insists on what we apparently most wish to deny: that we were all tiny, dependent babies once; that our lives are forever entwined with our early loves and hates, identifications and disappointments; and that virtually any human action may carry a great load of symbolic significance. So long as we repress these truths, they will return to haunt us and to upset our tidy theories and methods. If for no other reason, anthropology needs the psychiatrist.

Karl Marx

EIGHT

Social Structure and Personality

The approaches to be considered in this chapter share one important feature: They all reject the uniformity assumption—that a one-to-one relationship exists between a culture and a typical personality or character type. The authors of many of the works discussed are sociologists and social psychologists, not anthropologists. Nevertheless, their work is highly relevant to the development and future of psychological anthropology.

I have chosen the term *Social Structure and Personality* to distinguish this school of thought from Psychoanalytic Anthropology and from Culture and Personality (see Table 3-1). Within the Social Structure and Personality school, I recognize three major approaches: *materialist, positionalist,* and *interactionist.* Each approach has its distinctive concepts and methods. The three are united by the fact that they all address the psychological characteristics of groups or roles within a society or across several societies rather than characteristics alleged to be typical of entire societies.

MATERIALIST APPROACHES

The materialist view of the relationship between society and personality goes back at least to Karl Marx. In a famous passage in the *Critique of Political Economy*, Marx states:

> The mode of production of material life conditions the social, political, and mental life-process in general. It is not the consciousness of men that determines their being, but, on the contrary, their social being determines their consciousness. (Marx 1904:11)

Marx is asserting the primacy of material (economic) conditions as the source of a group's ideas and values, and rejecting the Hegelian idealism in which the world is viewed as a product of immaterial (spiritual) forces.

Throughout his works, Marx insists that social classes and class conflict are the dynamic basis of historical change. The "ruling class" in any complex society is the group that controls the means of production—land, machines, and other forms of capital. The beliefs and values of the ruling class are generally appropriate to its material interests, that is, to maintaining and increasing its power. Ruling-class ideology also includes elements contributing to the "mystification" of the masses, for the workers must be convinced that the ruling group *deserves* its position of privilege. Under the influence of the rulers and their accomplices, the lower classes are kept ignorant of their true (revolutionary) interests. They often develop a "false consciousness," which actually corresponds to the interests of the rulers, accepting their subordination as being the "will of God."

Ultimately, say the Marxists, *all psychology is class psychology* (Bukharin 1969:213). Individual differences within classes are unimportant; to a Marxist, what really matters is how people will behave in situations of class conflict, including revolutions. Especially at these times, material interests emerge as the real determinants of behavior. (Marx was, of course, more concerned with revolutionary action than with dreams or neuroses.)

What produces class psychologies and the ideologies that are their systematized forms? The primary force is awareness of shared material interests. This awareness is facilitated by certain *conditions of work*. For example, in their daily interactions with one another, industrial workers realize both the fact of their exploitation and the power that solidarity with fellow workers can bring them. The factory that draws hundreds or thousands of workers together in the production process inadvertently promotes class consciousness among them. Industrial workers differ in this respect from peasants who work in isolation from one another and who own small amounts of property. (See the discussion, below, of "peasant personality.")

A great deal of Marxist analysis is devoted to the psychology of the *bourgeoisie*—the class of capitalists who exploit the labor of the working class to produce commodities and to accumulate more capital. The bourgeoisie are much more mobile and innovative than the conservative feudal landholders whom they replaced as the ruling class in Western Europe and America. This is due to their conditions of work, which produce the following psychological characteristics: "*individualism*, a result of the competitive struggle, and *rationalism*, a result of economic calculation," together with a "*liberal* psychology . . . based on the 'initiative of the entrepreneur'" (Bukharin 1969:291). It follows that, as economic conditions change, class psychology also changes. Marx believed that "feelings, illusions, modes of thought, and views of life" were the *superstructure* that each class creates "out of its material foundations, as well as out of the corresponding social relations" (quoted in Bukharin, p. 292).

Marxist analysis cuts across the usual cultural units considered by anthropologists. From this perspective, it matters little if one is a Russian, a Japanese, or a Nigerian. What does matter is whether one is an industrial worker, a peasant, or a petit bourgeois (small-scale merchant). One's position in the social (class) structure largely determines one's beliefs and actions. As we shall see, positionalists and interactionists assume related points of view.

As noted earlier, some contemporary materialists believe that psychological concepts and personality variables are simply irrelevant to the understanding of cultural process. Most materialists do take account of individual differences in perception, motivation, and cognition, although they treat these distinctions as dependent variables to be explained by material factors. For example, a key concept in Marxist analysis is *alienation,* the estrangement of individuals from the material world and from themselves. Alienation is the result of a class structure that deprives individuals of access to the necessary means of production: "This separation from their work and the products of their work results also in their being alienated from nature and from themselves" (Lang 1964:19). The psychological state of alienation is thus a result of material conditions.

Much discussion of alienation is highly speculative (for example, Althusser 1970), but some empirical studies help to clarify the significance of this phenomenon. One such work is *The Hidden Injuries of Class* by Richard Sennett and Jonathan Cobb (1973), which provides rich data from long, sensitive interviews to illuminate the effects of the class structure on American blue-collar workers. Although their sample is small, the authors convincingly portray the deep ambivalence of their subjects toward their jobs, the possibility of mobility, and themselves:

> One aerospace worker pinpointed the paradox in the situation very well, in reflecting on his own daydreaming at work. The more a person is on the receiving end of orders, he said, the more the person's got to think he or she is really somewhere else in order to keep up self-respect. And yet it's at work that you're supposed to "make something" of yourself, so if you're not really there, how *are* you going to make something of yourself? (Sennett and Cobb 1973:94; compare Garson 1977)

A quite different variety of materialism is represented by the movement known as *sociobiology* (Wilson 1975; Barash 1977). Despite strong opposition from Marxists, sociobiology *is* a materialist theory, and it attempts to explain human and animal social behavior by means of a Darwinian model. Sociobiologists analyze the evolution of behavioral characteristics (aggressiveness, territoriality, altruism) and specific cultural practices (types of child care, kin groups, and marriage rules) as adaptations that maximize an individual's chances to pass on genes to future generations.

The sociobiological approach can to some extent account for group differences in such psychological characteristics as "jealousy" and parental "investment" of time and resources in child care. Sociobiology also provides a basis for quantitative studies and prediction of behavior, something that other approaches provide only in the vaguest ways. For example, since one's siblings and their children carry and can transmit some of a person's genes, though not as many as one's own offspring, it "makes sense" (in evolutionary terms) for people to favor nieces and nephews over nonrelatives, though not above their own children. See *The Selfish Gene* by Richard Dawkins (1978) for a lively discussion of the "evolutionary strategies" predicted by sociobiological theories.

POSITIONALIST APPROACHES

Positionalism denotes a body of research that shares with Marxism the materialist assumption that one's behavior is strongly influenced by one's position in the social structure. However, positionalist studies treat social class as only one of a number of social positions that influence individual behavior. Ethnic group, social role, age, occupation, and even birth order are among the positions that have been studied from this perspective.

While using the concepts of material interests and conditions of work as explanatory principles, positionalists extend these ideas to nonmaterial interests and to general conditions of living. They also suggest that the principal mechanism through which material conditions affect personality characteristics is *differential socialization*. This phrase refers to the hypothesis that behavioral and personality differences found in members of various groups and performers of different roles can be traced back to specific socialization practices in childhood and in later life.

Applied to social classes, the hypothesis of differential socialization suggests that a class psychology cannot simply by inferred from shared interests and conditions of work. The socialization practices characteristic of each class must be studied empirically and their consequences for adult behavior traced. For example, Urie Bronfenbrenner, whose comparison of Russian and American child rearing was mentioned in Chapter Five, has also examined class differences in socialization within the United States. He summarizes a number of different studies indicating that

> middle class parents especially have moved away from the more rigid and strict styles of care and discipline . . . toward modes of response involving greater tolerance of the child's impulses and desires, freer expression of affection, and increased reliance on "psychological" methods of discipline, such as reasoning and appeals to guilt, as distinguished from more direct techniques like physical punishment. At the same time, the gap between the social classes in their goals and methods of child rearing appears to be narrowing, with working class parents beginning to adopt both the values and techniques of the middle class. (Bronfenbrenner 1967:190)

Within each social class, however, Bronfenbrenner found that girls are exposed to more affection and less punishment than boys. Similar differences are found in the treatment of first-born versus younger children in a given family. Great use of "love-oriented techniques," although highly efficient in producing conformity with parental wishes, entails the risk of "oversocialization" of girls and eldest children, often producing individuals who are "anxious, timid, dependent, and sensitive to rejection" (p. 193). Differences in socialization of the sexes are most pronounced at lower-class levels;

they decrease as one moves upward in the social structure where "patterns of parental treatment for the two sexes begin to converge" (p. 195).

Bronfenbrenner's studies (together with more recent ones, which seem to confirm his general findings) depart from the uniformity assumption by recognizing (1) class differences within a society, (2) sex differences within the same class, and (3) changes in socialization practices over time. However, the positionalist approach is also applied to social categories that cut across cultural boundaries, for example, in studies of peasant personality. Oscar Lewis, in his work in a Mexican peasant community (1951), and Herbert Phillips, in his analysis of Thai peasant personality (1965), concentrated on the peasantry of a single nation or region. Other investigators have attempted to establish psychological characteristics common to *all* members of the peasant class.

The best-known of the anthropological characterizations is that of George M. Foster (1965). Foster argued that peasants in all societies share a common "cognitive orientation," which he calls the *image of limited good.* This is the shared (though usually unverbalized) assumption that the good things of life—wealth, health, land, prestige, and even pleasure—are strictly limited in quantity. Since nothing can be done to increase the resources that peasants divide among themselves, one person's gain is inevitably another's loss. (See Benedict's description of Dobu in Chapter Three.)

Foster claims that this shared cognitive orientation accounts for a great deal of otherwise puzzling peasant behavior. (For a similar argument, see Banfield 1958.) For example, people who believe that *good* is limited will understandably be secretive about their own successes and envious of others'; they will avoid cooperative work situations for fear of being cheated; and they will resist innovations that, in their view, cannot increase the available good. Foster argues that peasants as a class *are* secretive, envious, uncooperative, fearful, and tradition-oriented, regardless of their specific culture. He also believes that this "image" often persists into an era in which cooperation and acceptance of modern techniques could lead to a better life for all. Peasant communities have strong sanctions against innovation: "The villager who feels the need for Achievement and who does something about it, is violating the basic, unverbalized rules of the society of which he is a member" (Foster 1965:309).

John G. Kennedy (1966) questioned Foster's assumptions and thus his interpretations of peasant personality. He believes that Foster underestimated cultural differences among peasant communities, particularly with regard to familistic values, degree of stratification, and types of relationships with the elite class. According to Kennedy, "economic differentiation and differences in social ranking not only exist in some peasant societies, but ... they are associated with status-striving and achievement orientations" (1966:1217). Steven Piker (1966) and many others have offered quite different interpretations of peasant behavior, but continued controversy has failed to resolve any of the basic questions about peasant personality: Does it exist at all? If so, what is it like? Is it the result of a cognitive orientation, a culture of poverty, a rational "ethos," or differential socialization?

Recent research emphasizes the capacity of peasants for rapid change and their eager adoption of innovations when new opportunities in a developing economy make change clearly beneficial. It has been argued that a person's economic position and ability to take risks determine whether he or she will accept an innovation or participate in a revolution, and that peasant "personality" is irrelevant to these decisions (Cancian 1967; Scott 1976). As a result of these studies, some anthropologists have been drawn to a more materialist position—one that allows for a certain amount of "lag" between economic change and psychological change, but that emphasizes the ultimate dependence of psychological phenomena on material conditions.

Positionalists have also studied the personality types associated with various social roles and the socialization of adults for role performance. Classic studies by Max Weber and Robert Merton of the "bureaucratic personality" are examples of this concern. In Merton's formulation, the typical bureaucrat has chosen an occupation that offers security through conformity. The individual advances by avoiding conflict with superiors and by passively achieving seniority. Passing "objective tests of competence," usually involving knowledge of bureaucratic regulations and procedures, may also be necessary for advancement. Bureaucratic careers thus *attract* a certain type of person, but they also *reinforce* tendencies toward conformity and a narrow view of life. Under these circumstances, it is not surprising that bureaucrats are often more concerned with adhering to the rules than with getting a job done or satisfying a client (Merton 1957:123–124).

Unfortunately, few studies include many data on individual peasants, workers, or bureaucrats. To this extent they are open to the same criticisms leveled at Culture and Personality studies: Inferences made about personality from institutional data are not verified independently. Also, we cannot know whether timid, conformist, authoritarian individuals are attracted to bureaucracies or whether these traits are created by bureaucratic careers unless we have reliable data on individuals before, during, and after their acceptance (or rejection) of bureaucratic positions. Both mechanisms are probably involved. Some evidence, however, suggests that children are socialized somewhat differently in families where the father has a bureaucratic position than in families where he is an independent entrepreneur. (See Miller and Swanson 1966.) An early correlational study also indicates that children in agricultural societies are socialized for "responsibility," whereas pastoralists' children are trained for "independence" (Barry et al. 1959; cf. Edgerton 1971).

Only a few psychologically oriented studies of occupations provide rich individual data. Outstanding among these are the studies of eminent American scientists conducted by Anne Roe (summarized in Endleman 1967). Roe used projective tests, life-history interviews, and comparisons with other groups to understand the personalities of highly successful natural and social scientists (Nobel Prize winners and the like). She found that members of this group shared some background characteristics and psychological tendencies. For example, a large number of individuals in the group had been first-born children. Many of the scientists had experienced early loss of a parent (through death or divorce), and almost all reported a sense of personal isolation early in life. TAT protocols revealed notable differences among subjects in various disciplines, and Rorschach responses indicated that

> all of the types of eminent scientist show unusual capacity to see things in ways that are out of the ordinary and share a considerable load of anxiety, probably reflecting underlying insecurities which are presumably connected with their drive toward unusual achievement and the strength and persistence of their immersion in their work. (Endleman 1967:374)

Intermediate between general studies of class psychology and studies concerned with specific roles lies an area where relatively little research has been done, yet it was in this area that one of the most significant studies of social structure and personality was attempted. Building on data collected in earlier research, John Rohrer and Munro Edmonson directed a careful, interdisciplinary study of New Orleans blacks. Their work was first published as *The Eighth Generation* (1960), a title referring to the eight generations since the first slaves were brought to Louisiana. The study has many interesting features, including its sampling and interviewing methods; however, I am concerned here with the ideas that Rohrer and Edmonson developed to account for continuities between childhood experience and adult psychosocial adaptations. To understand these ideas, we must review the history of the study.

Allison Davis and John Dollard carried out fieldwork in New Orleans during the 1930s when "white supremacy" was still strong in the South, and when all Americans were feeling the effects of the Great Depression. The investigators argued that *social class was more important than race* in the experience of many blacks, and they demonstrated the influence of class on child training and school experience. Their staff interviewed nearly two hundred adolescents and in most cases the children's families as well. Their book, titled *Children of Bondage,* contained rich case studies of several youths from each social class.

Rohrer and Edmonson introduce their follow-up study with a detailed history of class and race relations in New Orleans, describing the many kinds of groups that exist within "New Orleans Negro Society," such as families, churches, schools, unions, and lodges. They next look at the ways that people *relate* to the groups available to them. The central thesis of *The Eighth Generation* is that individuals develop a series of role identifications—that is, they organize conceptions of their "selves" in terms of the role or group that has greatest importance to them at a given time of life. Furthermore, they become highly "ethnocentric" about their choices and hostile to opposed groups.

People may be aware of alternative identities (and may even choose differently later in life), but most individuals do have a clear *primary role identification.* Rohrer and Edmonson found that they could specify a primary role identification for most subjects, and that this identification was an essential part of the individual's psychic integration. Furthermore, they observe,

> these commitments are not unique or idiosyncratic but are characteristic of groups of individuals. For one group the primary role identification was with the middle class, and was suffused with the values associated with that class. For another it was the maternal role in the matriarchal family, and in this group sex becomes a more basic fact—even socially—than class. For a third group the primary identification was with older boys and men in more or less age-graded peer groups—gangs; while for a fourth being a family member was the most important of all roles and the family

became not only a focus but almost the total sphere of social life. (Rohrer and Edmonson 1964:299)

The authors argue that a clear role identity and a sense of individual ego identity (in Erikson's sense) are both necessary to achieving an adult level of personality integration. Rich case studies with longitudinal data going back twenty years support these interpretations, showing remarkable stability in the identifications achieved early in life. There was also a consistency of *marginality* in certain individuals:

> As would be expected, not all individuals are able to evolve unequivocal identifications of this type; some have only vague or conflicting role identifications. There is a corresponding diffusion or lack of mature integration in the psychic functioning of such individuals. (1964:299)

The approach developed by Rohrer and Edmonson, with its combination of cultural and individual data compiled by interracial and interdisciplinary teams, holds much promise. The authors criticize Davis and Dollard's overemphasis on class, and also take issue with a study of Negro "basic personality" (Kardiner and Ovesey 1951), arguing that both approaches oversimplify the complexity of black personality and adaptation. The concept of primary role identification is, I believe, especially important as a way to synthesize individual and social data. It has been neglected, partly because many psychological anthropologists are unfamiliar with the study, but also because having the kind of background data provided by the Davis and Dollard study is unusual. (See McClelland et al. 1978 for a preliminary report on a longditudinal study of the effect of child training on adult personality.)

INTERACTIONIST APPROACHES

The studies discussed in this section start from the positionalist assumption that one's place in society is the major determinant of behavior, and carry this assumption to its logical conclusion: *The self is an entirely social product.* Interactionists go beyond concepts such as *class psychology* and *primary role identification* to insist that one's sense of identity is continually constructed from ongoing interactions. They are more concerned with the effects of one's *immediate situation* on behavior than with alleged *continuities* of intrapsychic structures. Writers in this tradition seldom use such terms as *personality* or *character,* preferring such concepts as *social self* or *personal identity* (Carson 1969).

The speculative background of interactionism is found in the sociological works of Georg Simmel, Émile Durkheim, W. I. Thomas, and C. H. Cooley. American interactionism is also derived from the teachings of the University of Chicago social philosopher George Herbert Mead on the development of the self (1934). Fundamentally, Mead argued that we learn who we are only by observing how others respond to our actions and by "taking the role of the other" toward ourselves. This idea is similar to the Freudian concept of the superego as an "internalized parent," but Mead emphasizes the continuous operation of this process. Unlike the superego (which is formed in childhood), the self is constantly being modified by interaction with *significant others* as part of what we would today call a system with positive and negative feedback. Even when no one else is physically present, says Mead, we still take the attitude of a *generalized other* toward our own actions, approving or disapproving, and keeping ourselves in line. For Mead, the self is a *process,* not a "thing." (See Murphy 1947:479–522.)

An empirical offshoot of this Chicago tradition took the form of intensive field studies of occupations. During the 1950s, under the guidance of Everett C. Hughes, a generation of University of Chicago graduate students studied taxi drivers, furniture salesmen, dance musicians, and funeral directors at first hand. These investigators were less concerned with general "conditions of work" than with the concrete interaction situations that each job created and with the interpersonal dynamics of these situations.

Fascinating as some of these studies are, it remained for

someone to synthesize them and spell out their relevance to the problems of individual and society. This person was Erving Goffman. For the past twenty years, in a series of books and articles, Goffman has stimulated thought and research on a variety of topics, offering an important challenge to psychological anthropology and to many other disciplines. I believe that Goffman's work is as important to the study of interaction as Freud's has been to the study of dreams and the unconscious. (The parallel is deeper than most people realize, as we shall see.)

The title of Goffman's first book, *The Presentation of Self in Everyday Life* (1959), has many resonances. The "self" referred to is, like G. H. Mead's concept, a constant process of creation rather than a stable entity. Its "presentation" is a dramatic one, entailing the realization of a role in relation to an audience and in cooperation with backstage teammates. The title also alludes to Freud's early work *The Psychopathology of Everyday Life,* which, like Goffman's book, builds an elaborate interpretive framework out of mundane experience.

Taking his cue from Simmel (1950:307), Goffman points out that people who enter into "the presence of others" (that is, any social situation) are faced with a problem of information control. As in a theatrical performance, certain data must be revealed and others hidden. Each performer in a social situation implicitly claims to be a certain kind of person and expects to be treated as such (whether as a doctor, a cabdriver, a faithful spouse, a skilled mechanic, or an innocent bystander). He or she "projects a definition of the situation" in which these claims should be honored. Yet we know that claims to a social identity can be false, and terms such as "quack," "con man," or "traitor" are common labels for fraudulent performers in American culture.

Given the possibility of deception, Goffman asks what the implications of deception are for normal social interaction. Since people are *not* always what they claim to be, even legitimate performers must put on a kind of show to convince their audience that they are genuine. Real doctors and faithful spouses have the same *dramaturgical* problems as do quacks and faithless spouses. Indeed, the frauds may be more skillful than the legitimate performers at presenting a believable self! This is why Goffman uses many concepts and terms from the world of the stage and the sting.

Most of our everyday life with others is indistinguishable from a staged performance, including moments spent "backstage" with team members (people like our barbers, tailors, doctors, and spouses), who help us with our public presentations. This fact has important consequences for the relation of self to society. In several of his works, Goffman shows how social norms penetrate every aspect of individual behavior: Whether we wish to be considered authoritative, threatening, harmless, or just "normal," we must take constant care that a momentary slip doesn't "spoil the show," causing others to get the "wrong impression."

People who are very obviously not "normal," and people who have something to hide—the discredited and the discreditable, in Goffman's terminology—are excellent subjects for study from this perspective. In *Stigma* (1963), Goffman analyzes the situation of stigmatized persons (for example, the physically handicapped, the mentally retarded, ex-convicts, or ex-mental patients). He argues that the differences among kinds of stigmas are less important than the common dilemma faced by all stigmatized persons when they interact with "normals." He calls such interaction situations the "primal scene of sociology" (another Freudian allusion), and he documents the similarities among organized groups of stigmatized persons, from Alcoholics Anonymous to the NAACP.

Another significant Freudian parallel is found in Goffman's treatment of the relationship between persons who share the same stigma, whether or not they are organized into a political action group. Goffman characterizes this relationship as highly ambivalent: Stigmatized persons feel a common bond with their "own," yet they also want to be accepted by normals. Whether blind, diabetic, retarded, or born into a despised minority, they are torn between social identities, sometimes wishing to "pass" as normal, and at other times militantly defending their fellow sufferers. There is no solution to this dilemma. Stigmatized persons who become leaders of their "own" groups end up spending much time interacting with normals who consider them "different" from those they represent and/or "a credit to their people."

To me, the most fascinating point in *Stigma* is Goffman's demonstration that organized groups of the stigmatized rest, ultimately, on their *shared guilt*. Members of these groups frequently feel that they have done something terrible to deserve their stigma. They may also feel guilty about their ambivalence toward their "own," and may try to compensate by working for the cause or proclaiming pride in their handicap. Goffman comes close to suggesting that, since we are all stigmatized relative to some category of "normals," *guilt lies at the basis of all social organization* (1963:124–128). If Goffman were to accept my analysis, this least Freudian of sociologists would find himself advocating a position very like that expressed in *Totem and Taboo:* that participation in a "primal crime" is the precondition of human social cooperation (Brown 1966:13).

Goffman's other works deal with a wide variety of topics, but he always returns to the interpretation of interaction in specific social situations. In *Encounters* (1961a), he is concerned with the ways in which people express their involvement in, or distance from, the roles they perform. *Relations in Public* (1971) suggests how certain ideas developed in the study of animal behavior (ethology) can be fruitfully applied to human interaction. In *Frame Analysis* (1974), he borrows concepts from literary criticism and symbolic anthropology to analyze the ways in which people "frame" their experiences in order to attribute meaning to them. There are also several collections of essays (1961b; 1967; 1969) whose topics range from the situation of mental patients to behavior at the gaming tables of Las Vegas, and an analysis of sexual symbolism in advertising (1979). Goffman's work is important to psychological anthropology as a demonstration of the complex ways in which social norms influence behavior quite apart from "intrapsychic" (personality) factors. He has led many ethnographers to focus more carefully on details of interaction (see Chapter Nine).

Several other kinds of interactionist studies can only be mentioned briefly here. The term *symbolic interaction* has been applied to a variety of approaches that, like Goffman's, seek to interpret the meaning of social behavior in concrete situations (Blumer 1969; Hewitt 1976). A related approach goes by the rather awkward title of *ethnomethodology*. As developed by Harold Garfinkle and others, ethnomethodology focuses on details of behavior and written texts that reveal social actors *creating* the categories and rules that they live by, and *negotiating* their interpretations of what has happened. (See Turner 1974.)

A particularly clear example of this approach is found in Jack D. Douglas' book *The Social Meanings of Suicide* (1967). There is a long tradition in sociology of studying the official rates of suicide in various social groups (classes, religions, nationalities) and then interpreting the social causes of these rates. For example, Protestants appear to have higher suicide rates than do Catholics; this differential has been attributed to the Protestant emphasis on individual responsibility for sin as well as the alleged lack of forgiveness for individual failings in Protestant communities.

Douglas argues that such interpretations are invalid because the classification of a given death as suicide is strongly influenced by community attitudes. Actual rates of self-destruction may be the same for Protestants and Catholics, but the strong condemnation of suicide by the Catholic Church probably leads families, doctors, and other officials to classify uncertain cases as "accidental" or "natural" deaths. Differing suicide rates are thus seen as the result of *negotiated decisions,* not as objective *social facts.*

Ethnomethodology raises questions about all studies that rely on official statistics. In particular, the method of *epidemiology,* used to analyze possible causes of physical and mental illness, must be critically reviewed. Epidemiology involves identifying social groups between which incidence rates for a particular disease differ, and then inferring the contribution made by factors such as diet, stress, or climate to the rates. The method is extremely useful in tracing the causes of clear-cut physical illnesses such as heart disease or tuberculosis, but serious problems arise when it is applied to mental illness, for which the official statistics are less reliable.

For example, if one uses the rate of admission to mental hospitals as a measure of illness, some strong correlations between psychosis and social class are revealed. But what happens when we ask (as Douglas did of suicides) *who decides* whether a given patient will be admitted (or committed) to a mental hospital? It is now well established that upper-class sufferers tend to receive private psychotherapy and to stay at home (or in private "rest homes"), whereas lower-class sufferers with objectively similar symptoms often get into trouble with the law and end up being committed to state institutions. Thus, some of the correlations between illness and social class disappear when we determine the *meaning* of official hospital statistics.

One significant study in social psychiatry clearly showed the danger of relying on official statistics. The Hutterites are members of a large, communal Anabaptist sect that settled in western Canada about a hundred years ago after centuries of persecution in Europe. They are highly conservative in speech, dress, and customs, though they accept modern agricultural techniques and have become successful farmers (to the envy of their neighbors). Because few Hutterites entered mental hospitals, it was long believed that Hutterite society had an extremely low rate of mental illness; this characteristic was usually attributed to the stability and security of their way of life.

Intensive, first-hand studies by anthropologists and psychiatrists, however, revealed that rates of mental illness in Hutterite society were *not* very different from those in neighboring communities (Eaton and Weil 1953; Kaplan and

Plaut 1956). The low rate of hospital admissions can be explained by Hutterite cultural values, which encourage sheltering and supporting afflicted persons rather than expelling them from the community (cf. Cumming and Cumming 1957). For example, a common form of adult depression, called by the Hutterites *Anfechtung* ("temptation by the devil"), is met with sympathy and emotional support. Afflicted persons are patiently counseled by Hutterite ministers, who assure them that many people experience similar temptations. In most cases, the depression passes and the person resumes a normal pattern of life.

Social psychiatry is a rapidly growing discipline in which anthropologists often play important roles (Opler 1959). Whether carried out in large urban centers (Srole et al. 1962) or in depressed rural areas (Leighton et al. 1963), within a single society or across several cultures, studies of mental health and illness often benefit from the specialized knowledge and interviewing skills of anthropologists. A survey of this field by Ransom J. Arthur (1971) indicates the range of topics it embraces. In addition to epidemiology, Arthur discusses social class and psychiatric disorder, social factors in the onset of disease, studies of mental hospitals, community psychiatry, and transcultural psychiatry (see also Kiev 1972). Although the two share many interests and methods, social psychiatry and psychological anthropology differ in that practitioners of the former are oriented toward *healing* as well as research. But many anthropologists have participated in cross-cultural studies of mental illness, and others have described mental disturbances specific to certain societies or regions (see Barnouw 1979:333–360; Bourguignon 1979:270–297).

SUMMARY

We have seen that the Social Structure and Personality school presents an alternative to both Psychoanalytic Anthropology and to Culture and Personality. Materialist and positionalist approaches reject the uniformity assumption, looking rather at the psychological correlates of social classes, roles, and occupations that are not limited to single societies. Interactionist approaches reject the continuity assumption, and focus instead on factors in the immediate situation that produce regularities in behavior. In this view, the self is a continual creation of social interaction; its apparent consistency is due to the fact that people tend to play the same interaction "games" throughout life (Berne 1964), but when placed in unusual, or "extreme," situations, much of this consistency disappears (Bettelheim 1943). In the next chapter, we examine some recent anthropological studies that also deemphasize the concept of personality in favor of empirical observations of behavior in the "here and now."

Bronislaw Malinowski

NINE

Focusing on the Here and Now

Starting in about 1960, several new approaches in psychological anthropology were developed based on the *intensive observation of human behavior in natural settings*. Some of these developments were responses to criticisms of the cross-cultural approach (Chapter Six). Others were stimulated by naturalistic studies of animal behavior (ethology), while many showed the influence of interactionist theories, especially in their emphasis on situational variables and their questioning of the continuity assumption.

Similar interactionist tendencies appeared in popular psychotherapies of the same era. Gestalt therapy, transactional analysis, and related movements all encouraged patients to deal with their feelings and conflicts by focusing on "the here and now" rather than by reliving the past or probing the unconscious. In these theories, neurosis and character structure were no longer viewed as entities but as interaction "games" that people play, sustained by the responses of other people (Berne 1964). The 1960s were also years in which experimentation with psychotropic drugs was widespread and interest in "altered states of consciousness" was growing. All these factors contributed to the development of the approaches surveyed in this chapter.

SIX CULTURES

One way of meeting criticisms of cross-cultural studies was to train investigators in observational methods and have them collect first-hand data on a diverse sample of societies. These data could be used to test hypotheses concerning the effect of variables such as age, sex, or culture type on behavior, eliminating the need to infer measures from ethnographies collected for other purposes (see Chapter Six). In the "Six Cultures Project," directed by John Whiting and his wife, Beatrice Whiting, six pairs of investigators (most of them husband-wife teams) were used to observe six communities, widely distributed from Africa to Okinawa. Special attention was given to the behavior of children between three and eleven years old as they interacted with peers, infants, and adults.

The theory guiding the project derived from the earlier cross-cultural work of Whiting and Child (1953). It differs from this approach mainly in its emphasis on the children's *learning environment,* which is viewed as mediating between cultural institutions and personality (see Figure 9-1). As John Whiting did in his study of the Kwoma (1941), Whiting and Whiting wished to discover exactly how culture impinged on children's lives.

The findings of the project were published in three major books. In *Six Cultures* (B. Whiting, ed. 1963), brief ethnographies of the communities were presented together with the "Field Guide for a Study of Socialization" used by the investigators to make their observations more comparable. *Mothers of Six Cultures* (Minturn and Lambert 1964) was based primarily on data from questionnaires given to mothers in each community. It reveals the diversity of cul-

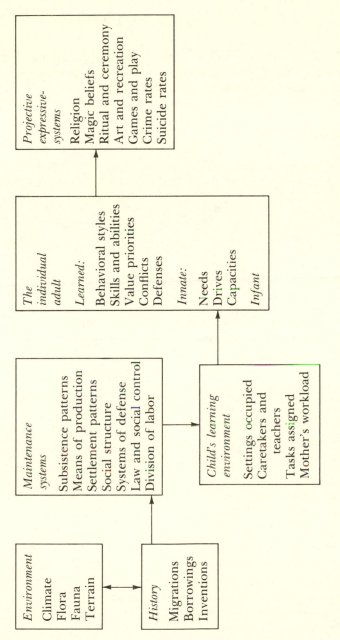

Figure 9-1 A model of psychocultural research. (From *Children of Six Cultures* by Beatrice Whiting and John W. M. Whiting. Cambridge: Harvard University Press. Copyright © 1974 by the President and Fellows of Harvard College.)

tural norms regarding child rearing in the six societies (for example, adult attitudes toward child obedience, responsibility for chores, treatment of aggression, and discipline). Finally, *Children of Six Cultures* (Whiting and Whiting 1974) presents data on child behavior in relation to selected variables. As the authors note,

> We try to combine cross-cultural and intracultural approaches. The same children were compared with other children within their culture as well as those of different cultures. It must be admitted that with but six cultures and sixteen to twenty-four boys and girls in each varying from three to eleven years in age . . . we had the barest minimum of cases to test our hypotheses. . . . Despite this defect, the opportunity . . . of testing the same hypotheses both within and across cultures . . . makes up to some degree for the inadequacy resulting from small sample size. (Whiting and Whiting 1974:2–3)

This project differed from earlier cross-cultural studies in several other ways:

1. It relied on direct observation of child behavior in natural settings. Precautions were taken to avoid bias in observations: A total of at least fourteen five-minute observations were made on each child; the ethnographer recorded general interaction and a bilingual assistant transcribed all verbal communications (p. 41).

2. Behavior was used as an "index of personality" (p. 5). Projective tests were not employed, and inferences from "projective-expressive systems" to adult personality were avoided. No assumptions were made about continuity from early experience to later character.

3. Child behavior was observed in different settings (home, garden, and school), during various kinds of activities (play, work, learning), and when different kinds of groups were present.

4. Quantitative data on intracultural variability as well as intercultural differences were preserved and pub-

lished. Independent judges were used to classify reported behaviors into categories for statistical analysis, but subjective ratings by judges as to presence, absence, or intensity of customs were not necessary.

Despite all these methodological improvements, the results of the project are disappointing. The six ethnographies are presented in uniform style for easy comparability, but they are not really that easy to compare. The categories and procedures used by the judges to classify behavior frequently seem arbitrary. For example, as any parent knows, it is often difficult to distinguish behavior that "seeks help" from that which "seeks attention," and such actions can also be confounded with behavior that "seeks dominance"; yet these types of behavior are three of the twelve categories used in the analysis. Reliability of the original observations must be questioned when we read that, "since only one [bilingual] assistant was available at any one time at a field site, it was impossible to make simultaneous observations; hence the question of reliability must be taken *on faith*" (p. 42; italics added).

The conclusions of the Six Cultures study hold few surprises. Age, sex, setting, and culture type (for example, whether agricultural or pastoral) can all be shown to affect child behavior under certain circumstances. A given child's behavior shows variation depending on the setting and whether the child is interacting with infants, peers, or adults, but enough consistency is present to indicate a "personality" factor at work:

> Above all, the findings of this study suggest that none of the traditional theories alone can account for the social behavior of children. That boys are more aggressive and less nurturant than girls cannot be completely explained by either a biological or a cultural model. The children of each culture are unique in some respects but indistinguishable in others. Differences in learning environments produce differences in children's social behavior; despite this all children seek help and attention from adults and offer help and support to infants. (pp. 184–185)

This conclusion does not really represent a great deal of new information, considering the time, effort, and expense such an undertaking requires.

In another use of intensive on-site observation, adults in four East African societies were studied by members of the UCLA Culture and Ecology Project. Because each society had both farming and pastoral populations, the investigators were able to make comparisons among the four societies and also between farmers and pastoralists across cultures. An elaborate test-interview was conducted with a total of 505 men and women, but despite considerable methodological ingenuity, the results of this project are also rather disappointing (Edgerton 1971). What are the problems with these approaches and where can we look for alternative methods of study?

HUMAN ETHOLOGY

One of the problems in any observational study of behavior is finding the appropriate language to describe what one observes. Even when high-quality video tapes are available for repeated viewing, at some point the analyst must describe what is happening. This usually means breaking up the continuous "stream of behavior" into *units* that can be classified, counted, and compared.

In the Six Cultures Project, a subset of English verbs and adjectives was used, and these terms were later classified under twelve categories, from "acts sociably" to "assaults." Similar classifications have been used for many years in experimental studies of small-group interaction (Bales 1950) and in psychological studies of the "stream of behavior" (Barker and Wright 1954). Unfortunately, the use of ordinary English for description introduces a cultural bias, because actions that can be most easily named (codified) are most easily noticed or remembered by the observer. Some categorization is surely necessary, but it should not be arbitrarily imposed upon the data.

Faced with these problems, many anthropologists have looked to ethology, the scientific study of animal behavior, for ideas. A recent review article cited 178 studies relevant to "human ethology." In defining this field, Fox and Fleising state:

> The essence of the ethological approach is the acceptance of the synthetic theory of evolution as the master paradigm for the analysis of all life processes, including such uniquely human processes as language and culture. Human behavior then, like the behavior of any life form, must be analyzed in terms of its evolution and *patterns of adaptation*. (Fox and Fleising 1976:265)

Human ethologists use concepts and methods developed in the study of animal behavior. For example, child ethologists try to identify a list of objectively defined behavior units and then study their organization and development in a sample of children (Blurton Jones 1972). Because the quantity of data in such studies can be enormous, mathematical techniques such as sequence and factor analysis are employed to discover relationships and identify causal factors.

Some of the most impressive results of human ethology have been achieved by Paul Ekman and his associates in their cross-cultural studies of facial expression. They wanted to test ideas first suggested a century ago by Charles Darwin. Darwin believed that facial expressions were universal in the human species, and that they had evolved from muscular responses of lower animals. However, many anthropologists who were impressed with the way culture could shape nonverbal behavior argued against Darwin's views. Some took the extreme position that all expressions of emotion were learned—that smiles, frowns, grimaces, and gestures were culture-specific. Others, while not denying the contribution of universal biological factors, pointed to the role of culture in shaping or "masking" the expression of joy, anger, or grief. That is, in every society some emotions are subject to *display rules,* "norms regarding the expected management of facial appearance" (Ekman 1973:176).

Ekman and his colleagues used two basic approaches to resolve this dispute. First, they filmed the facial expressions "shown in a particular situation by people in two or more cultures" and made careful measurements of the muscular movements to determine similarities and differences (p. 187). The second method involved showing photographs to people in various societies to find out "whether people from different cultures will judge the same emotion when viewing the same facial appearance" (p. 188). The *judgments approach* was the more successful.

The investigators found remarkable agreement within and across five literate societies (the United States, Brazil, Chile, Argentina, and Japan) in judgments of photos representing six basic emotions. More than 85 percent of all subjects agreed on the photos showing happiness, disgust, or surprise, and a large majority also agreed in their judgments of sadness, anger, and fear. Furthermore, when asked to "rate each facial expression on a seven-point intensity scale," no significant differences were found between North American and Latin American subjects. (The Japanese were not tested on this scale.) Other studies verified these findings (for example, Izard 1971).

Although members of literate cultures made similar judgments of emotions, one "loophole" remained: the similarities might be due to common visual experiences (for example, in the mass media). After all, "I Love Lucy" is a great favorite on Japanese television! But where can one today find people who are "visually isolated" from these ubiquitous stimuli? To overcome this problem, they went to New Guinea to study the Fore, a society that had been isolated from Western influence until a few years ago. They carefully selected only Fore subjects who had "seen no movies, neither spoke nor understood English or Pidgin, had not lived in any of the Western settlements or government towns, and had never worked for a Caucasian" (p. 211).

A form of the judgment task suitable for nonliterate people was administered to 189 Fore adults and 130 children. On most of the photographs, high levels of agreement with the other samples were found, although the Fore had some difficulty distinguishing "fear" from "surprise." Conversely, video tapes of Fore adults posing the basic emotions were accurately judged by American college students. These studies led Ekman to declare the need for a *neurocultural* theory to "account for both the universal elements (neurally determined) and the culture-specific (learned) element in facial expression" (p. 219). Universal elements do exist, and some of them have now been objectively measured. But we have yet to understand their adaptive basis or to discover the display rules that mask or distort them in specific societies. (For a popular account of this research, see Ekman and Friesen 1975.)

ATTACHMENT, SEPARATION, AND CROWDING

Clues to important behavioral regularities in human interaction have also been revealed by studies of nonhuman primates (apes and monkeys). These sources include the famous experimental studies conducted by Harry Harlow and the well-known field studies of Jane Goodall. Many less well-known works may be important to our understanding of human socialization. For example, studies of macaques (a genus of Old World monkeys) have shown a typical sequence of mother–infant interactions:

> At birth and for some time thereafter . . . the mother and infant are very close, physically and otherwise. A stage follows in which the infant makes efforts to disengage from the mother, but these efforts are frequently thwarted as the mother attempts to keep the infant close. Following this, however, there is a progressively greater apartness of the pair, which the mother either encourages or allows. The infant spends more and more time away from the mother, involved in play, increasingly with peers, as it develops autonomy and acquires the skills of its species and gender. (Kaufman 1975:133)

This general developmental sequence obviously bears strong similarities to mother–child interaction among humans. Intensive studies of two macaque species by I. Charles Kaufman and his colleagues have demonstrated that, although the bonnet macaque and the pigtail macaque share many behaviors (including those described in the extract above), these species differ in three major ways:

1. Bonnets tend to huddle in close physical contact with one another, even when sleeping, whereas pigtails do not often touch one another unless involved in social interactions such as grooming, mating, or fighting.

2. When a mother macaque of either species is removed from the pen containing her four- to six-month-old infant, the infant becomes "agitated." Bonnet infants are quickly comforted and cared for by other adult females or by their own fathers. Pigtail infants seek comfort but receive no attention from other females or their fathers, and they may even be abused by the adults. Within a day or so, these infants show signs of intense depression similar to that displayed by human infants separated from their mothers. When the pigtail mother is returned to the pen, "there is usually a very intense reunion with increased closeness between mother and infant lasting for as many as three months after reunion. The reunion behavior is much less intense when a bonnet mother is returned" (Kaufman 1975:134).

3. When groups of macaques are observed for several generations, it becomes apparent that pigtails interact much more with their "clanmates" (descendants of the same female ancestor) than do bonnets. This probably follows from the exclusive and intense contact between pigtail infants and their own mothers. Bonnet mothers, on the contrary, allow unrelated females to interact with their infants; while they provide good care of their infants, "bonnet mothers are less restrictive and more

tolerant, that is, they allow infants to go and to return" (p. 138).

These observations suggest that the bonnets develop greater security than the pigtails due to the "multiple mothering" that is part of their social structure. Apparently, their feelings of security make it possible for them to move away from the mother sooner and to establish "initiative" and "autonomy," though they also display some emotional "shallowness" in reunions (cf. M. Mead 1949; Erikson 1950). Kaufman himself relates the species differences to some of Margaret Mead's ideas regarding styles of mothering and their consequences for child development, though he cautions us not to take monkeys *too* literally as models for human behavior (pp. 139–140).

It is much easier to carry out many hours of detailed observations on penned monkeys than on free humans, yet a few anthropologists have managed to collect behavioral data of great richness. For example, Patricia Draper has spent many months in the field intensively observing social interaction among the !Kung Bushmen of southern Africa. Fortunately for the anthropologist, these hunter-gatherers live mainly in the open, using their small brush shelters only for storing food, skins, and tools:

> Each hut, with its own hearth, is a marker signifying the residence of one nuclear family. Typically huts are so close that people sitting at different hearths can hand items back and forth without getting up. Often people sitting around various fires will carry on long discussions without raising their voices above normal conversational levels. (Draper 1973:302)

Despite the extremely low population density of the !Kung territory (approximately 1 person per 10 square miles), Draper found that the Bushmen choose to crowd together in their camps, using an average area of only 188 square feet per person (compared with the 350 square feet minimum recommended for Americans by the American Public Health Association). Furthermore, the !Kung showed none of the symptoms of stress usually produced by such crowding: "Blood pressures are low and do not rise with age, and serum cholesterol levels are among the lowest in the world" (p. 302).

Bushman children sometimes accompany their parents on foraging trips, but more often they are left at the base camp where they can be supervised by adults who are not working that day. Draper comments that "the single most striking feature of !Kung childhood is the extraordinary close association between children and adults" (p. 302). Her detailed observational data make possible statements such as the following:

> In a series of 165 systematically collected, randomized spot observations of 30 children living in the bush, girls (14 years and under) showed an average score of .77 on being inside the circle of huts. (In this usage, a "score" for each child is the proportion of spot observations during which the given behavior was observed.) Boys of the same age range had an average score of .50 on being inside the circle. One or more adults . . . was always present with the children within the village circle. (p. 303)

Spot observations of physical contact revealed that all !Kung touch each other a great deal. This characteristic is most pronounced in children: Girls were touching at least one other person in 57 percent of the observations, while the average for boys was 35 percent. (See also Konner 1976.)

While Bushmen can evidently live in close quarters without experiencing stress, it should be remembered that they are still located in the "wide open spaces" of the Kalahari Desert, and that, if tensions develop in a camp, any !Kung family can easily move to a different camp containing friends and relatives. Much of Draper's later work deals with behavioral changes that occur when Bushmen abandon the nomadic life and congregate in sedentary villages. She has shown the enormous impact of this situational change on socialization, findings of great importance to our understanding of the human condition in a rapidly urbanizing world.

Related studies have been carried out in other disciplines. The British psychiatrist John Bowlby (1973) has written eloquently of mother–child interactions, and especially of the traumatic effects on human children at certain ages of separation from the mother. In research combining psychoanalytic theory with ethological methods, Mahler, Pine, and Bergman (1975) established substages in infant development as indicated by the child's responses to brief separations from the mother. Other investigators have focused on the details of nursing behavior or of infant smiling (Freedman 1974). Still others, often influenced by linguistics or ethnomethodology, have concentrated on details of verbal and nonverbal interaction among adults in experimental or therapeutic groups (Scheflen 1974).

Some of these works follow the Six Cultures Project in treating behavior as an "index" of personality. Others dispense with the concept of personality entirely, striving instead for objective observations of behavior that can be analyzed quantitatively. These are important developments in method, but one wonders if the "repressed" concept of individual continuity (personality) may not return to haunt behavioral studies in another form (cf. Bettelheim 1971:247).

ALTERNATIVE STATES OF CONSCIOUSNESS

While anthropologists were learning to observe external behavior objectively in the here and now, many of their students were "tuning in" to their own inner experience and questioning the validity of "normal" perceptions of the world. Timothy Leary arrived at Harvard University in 1960 and proceeded to "turn on" both colleagues and students. There followed a decade of intense experimentation with drugs and other mind-expanding techniques that is still influencing psychological anthropology. For a brief time there even existed an International Society for Psychedelic Anthropology. This group called for a new approach that could transcend "the crippled thought of current Aca-

demia," and lead to "a consciousness capable of understanding its own concern with cosmic history" (Coult 1977:3).
Less radical scholars recognized the need to study the drug
experience cross-culturally and to reexamine our conventional ideas about shamanistic practices, dreaming, learning,
and the limits of human thought.

Among the works that stirred public interest in these
topics was *The Teachings of Don Juan: A Yaqui Way of Knowledge* (1968) by Carlos Castaneda. This book was followed (in
1971, 1972, and 1974) by three other works on the same
theme. The Castaneda "tetralogy" purports to be an account
of the author's apprenticeship to a Yaqui Indian shaman.
Over several years, Don Juan allegedly taught Castaneda
how to experience an alternative reality and how to take
charge of his own life—to live as a "warrior" and a man of
knowledge. (A fifth book has since appeared and a sixth is
rumored.)

As Jacques Maquet recently commented, "a Ph.D. dissertation that expands into a series of four best-sellers relating a
shamanistic apprenticeship is an unusual event; yet the reaction of the profession has been, on the whole, silence and
uneasiness" (1978:362). Many anthropologists question the
authenticity of Castaneda's account, but even those most
knowledgeable about Yaqui culture seem reluctant simply to
call it a fraud. For example, Ralph Beals (1978:357) declared
that, whatever he may be, Don Juan is not culturally a Yaqui,
and surely not a shaman or sorcerer in the anthropological
sense. However, Beals does not deny that Castaneda may
have received parts of an esoteric tradition from someone in
the Sonora region.

Personally, I do not feel that it matters whether Don Juan
exists or not. The Castaneda books constitute a fascinating
cultural phenomenon whatever their grounding in "reality."
If, as I suspect, Castaneda has imaginatively transported a
Japanese Zen master to the Sonoran desert, presenting par-
ables as real events and *koans* (Zen riddles) as the wise say-
ings of an old Indian, the cumulative effect is still quite ap-

pealing as literature. Castaneda's descriptions of his experiences with peyote, datura, and a psychotropic mushroom apparently correspond to the experiences of many of his readers. However, he and Don Juan insist that the drugs merely help to start one on the "path of power," and that other teaching techniques are essential to becoming a "man of knowledge."

Independent research in Central and South America has confirmed the importance of drugs in New World shamanistic practice. In particular, the writings of Michael Harner on the use of hallucinogens by the Jivaro contribute to our understanding of alternative states of consciousness. Jivaro Indians regularly take large quantities of a drug called *natemä* (*Banisteriopsis* sp.), and Jivaro shamans learn, by using this drug, to summon and control animal spirits. These spirits can be used to kill or to cure, and may also protect their master against attack from other hostile spirits. According to Harner,

> any adult, male or female, who desires to become such a practitioner, simply presents a gift to an already practicing shaman, who administers the *Banisteriopsis* drink and gives some of his own supernatural power to the apprentice. These spirit helpers . . . are the main supernatural forces believed to cause illness and death in daily life. To the non-shaman they are normally invisible, and even shamans can perceive them only under the influence of *natemä*. (Harner 1973:17)

In their drawings, Jivaro men show considerable agreement about the appearance of the spirits; some appear as jaguars, others as snakes or birds, and the shaman himself is seen by others drinking *natemä* to have his head surrounded by a halolike crown. Cultural expectations concerning the animal spirits doubtless affect the drug-induced fantasies, but it also seems possible that certain drugs produce specific kinds of visual, auditory, and kinesthetic effects. Harner, who took these drugs, reported experiences very like those described by Jivaro shamans, as did a number of non-

Indians who knew nothing about the usual effects of the drug (Harner 1973:151–190).

Visions can be induced by a number of other means: fasting, chanting, drumming, dancing, fixating the gaze, or combinations of these. Such "techniques of ecstasy" have been used throughout the world to promote successful hunting or warfare, to increase the fertility of fields or women, and especially to heal the sick. Native healers employ curative herbs as well as ritual techniques, and they are often able to relieve their patients' symptoms (Bock 1979:204–209).

The careful reader may have noticed that I use the phrase "alternative states of consciousness" rather than the usual "altered states." I do this to avoid the presumption that our (my) everyday way of experiencing the world is "unaltered" or normal in any absolute sense (see Price-Williams 1975:91). We do not really know what the world is like to members of very different societies, or to people who speak different languages. Nor do most of us know how the world would appear if we fasted for four days. Many American adults have rather large quantities of nicotine, caffeine, alcohol, or less legal substances periodically circulating in their bloodstreams. What would our consciousness be like without these chemicals, or without the constant crowding and noise pollution of urban life? How does the natural landscape appear without roads, fences, or power lines cutting across it? What are the long-term effects of microwave radiation or even of "background music" on our thinking? No one yet knows the answers to these questions, but studies of brain functioning and "meditative states" indicate that ordinary waking consciousness is just one of several alternative mental states available to most humans without the use of drugs (Sugerman and Tarter 1978).

The most common of these states is *dreaming*. Anthropologists have long known that societies attribute different kinds and degrees of importance to dreams. A few representative examples of social attitudes were summarized by Dorothy Eggan as follows:

> Huron Indians believed that dreams were a revelation of the secret and hidden wishes of the soul, while the Trobriand Islanders reversed this belief and thought that magically induced dreams could *produce* a wish in the dreamer, and thus influence his waking conduct. The Naga of Assam dismissed much of the manifest content and looked for symbols. Other groups, such as the Hopi and Navaho Indians, treated the manifest content at face value, interpreting it loosely, depending upon the dreamer's emotional and physical reaction on awakening. . . . The Navaho treated a bad dream as they did any illness, by religious ceremony and native medicine. (Eggan 1961:553; see also Wallace 1958)

Documenting such cultural differences is an important part of psychological anthropology, but many problems of theory and method remain. Should cross-cultural analysis of dreams attempt dynamic interpretations, combining "the couch and the field" (LeVine 1973:203–215)? Or should it deal only with manifest dream content? To what extent are dreams personal and to what extent are they shaped by cultural expectations or universal symbolism? Since dreaming appears to be universal in human experience, what are its adaptive functions for the individual and for his group?

Freud, Róheim, Devereux, and other psychoanalytic anthropologists used dream material in their cultural studies. But while dreams provide special kinds of information about an individual, even collecting a representative sample of dreams may present great difficulties: It calls for close rapport between anthropologist and dreamers, a willingness on the part of the dreamers to record or tell their dreams, an avoidance by the collector of "cultural standardization" of the contents as well as a sensitivity to linguistic and symbolic meanings. For example, the Hopi believed that "a bad dream required immediate confession and action, while a good dream had to be remembered but not told until it came true" (Eggan 1961:567). Obviously, this attitude might bias the sample available in Hopi society. Nevertheless, with persistence and imagination, a great deal can be learned from cross-cultural dream analysis. Dorothy Eggan's own work with the Hopi and George Devereux's extended case study of a "Wolf" Indian man (1969) are examples of what can be accomplished in this area. (For a good introduction to research on sleep and dreaming, see Dement 1974; also Abel and Métraux 1974:235–253; O'Nell 1976; D'Andrade 1961.)

Abundant evidence exists to show that intense mental activity goes on during sleep. Solutions to personal or intellectual problems often come into dreams, as do poems, melodies, and visual images that may be developed into works of art (Dement 1974:95–102). These facts should make us aware that some kinds of learning cannot be accounted for entirely by mechanical stimulus-response connections. Some kinds of learning appear to have quite special characteristics.

Anthony Wallace calls one special type *ritual learning* to refer to the rapid reorganization of experience under conditions of stress resulting in far-reaching cognitive and emotional changes (1966:239–242). Such learning may be found in tribal initiations, individual conversions, and in the bizarre "restructuring of behavior" that often accompanies recruitment to messianic cults (Katcher and Katcher 1968). Some people would argue that becoming a nuclear physicist, a communist, or a Freudian involves a similar reorganization of experience under stress (Whyte 1974). The techniques of "thought reform" developed in China and methods of intensive persuasion (such as those used in Reverend Jim Jones' People's Temple) combine situational and interpersonal factors to produce special kinds of learning and unlearning (Lifton 1961; Frank 1963; see also Holloman 1974). One does not have to approve of those methods to recognize their potency.

OF HUMAN THOUGHT

Scientific reports about the effects of sensory deprivation and recent research into the different functions of the brain's two hemispheres should by now have convinced us that we do not know the limits of human thought. Freud taught that consciousness is but a small part of our total psychic functioning. His famous dictum "Where id is, there shall ego be," points to the possibility of a greatly expanded awareness to be achieved through psychoanalysis. But other pathways to self-knowledge exist, and, as Douglass R. Price-Williams has wisely suggested, it would be a mistake to evaluate shamanistic, Yogic, or Tantric doctrines exclusively from the standpoint of Western science, for "these schemes appear to be more in the nature of a chart or map through which people, following them, are able to share experiences" (Price-Williams 1975:89). Many lines of research lead us back to the problems of primitive and civilized mentality with which this book began. We shall consider these topics further in the final chapter.

Claude Lévi-Strauss

TEN

Cognitive Anthropology

To what extent can cultural differences be explained by differences in the thought processes of people in diverse societies? If such cognitive differences exist, are they due to biological or environmental factors? To what degree are they modifiable by experience? And what can the cross-cultural study of cognition teach us about our own habits of thought? Anthropologists have long been interested in such questions. In Chapter One, we considered the views of Tylor, Frazer, Wundt, Lévy-Bruhl, and Boas on the question of "primitive mentality." Many influential anthropologists have expressed interest in "how the natives think." For example, in a famous passage, Bronislaw Malinowski wrote that the final goal of ethnography should be "to grasp the native's point of view, his relation to life, to realize *his* vision of *his* world" (1961:25).

Like Boas, Malinowski believed that language was an important key to understanding native thought, and he stressed the collection of *texts* in the native language. One modern heir to this approach was the late Dorothy Lee. Her sensitive essays suggested ways that differences among languages affect the individual's sense of self, of time, and of causation (Lee 1959). Her style of writing and her attempts to synthesize data of various types are reminiscent of Ruth Benedict and Edward Sapir; however, like Irving Hallowell, Lee fits into no particular school or approach, and her influence has been mainly transmitted by a small group of students.

Although other issues dominated the field after World War II, interest in primitive thought never completely vanished from American anthropology. Starting in the mid-1950s, however, concern with human thought' processes reappeared in several different quarters, leading to the emergence of a school of Cognitive Anthropology (Tyler 1969). In the following sections, we shall trace the emergence of this school and its relation to developments in other disciplines.

ETHNOSEMANTICS

For many decades, American linguistics was a formal, descriptive science concerned largely with sound systems and syntax to the neglect of semantics. Anthropologists trained in this discipline used language as a practical research tool, and some improvised ways of using the native language to explore unique cultural meanings (see Hymes 1964). When new methods were developed in linguistics for analyzing semantic relationships, anthropologists were quick to take an interest in and to use these methods for their own purposes.

This approach to understanding native systems of meaning through language became known as *ethnosemantics*. In the hands of skilled ethnographers such as Harold Conklin, Ward Goodenough, and Charles Frake, a variety of topics was studied. Ethnosemanticists set themselves the goal of understanding how cultural knowledge is organized (Spradley 1972). They systematically investigated *semantic domains* (areas of meaning) such as kinship terms, disease categories, and color terminology, carefully defining individual terms and showing each term's relationship to other terms in the domain. They also compared the structure of semantic domains within and across languages, and sought to understand how people *used* such cultural knowledge to interpret behavior and make decisions.

Even the simple task of "getting names for things" turned out to be much more complicated than had been suspected. The ethnosemanticist must learn to ask the right kinds of questions if the informants' answers are to be really meaningful. As Frake observed,

> an ethnographer should strive to define objects according to the conceptual system of the people he is studying. [One should] look upon the task of getting names for things not as an exercise in linguistic recording, but [as] a way of finding out what are in fact the "things" in the environment of the people being studied.... The analysis of a culture's terminology will not ... exhaustively reveal the cognitive world of its members, but it will tap a central portion of it. (Frake 1962:74–75)

One technique used in the study of semantic domains is called *componential analysis.* This technique helps the analyst to discover the "dimensions of meaning" that differentiate the terms in a domain and to display the relationships of contrast and hierarchy among the terms. For example, the English subject pronouns contrast in terms of the dimensions of *person* (first, second, third), *number* (singular, plural), and, in one case, *gender* (masculine, feminine). This information is presented in Table 10-1.

French subject pronouns use these three dimensions, extending the gender contrast to the third person plural pronouns *(ils, elles).* The French pronouns also include two different forms for second person singular *(tu, vous)* that introduce an additional dimension of meaning, usually called *intimacy* (familiar, formal), as shown in Table 10-2. This display is quite similar to the previous one, for English and French

Table 10-1   Subject Pronouns in English

| | Person and Gender | | |
Number	First	Second	Third
Singular	I	You	He (m.), She (f.)
Plural	We	You	They

Table 10-2   Subject Pronouns in French

| | Person, Intimacy Level, and Gender | | |
Number	First	Second	Third
Singular	*Je*	*Tu, Vous*	*Il* (m.), *Elle* (f.)
Plural	*Nous*	*Vous*	*Ils* (m.), *Elles* (f.)

are closely related languages; nevertheless, there are significant differences between them.

The "components" of a componential analysis are the semantic values of a term on each relevant dimension of meaning. For example, the components of *she* are third person, singular, and feminine on the dimensions of person, number, and gender, respectively. Anthropologists have used componential analysis to discover the dimensions of meaning in the domain of kinship terms (see Tyler 1969). In English, for example, the terms *grandfather, father, son,* and *grandson* contrast with one another on the dimension of *generation,* and the entire set contrasts with the terms *grandmother, mother, daughter,* and *granddaughter* on the dimension of *sex*. These eight terms may be displayed to bring out their contrasts and similarities as in Table 10-3; however, it is only when they are contrasted with all the other English terms (including *cousin* and *sister-in-law*) that the full range of components is realized. In other languages, quite different dimensions and components may be used to contrast kinship terms (see Burling 1970).

Table 10-3 Contrasts Among Some English Kinship
Terms on Two Dimensions (Generation and Sex)

	Sex	
Generation	Male	Female
+2	Grandfather	Grandmother
+1	Father	Mother
−1	Son	Daughter
−2	Grandson	Granddaughter

Besides contrasting on one or more dimensions of meaning, many terms in a semantic domain stand in *hierarchical
relations* to one another. For example, a *father* is a kind of
parent, and a *parent* is a kind of *relative.* This species-genus
(or class inclusion) relationship can be displayed in a tree
diagram such as Figure 10-1, where the general terms are
connected by lines to the specific terms they include. (For a
formal method of generating such trees and their components, see Bock 1968.) Terms on the same horizontal level in
such a diagram contrast with one another on dimensions of
meaning (sex, generation, and the like), but terms on
different levels do not directly contrast with one another.
Instead, lower-level terms are related to higher-level terms as
species to genus, part to whole, ingredient to mixture, and so
forth, depending on the specific domain.

Ethnosemantic studies of anatomy investigate cultural
conceptions of the human body, its parts and their functions.
These studies have shown that societies do not all divide up
the body in the same way. Our notion of what constitute
body parts (for example, shoulder, hip, or foot) and of how
these parts relate to one another (*finger* is part of *hand,* which
is part of *lower arm*) are far from universal. For example, the
Kewa of New Guinea have terms for body parts that we
would roughly translate as *back, chest,* and *arms,* but these
parts are considered parts of a unit called *kádésaa,* a term

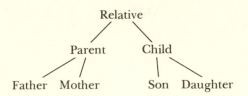

Figure 10-1 Hierarchical relations among some English kinship terms.

that has no simple English equivalent (Franklin 1963). Kewa body parts are also associated with distinctive physiological and spiritual functions peculiar to Kewa culture.

One of the most interesting studies of this domain is the Navajo anatomical atlas compiled by Oswald Werner and his colleagues, a work that demonstrates the remarkable amount of anatomical knowledge accumulated in traditional Navajo culture. It specifies hundreds of different terms (some for minute bodily structures) and complex relations among them. This Navajo ethnoscience is only in error where the Navajos have transferred to human anatomy structures that they learned about in butchering sheep and other mammals. (These are exactly the kinds of errors that persisted in European anatomy books for hundreds of years, including the centuries when dissection of human cadavers was forbidden by the Roman Catholic Church.)

Another area of continuing interest is the ethnosemantic analysis of *color terminology*. Each language has a set of terms that partitions the domain of color, but languages differ in the number of basic terms and the range of colors to which each term refers. In reaction to simplistic (and racist) notions about "primitive languages," American anthropologists usually argued that the size of a color lexicon was unimportant, since all such systems were arbitrary and one way of partitioning the visible spectrum was as good as the next.

During the 1960s, however, anthropologists at the Language Behavior Laboratory at Berkeley began to uncover a fascinating pattern in the color terms found in hundreds of languages. When one examines the *basic* color terms (words such as *red* or *blue,* but not *scarlet, rust,* or *sky blue*), it appears that the number of such terms in a language is closely related to the kinds of colors they designate. Brent Berlin and Paul Kay published an exciting study, *Basic Color Terms* (1969), suggesting that color terminology *evolves* from simple to complex, with new terms being added in a fixed order. In the few languages that have only two basic color terms the domain is simply divided into "light" and "dark," but languages that have three basic color terms *always* refer to white, black, and red. Five-term systems always have these first three plus yellow and green, and the sixth term added is always blue, which takes over some of the hues formerly included in black and green. In seven-term systems, brown is added, and this term is found only in systems that have at least six other terms. There are four other basic terms (gray, pink, orange, and purple), but these do not appear to be added in any particular order.

Minor modifications have been made in the Berlin and Kay analysis since it first appeared, but controversy continues over its significance. What produces these regularities in color lexicons? Could they be due to biological universals? The regularities are too widespread to be entirely accounted for by the historical diffusion of words or ways of categorizing. Furthermore, an undeniable correlation exists between size of color lexicon of a language and level of social and technological complexity of its speakers. As summarized by Robbins Burling,

> languages with two terms are confined to people with the simplest level of technology, such as the New Guinea Jalé. At the other extreme, the only languages known to have terms for all eleven [basic colors] are from Europe and east Asia where the people have long histories, and great complexity in

their culture and technology. Between these extremes are people like the Tiv, a rather simple African tribe of Nigeria with three terms, the Hanunóo tribe of the Philippines with four, the Eskimo with five, some rather complex African tribes with six, the Malayalam of southern India and the Burmese with seven. (Burling 1970:48)

Other studies suggest that there may be a physiological basis for the distribution of color terminologies. Marc H. Bornstein (1975) draws on recent work in color vision indicating that people with dark retinal pigmentation have impaired vision in the blue-green part of the spectrum, whereas light-eyed people are relatively more sensitive to color differences. Bornstein demonstrates that societies with small color lexicons cluster in the latitudes near the equator, where populations with high frequencies of dark eye pigmentation are found. Melvin Ember has recently shown that latitude and level of social complexity appear to interact (statistically) in determining the size of color lexicons:

> High societal complexity predicts large basic color lexicon *only* in the relatively higher latitudes . . . and high latitude predicts a large basic color lexicon *only* where social complexity is high. [These facts] suggest that we have an example here of cultural and biological factors interacting as determinants of a semantic domain. (Ember 1978:366–367)

Retinal pigmentation also seems to affect susceptibility to optical illusions such as the Müller-Lyer illusion, so this issue too may have to be reconsidered (see "Perception, or 'Do You See What I See?'" in Chapter One).

The color-term controversy will doubtless continue for many years. It is a good example of the way in which ethnosemantic studies can lead to hypotheses about human cognition. We cannot *assume* that differences among languages correspond to group differences in perception or thinking, but imaginative ways are being found to test ideas about these topics. Intensive field studies of native systems of classification ("folk taxonomies") have focused on plants, animals, body parts, color terms, and classifications of every-day objects (Conklin 1972; Rosch 1975). All such studies can contribute to our understanding of human thought, but they must be interpreted with great caution.

COGNITIVE DEVELOPMENT:
STAGES, STYLES, AND MAPS

A second group of approaches in cognitive anthropology is concerned with development and functioning. Most of them address differential development of thought processes in various cultures and environments. Topics studied range from perceptual learning to mathematical and moral reasoning, but all have been influenced by the work of the great Swiss psychologist Jean Piaget.

Piaget's studies of cognition began in the 1920s, and include major books on play, imitation, and the development of moral judgment as well as children's conceptions of time, space, number, and logic. Piaget is best known to American psychologists and educators for his work on stages of intellectual development. His concepts of *sensory-motor schema* and *operational intelligence* have become as popular in some circles as many Freudian concepts once were. Much of contemporary cross-cultural psychology is intended to validate or modify Piaget's ideas.

Essentially, Piaget holds that knowledge is not a "passive copy of reality," but rather an active construction that the individual achieves in the course of time:

> Knowing an object does not mean copying it—it means acting upon it. It means constructing systems of transformations that can be carried out on or with this object. . . . Knowledge, then, is a system of transformations that become progressively adequate. (Piaget 1971:15)

Piaget believes that there are *universal stages of cognitive development,* that is, that children learn about reality first by perceptual and motor exploration of their world and then by acquiring mental operations, such as seriation, conservation, and propositional thought, that enable them to transform their experience without necessarily manipulating the environment. All normal children are said to master these operations in the same order, though at somewhat different ages (Murray 1972).

When claims about universal cognitive stages are based primarily on experiments with members of a single society (Swiss school children), they must be validated by cross-cultural research. Piaget was fully aware of this, and in *The Child and Reality* he posed these important questions: "Does the life cycle express a basic biological rhythm, an ineluctable law? Does civilization modify this rhythm and to what extent? In other words, is it possible to increase or decrease this temporal development" (Piaget 1973:1–2)? Most research on these questions has been carried out by cognitive psychologists rather than by psychological anthropologists, but the results are highly relevant to anthropological problems (see Dasen 1972). We wish to know whether Piaget's stages are indeed universal and, if so, how they are modified by social experience (culture).

A great deal of attention has been devoted to Piaget's concept of *conservation,* that is, the child's recognition that some things remain "the same" despite transformations of physical properties. For example, to study conservation of volume, the experimenter may pour liquid from a short, wide beaker (A) into a tall, narrow one (B). Children can see that all the water in A has been poured into B, but up to the age of about six they will usually insist that there is a different amount of water in the second beaker. When children learn to judge the volume of water to be equal despite the transformation of shape, they are said to have mastered the concept of conservation of volume.

A number of studies seem to indicate significant cultural differences in the mastery of such basic concepts. For example, conservation concepts that most American children learn by age seven (when they have entered elementary school) may be learned several years later by non-Western children, especially in societies that have no formal educational institutions. However, as Cole and Scribner comment, even within a single society, "performance depends on how the task is presented and the particular past experiences of the subjects (as for instance, whether they live in a rural town or the city, and whether or not they attend school)" (Cole and Scribner 1974:151). Before leaping to conclusions about primitive mentality, we must carefully consider such factors as the content of tests and the familiarity of test materials.

Another of Piaget's conservation tests involves two identical balls of clay. When one of the balls is rolled out into a long "sausage," children who lack the conservation concept report that the amounts of clay are now different. To assess the effect of familiarity with test materials on outcome, Price-Williams, Gordon, and Ramirez (1969) went to a Mexican village where many families of potters lived. They tested seventy-six children between six and nine years old, half from potter families and half from nonpotter families. As might be expected, children of potters did much better on the tests using clay than did the other children. (They also did somewhat better on other conservation tests.)

It has been difficult to correlate performance on conservation tests with other cognitive skills; however, as in Piaget's original work, many valuable data do not appear in the summaries of results. Piaget developed subtle ways of interviewing that reveal the *kinds of reasoning* that lie behind a child's actions or judgments. The Piagetian method of inquiry has as much to offer to psychological anthropology as do his proposed developmental stages. (The same might be said of psychoanalysis.)

The French anthropologist Claude Lévi-Strauss is another European scholar who has written about universals of human cognition. Like some psychoanalytic anthropologists, Lévi-Strauss works from cultural rather than individual data, attempting to infer properties of the human mind from myths and from social structures.

In his best-known book, ironically titled *The Savage Mind,* Lévi-Strauss asserts that no significant differences exist between the mental capacities of civilized and primitive peoples. He argues, rather, that many preliterates employ a "style of thinking" in which the *sensible* qualities of objects and organisms (size, color, odor, and the like) are used in the construction of categories and the performance of logical operations, rather than the *abstract* qualities that Western science has found useful (mass, frequency, acceleration, and so on). Use of this style is not evidence of confused thinking. Magic and mythical thought have a logic as rigorous as that of science, and they are based on "a complete and all-embracing determinism" (Lévi-Strauss 1966:11). The accomplishments of mythical thought are also to be admired; the development of pottery, weaving, agriculture, and animal domestication all "required a genuinely scientific attitude, sustained and watchful interest and a desire for knowledge for its own sake" (p. 14).

In the same book, and from a perspective closer to Piaget's than Freud's, Lévi-Strauss takes up the topic of totemism and its relationship to food taboos. He suggests that, since totemic societies have already used differences among animal species to create differences among themselves (that is, among clan groups named for different species), they use food taboos to *deny man's animal nature* (1966:108). Taboos function to support essential distinctions between categories: human versus animal, man versus woman, friend versus enemy, and so forth. Those who employ mythical thought encounter exactly the same intellectual problems that have troubled Western philosophers for centuries in trying to comprehend the mystery of human origins and our place in the universe.

The phrase *cognitive style* is most closely associated with H. A. Witkin's theory concerning general modes of psychological functioning. Witkin (1967) suggests that individuals differ in their approaches to cognitive and perceptual tasks:

People with a "global" style respond to the general characteristics of a situation, whereas those with "articulated" styles are more able to differentiate component features of their environments. (For an early discussion of global versus differentiated perception, see Murphy 1947:331–361.)

Witkin also introduces the concepts of *field-dependence* and *field-independence* to denote the perceptual abilities of global and articulated thinkers, respectively. Field-dependent people have difficulty picking out geometric forms embedded in complex figures, whereas field-independent people are better at decomposing such configurations. Both environmental and cultural factors (child training) have been shown to contribute to cognitive articulation. (See Cole and Scribner 1974:82–90; Berry 1976; Serpell 1976:51–54.)

The concept of *cognitive maps* is somewhat less elusive than the notion of cognitive styles. It was first formulated by Edward C. Tolman in the classic paper "Cognitive Maps in Rats and Men" (1948). Tolman noted a number of behavioral phenomena that the mechanistic behaviorism of his time could not explain. For example, hungry rats who had run through a maze ten times without receiving a food reward at the exit seemed to learn very slowly compared with rats who were rewarded. However, if the first group was rewarded on the eleventh trial, they showed a sudden marked improvement in performance from then on. Tolman argued that the unrewarded rats had nevertheless built up cognitive maps of the maze while exploring it on the first ten trials; when the reward was offered and incentive provided, these maps enabled them to perform quickly and with few errors.

Other experiments seem to confirm the idea that organisms develop maplike concepts of their environments, and that these maps include many features they have never been rewarded for learning. Cognitive maps are not just narrow "strips" showing starting point, route, and destination, but are often broad and "comprehensive." Tolman asks what conditions favor narrow maps in rats and in humans. He lists four factors that induce narrowness (1958:261); these are:

1. Brain damage.

2. Inadequate environmental cues (what we would today call an "impoverished environment").

3. Overlearning by repetition in early training.

4. Overmotivation or intense frustration.

Assuming that one favors broad, comprehensive knowledge, these points have obvious implications for child training and education. Tolman also suggests that the Freudian defense mechanisms of regression, fixation, and displacement are instances of people adopting (or returning to) extremely narrow cognitive maps under conditions of strong motivation or intense frustration. (Compare Dollard and Miller 1950.)

The concept of cognitive maps was used and reinterpreted by a number of anthropologists in the 1960s. In ethnosemantic studies the term refers to the contrastive and hierarchical relationships between the categories of a semantic domain. For example, Charles Frake wrote that "the selection of one statement over another in a particular sociolinguistic context . . . points to the category boundaries on a culture's cognitive map" (1962:77). Anthony Wallace stayed closer to Tolman's meaning; he incorporated the term into his own concept of the *mazeway*, defined as "the sum of all the cognitive maps which at any moment a person maintains" (1965:277). Wallace argued that even simple tasks such as tending a fire or driving to work require a high level of cognitive complexity, including action plans and rules, control operations, monitored information, and organization. (George Foster's "image of limited good," discussed in Chapter Eight, is also a kind of cognitive map that can be used to account for peasant behavior.)

Kevin Lynch, an architect at MIT, used the map concept quite literally in his book *The Image of the City*. His detailed interviews with the inhabitants of three cities revealed systematic differences in the cognitive maps these people had of their respective urban environments. There were differences in the degree to which each group cognized its city in terms of landmarks, districts, paths, edges, or "nodes," and in their use of these elements to orient themselves when traveling (Lynch 1964:46–90). Dean MacCannell (1976) used a similar approach to study the role of *tourism* in the development of people's cognitive maps of the modern world.

The most useful recent treatment of this topic is Ulrich Neisser's book *Cognition and Reality* (1976:108–127). Neisser argues that cognitive maps are not just passive images of the environment; rather, they are active, information-seeking structures that *direct* our perceptual exploration of the world. Guided by our general maps and the specific "perceptual schemata" embedded in them, we *sample* the information present in the environment; this process frequently leads us to *modify* our conceptions of the world. Our new conceptions then direct renewed exploration, creating a continuing cyclical process (see Figure 10-2).

Neisser's treatment of cognitive maps and perceptual schemata is highly compatible with my own views on the relation of culture to behavior. For many years I have argued that culture consists of *categories of experience* associated with *plans for action* (Bock 1979). We can infer the existence and structure of these categories and plans from the regularities of verbal and nonverbal behavior they produce. The capacity to learn the conventional categories and plans of one's community is fundamental to a human level of existence.

These cultural structures *influence* but do not completely determine behavior, and they can be modified by experience. Furthermore, I believe that the *meaning* of a cultural element, be it a word, a social role, or an artifact, is defined by its contrastive relations with similar types of elements and by the types of situations in which it is expected to occur (Bock 1964). This theory of culture is "psychological" in that it explicitly presupposes that all humans share certain cognitive capacities. I fully endorse Neisser's statement that "actions are hierarchically embedded in more extensive actions and are motivated by anticipated consequences at various levels of schematic organization" (1976:113; see Serpell 1976:18).

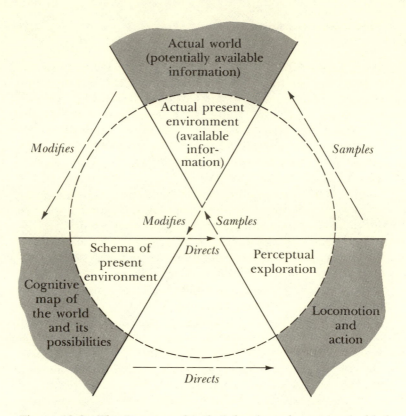

Figure 10-2 The "perceptual cycle," showing schemata embedded in cognitive maps, directing perceptual exploration of the environment, and being modified by the results of that exploration. (From *Cognition and Reality* by Ulric Neisser. W. H. Freeman and Company. Copyright © 1976.)

RACE, CULTURE, AND INTELLIGENCE

All normal people do acquire the basic cognitive skills necessary for social life in their respective cultures. This fact does not logically exclude the possibility of significant group differences in mental capacity, but most attempts to document such differences have met with great difficulties. Since investigators now agree that *there is no such thing as a culture-free test of intelligence,* any claims about ethnic, class, or racial differences in intelligence must be examined with great caution. For a comprehensive review of research on this topic, the reader should consult Loehlin, Lindzey, and Spuhler (1975). However, for a brief and thoughtful discussion of the issues, I know of no better source than Douglass R. Price-Williams' chapter, "The Cultural Relativism of Intelligence" (1975:51–64). I shall draw heavily on this essay in the following pages.

To avoid the problem of defining intelligence, many psychologists subscribe to the circular statement "Intelligence is whatever intelligence tests measure." But no intelligence test can do more than *sample* the cognitive abilities of those who take it. Furthermore, an intelligence test is itself the product of a particular cultural tradition in which certain cognitive styles and skills are valued while others are disparaged. Even within a complex society some groups may place more emphasis on skills such as rote memory or rapid arithmetical calculations than do other groups. Are any of these skills valid indices of intelligence for all people?

Using tests constructed for and validated on Western populations to assess non-Westerners introduces enormous problems of interpretation. Cross-cultural studies must be especially sensitive to the multitude of factors that can influence performance (see "Perception, or 'Do You See What I See?'" in Chapter One). According to Price-Williams,

> psychologists seem to have followed just the wrong sequence in probing other cultures. Instead of first exploring the social environment of the tested and examining cognitive skills such as classification, sorting and discrimination, and then constructing tests to accommodate such background knowledge, the tendency has been to impose tests already constructed for another culture. Then the researcher finds out what should have been modified, excluded or otherwise altered in the tests, and only afterward does he look around for influencing social factors. (Price-Williams 1975:55)

Social change is another factor that may interfere with attempts to measure intelligence. Industrial technology makes certain demands on the populations that use it, and in the process of meeting these demands, school systems in developing countries become homogeneous. Western intelligence tests assess readiness for this type of schooling—indeed, that is what they were invented to do. For this reason they may be of use in industrializing societies, but this does not mean that they measure any *general capacity* of individuals. In fact, there is ample evidence that IQ scores bear little relationship to occupational success or creative achievement in our own society.

Remember that the dominant Anglo-American culture is exceptionally individualistic in its values and practices (see "The Lonely Crowd," Chapter Five). In consequence, we evaluate intelligence with a strong individualistic bias. However, we should be aware that

> many societies do not go about solving problems individually but in groups; that tackling artificial tasks in the abstract is an alien challenge; that methods of instruction and the subsequent learning process are not to be differentiated from the rest of living; that the notion of doing something within a predetermined time, let alone with haste, is again foreign. (Price-Williams 1975:58)

There are, then, different styles of intelligence and perhaps even qualitatively different kinds of intelligence.

The concept of intelligence is itself a social product. An ethnosemantic investigation of this domain might begin with the analysis of words used in different cultures to refer to cognitive abilities. For example, the exceptionally intelligent child in American society is usually said to be "bright," while the exceptional French child is described as "wise" (*sage*); the corresponding term in Mexico means "ready" (*listo*). In the Shona language of Rhodesia the word closest to our "intelligence" is *ngware,* but this term also carries the connotations of "caution, prudence and wisdom, particularly in social matters" (p. 60).

Even at this superficial level we seem to be dealing with four quite different conceptions of intelligence. This obser-

vation does not mean we should abandon cross-cultural research, but it should put us on guard against "a facile comparison, based on category schemes that are not sufficiently
representative of the cognitive domains of any one of the
cultures being compared" (p. 64). These cautions also apply
to research on racial and ethnic differences within a complex
society.

TOWARD A NEW SYNTHESIS

Cognitive anthropologists and cross-cultural psychologists
will certainly continue to work on problems of cognitive development, intelligence, and the organization of cultural
knowledge, but ways must also be found to relate research
on these contemporary issues to traditional anthropological
problems. I believe that we can anticipate a new synthesis in
psychological anthropology, one that will emphasize cognitive processes without neglecting the importance of emotion.
Cross-cultural correlations will be used to suggest hypotheses, but these hypotheses will be evaluated by intensive observations of behavior in natural settings and, whenever
possible, by experiments. The synthesis will be concerned
more with human universals than with sociocultural differences, but its methodology will be relativistic, in recognition of the range of human adaptations and the pervasive
influence of culture on human behavior.

Where will the new synthesis come from? Probably it will
emerge from some major institution where the right "mix"
of personnel and resources is ready to be ignited by the
spark of an idea. Past syntheses have come from Columbia,
Yale, and Chicago. At present, the most likely locus for a
new synthesis is southern California, where faculty members
at two major universities (UCLA and UC, San Diego) have
the imagination and energy needed to maximally stimulate
one another as well as their students. Other locations are
possible (for example, Rockefeller University, Pittsburgh, or

Connecticut), and we should not exclude the chance that nonacademic institutions or individuals might provide the spark. But as Robert Edgerton insists, any synthesis of anthropology and psychology must combine naturalistic observation with experimentation:

> Such a fusion may be possible but it will not come about easily until we who work in cross-cultural psychology realize that . . . we must reconcile two paradigms—experimentalism and naturalism—with all their irreconcilable ideas about how human beings behave, think, and feel. It may take a revolution in Kuhn's [1962] terms to achieve such a reformulation, but until we do, the fields of cross-cultural psychology and psychological anthropology are more likely than not to diverge and to lose the opportunity for significant collaboration or fusion. (Edgerton 1974:64)

If no new synthesis develops, psychological anthropologists may simply stumble along, working on narrow problems and losing talented researchers to disciplines possessing more comprehensive cognitive maps. The consequence will be an era of *banalysis*—research that merely goes through the motions of scientific analysis. Our generation desperately needs a new paradigm in order to overcome the false dichotomy between culture and personality and to recognize the mutual relevance of social and individual phenomena (Bateson 1972).

POSTLUDE

All Psychology Is Cultural

I began this book with the intentionally provocative statement "All anthropology is psychological." I then offered arguments (some of which I believe to be correct) to support that position. Now it is time to turn the tables and ask, "To what extent is psychology cultural?"

To begin with, psychology as an academic discipline has the features of any cultural movement: It has a complex social structure and technology, and a language that, at its worst, is virtually incomprehensible to outsiders. It also has mighty founding figures—quasi-totemic ancestors whose emblems are the rat, the pigeon, the couch, and the mandala. Within this discipline, subcultures have emerged and disappeared, each with its own ideology and true believers. Commitment to particular schools of psychology, from psychoanalysis to behaviorism, can be explained by the same principles that explain participation in esoteric "suicide cults" or patriotic wars. Also, as Richard A. Shweder has recently demonstrated (1977), "magical thinking" is as prevalent in clinical judgments of personality as it is in shamanistic performances and folk science.

Next, what we have called "psychology" in this book is actually a very limited class of theories, derived exclusively from European and American research. Other psychologies and psychotherapies exist, arising from quite different cultural roots (see Murphy and Murphy 1968). For example, as Alan W. Watts has written,

> historically, Western psychology has directed itself to the study of the psyche or mind as a clinical entity, whereas Eastern cultures have not categorized mind and matter, soul and body, in the same way as the Western. [Western psychotherapists are] interested in changing the consciousness of peculiarly disturbed individuals. The disciplines of Buddhism and Taoism are, however, concerned with changing the consciousness of normal, socially adjusted people. (Watts 1969:16)

Failure to recognize the origins of Western psychology in our own cultural tradition, with its unconscious values, biases, and habits of thought, is the crudest kind of ethnocentrism. Besides being biased by their own culture, most Western psychologists introduce further biases into their results by using experimental subjects exclusively from their own societies. Robert Serpell has observed that

> a science of behaviour which can account only for the behaviour of a minority of the world's population is far more appropriately designated a limited specialty than the search for explanations which account for the full range of human behaviour patterns around the world. (1976:16)

This argument is not intended to deny the possibility of a *transcultural psychiatry* that would transcend the biases of a particular tradition to define the parameters of healthy human functioning, but it should serve to caution us against mistaking our own culture's implicit ideals for ultimate truths. (See Endleman 1967:576–598.)

Still another argument for the social—or cultural—basis of all psychology is found in the following statement:

> In the individual's mental life someone else is invariably involved, as a model, as an object, as a helper, as an opponent;

and so from the very first individual psychology [is] social psychology as well.

Most students are surprised to learn that this is a quotation from Sigmund Freud (1959:1), but the "first Freudian" clearly recognized the influence of social relations and group allegiances upon individual mental processes. Erik Erikson has extended psychoanalytic thought by insisting on the relevance of history and culture to the individual's sense of identity, while Rohrer and Edmonson's (1964) combination of social structure and individual striving in their concept of "primary role identification" indicates another way that culture may be "incorporated" into one's personality (Spiro 1951).

We saw in Chapter Ten that concepts of intelligence are relative to particular cultural contexts. This is true of many other psychological ideas, including concepts of self and of personality (Lee 1959:131–153). Gardner Murphy has cautioned us that the Western concept of personality as a self-contained unity can be traced back at least to Platonic idealism. According to Murphy, most of us prefer this "encapsulated" view of the individual to a social or interactionist view for reasons that are basically *moralistic:*

> People can be relied on if their boundaries are definite and fixed; you know where to put them; you know they will stay put. Above all, they can be held responsible. A society made up of persons of this sort . . . can be conveniently managed from above. (1947:10; see also Brown 1966:90–161)

The cultural basis of our psychological conceptions has been further revealed by a number of contemporary writers. The British psychiatrist R. D. Laing has written persuasively on the *political* basis of concepts of madness, suggesting that for many persons schizophrenia can be a healthy response to an insoluble dilemma. Thomas Szasz (1961) has argued that "mental illness" is a *myth* that should be replaced by more humane understanding based on the analysis of the communication process. (Cf. Siegler and Osmond 1974.) And sociologist Philip Rieff (1966) has pointed out the moral implications of contemporary notions of therapy, especially as they relate to individual responsibility and initiative. All these writers indirectly support Ruth Benedict's ideas about the *relativity of normality* ("Configurations of Culture," Chapter Three). Psychological anthropology must continually sensitize itself to the ways that a society's basic values influence the behavior and cognition of its members; and, in this case, clarity begins at home.

Viewed over the first century of its existence, psychological anthropology exhibits two complementary tendencies: It examines in ever finer detail the cultural and interactional constraints on individuals' behavior while simultaneously considering the widest possible context for any action (Price-Williams 1975:18). Our survey of issues and approaches in psychological anthropology brings us to this question: *Why does a particular society, or school of thought, or individual choose at some point in history to attribute behavior to a particular set of causes?* To answer this question we would need a psychohistory of the behavioral sciences (see Devereux 1978:373–375; Coles 1970). Difficult as this sounds, it may be a necessary prolegomenon to any future synthesis.

Only the most tentative answers to our master question are now available. In this book we have surveyed a series of scientific approaches that attribute behavior to every sort of cause, from early psychic trauma to the immediate interaction situation and from patterns of child training to "the selfish gene." In the cases of a few individuals (Sapir, Benedict, Bettelheim) and of several approaches (modal personality, cross-cultural correlations, interactionism), I have been able to trace the personal experiences and institutional arrangements that shaped their respective points of view. I believe that we *can* understand why individuals and groups are drawn to particular theories of "human nature," but I also believe that if we repress the motives for our own studies we are certain to fail. It was not Freud, but George Santayana who wrote, "Those who cannot remember the past are condemned to repeat it."

REFERENCES

Most citations are to recent, inexpensive editions. When the publication date of the new edition is more than ten years later than that of the original publication, the earlier date is shown in parentheses.

Abel, Theodora M., and Rhoda Métraux

1974   *Culture and psychotherapy.* New Haven: College and University Press.

Aberle, David F.

1960   The influence of linguistics on early culture and personality theory. In *Essays in the science of culture,* ed. G. E. Dole and R. L. Carneiro, pp. 1–29. New York: Crowell.

Adorno, Theodore, et al.

1950   *The authoritarian personality.* New York: Harper & Row.

Althusser, Louis

1970   *For Marx.* New York: Vintage.

Aronson, Eliot

1976   *The social animal.* 2d ed. San Francisco: W. H. Freeman and Company.

Arthur, Ransom J.

1971   *An introduction to social psychiatry.* Baltimore: Penguin.

Ayres, Barbara

1967   Pregnancy magic: A study of food taboos and sex avoid-
         ances. In *Cross-cultural approaches,* ed. C. S. Ford, pp.
         111–125. New Haven: HRAF Press.

Bales, Robert Freed

1950   *Interaction process analysis.* Cambridge: Addison-Wesley.

Banfield, Edward

1958   *The moral basis of a backward society.* New York: Free
         Press.

Barash, David P.

1977   *Sociobiology and behavior.* New York: Elsevier.

Barker, R. G., and H. F. Wright

1954   *Midwest and its children.* Evanston: Row Peterson.

Barnouw, Victor

1979   *Culture and personality.* 3d ed. Homewood, Ill.: Dorsey.

Barry, H., M. K. Bacon, and I. L. Child

1959   The relation of child training to subsistence economy.
         American Anthropologist 61:51–63.

Bartlett, F. C.

1923   *Psychology and primitive culture.* New York: Macmillan.

Barzini, Luigi

1964   *The Italians.* New York: Atheneum.

Bateson, Gregory

1958   *Naven.* 2d ed. Palo Alto, Calif.: Stanford University
         Press.

1972   *Steps to an ecology of mind.* New York: Ballantine.

Bateson, Gregory, and Margaret Mead

1942   *Balinese character: A photographic analysis.* Publications of
         the New York Academy of Science, vol. 2., New York.

Beals, Ralph L.

1978   Sonoran fantasy or coming of age? *American Anthropologist* 80:355–362.

Befu, Harumi

1971   *Japan: An anthropological introduction.* San Francisco: Chandler.

Benedict, Ruth F.

1923   The concept of the guardian spirit in North America. *Memoirs of the American Anthropological Association* 29: 1–97.

1928   Psychological types in the cultures of the Southwest. *Proceedings of the 23d International Congress of Americanists,* New York.

1932   Configurations of culture in North America, *American Anthropologist* 34:1–27.

1934   Anthropology and the abnormal. *Journal of General Psychology* 10:59–82.

1946a   *Patterns of culture.* New York: Mentor Books.
(1934)

1946b   *The chrysanthemum and the sword.* Boston: Houghton Mifflin.

Bennett, John W.

1946   The interpretation of Pueblo culture: A question of values. *Southwestern Journal of Anthropology* 2:361–374.

Berlin, Brent, and Paul Kay

1969   *Basic color terms.* Berkeley: University of California Press.

Berne, Eric

1964   *Games people play.* New York: Grove Press.

Berry, J. W.

1976   *Human ecology and cognitive style.* New York: Halsted.

Bettelheim, Bruno

1943   Individual and mass behavior in extreme situations. *Journal of Abnormal and Social Psychology* 38:417–452.

1962   *Symbolic wounds.* Rev. ed. New York: Collier.
(1954)

1967   *The empty fortress.* New York: Free Press.

1969   *The children of the dream.* New York: Avon.

1971   *The informed heart.* New York: Avon.
(1960)

1974   *A home for the heart.* New York: Knopf.

1976   *The uses of enchantment.* New York: Vintage.

Blumer, Herbert

1969   *Symbolic interactionism: Perspective and method.* Englewood
            Cliffs, N.J.: Prentice-Hall.

Blurton Jones, N. G., ed.

1972   *Ethological studies of child behavior.* Cambridge: Cam-
            bridge University Press.

Boas, Franz

1939   *The mind of primitive man.* New York: Macmillan.
(1911)

1966   *Race, language and culture.* New York: Macmillan.
(1940)

Bock, Philip K.

1964   Social structure and language structure. *Southwestern
            Journal of Anthropology* 20:393–403.

1967   Love magic, menstrual taboos, and the facts of geog-
            raphy. *American Anthropologist* 69:213–217.

1968   Some generative rules for American kinship terminol-
            ogy. *Anthropological Linguistics* 10:1–6.

1974   *Modern cultural anthropology.* 2d ed. New York: Knopf.

1976   "I think but dare not speak": Silence in Elizabethan cul-
            ture. *Journal of Anthropological Research* 32:285–294.

1979   *Modern cultural anthropology.* 3d ed. New York: Knopf.
(1969)

n.d.   Oedipus once more. *American Anthropologist,* forthcom-
            ing.

Bodley, John

1975   *Victims of progress.* Menlo Park, Calif.: Cummings.

Bornstein, Marc H.
  1975   The influence of visual perception on culture. *American
          Anthropologist* 77:774–798.

Bourguignon, Erika
  1979   *Psychological anthropology.* New York: Holt, Rinehart and
          Winston.

Bowlby, John
  1973   *Attachment and loss.* 2 vols. New York: Basic Books.

Brain, James L.
  1977   Sex, incest and death: Initiation rites reconsidered. *Cur-
          rent Anthropology* 18:191–208.

Briggs, Jean L.
  1970   *Never in anger.* Cambridge: Harvard University Press.

Bronfenbrenner, Urie
  1967   The changing American child—a speculative analysis.
          In *Personality and social life,* ed. R. Endleman, pp. 189–
          201. New York: Random House.
  1973   *Two worlds of childhood: US and USSR.* New York: Pocket
          Books.

Brown, Norman O.
  1959   *Life against death.* New York: Vintage.
  1966   *Love's body.* New York: Vintage.

Bukharin, Nikolai
  1969   *Historical materialism.* Ann Arbor: University of Michi-
  (1931) gan Press.

Burling, Robbins
  1970   *Man's many voices: Language in its cultural context.* New
          York: Holt, Rinehart and Winston.

Calogeras, Roy C.
  1971   Géza Róheim: Psychoanalytic anthropologist or radical
          Freudian? *American Imago* 28:146–157.

Cancian, Frank
   1967   Stratification and risk taking. *American Sociological Review* 32:912–927.

Carson, Robert C.
   1969   *Interaction concepts of personality.* Chicago: Aldine.

Carstairs, G. Morris
   1957   *The twice born.* London: Hogarth Press.

Castaneda, Carlos
   1968   *The teachings of Don Juan.* Berkeley: University of California Press.
   1971   *A separate reality.* New York: Simon & Schuster.
   1972   *Journey to Ixtlán.* New York: Simon & Schuster.
   1974   *Tales of power.* New York: Simon & Schuster.

Cazenueve, Jean
   1972   *Lucien Lévy-Bruhl.* New York: Harper & Row.

Chein, Isidor
   1972   *The science of behavior and the image of man.* New York: Basic Books.

Cohen, Yehudi A.
   1961   *Social structure and personality: A casebook.* New York: Holt, Rinehart and Winston.
   1964   *The transition from childhood to adolescence.* Chicago: Aldine.

Colby, B. N.
   1966   The analysis of cultural content and the patterning of narrative concerns in text. *American Anthropologist* 68:374–388.

Cole, Michael, and Sylvia Scribner
   1974   *Culture and thought: A psychological introduction.* New York: Wiley.

Coles, Robert
   1970   *Erik H. Erikson: The growth of his work.* Boston: Little, Brown.

1973   *The old ones of New Mexico.* Albuquerque: University of New Mexico Press.

Conklin, Harold C.

1972   *Folk classification (a bibliography).* New Haven: Yale University Department of Anthropology.

Costigan, G.

1965   *Sigmund Freud.* New York: Macmillan.

Coult, Allan D.

1977   *Psychedelic anthropology.* Philadelphia: Dorrance.

Cumming, Elaine, and John Cumming

1957   *Closed ranks.* Cambridge: Harvard University Press.

D'Andrade, Roy G.

1961   Anthropological studies of dreams. In *Psychological anthropology,* ed. F. L. K. Hsu, pp. 296–332. Homewood, Ill.: Dorsey.

Dasen, P. R.

1972   Cross-cultural Piagetian research: A summary. *Journal of Cross-cultural Psychology* 3:23–40.

Davis, Allison, and John Dollard

1964   *Children of bondage.* New York: Harper & Row.
(1940)

Dawkins, Richard

1978   *The selfish gene.* New York: Oxford University Press.

Dement, William C.

1974   *Some must watch while some must sleep.* San Francisco: W. H. Freeman and Company.

Devereux, George

1969   *Reality and dream: Psychotherapy of a Plains Indian.* Garden City, N.Y.: Anchor.
(1951)

1978   The works of George Devereux. In *The making of psychological anthropology,* ed. G. Spindler, pp. 361–406. Berkeley: University of California Press.

Dollard, John, et al.

    1939   *Frustration and aggression.* New Haven: Yale University Press.

Dollard, John, and Neil Miller

    1950   *Personality and psychotherapy.* New York: McGraw-Hill.

Douglas, Jack D.

    1967   *The social meanings of suicide.* Princeton: Princeton University Press.

Draper, Patricia

    1973   Crowding among hunter-gatherers: The !Kung Bushmen. *Science* 182:301–303.

Driver, Harold

    1966   Geographical-historical *versus* psycho-functional explanations of kin avoidances. *Current Anthropology* 7:131–182.

DuBois, Cora

    1961   *The people of Alor.* 2 vols. New York: Harper & Row.
    (1944)

Dumont, Louis

    1970   *Homo hierarchicus.* Chicago: University of Chicago Press.

Dundes, Alan

    1962   Earth-diver: Creation of the mythopoeic male. *American Anthropologist* 64:1032–1051.

Eaton, J. W., and R. J. Weil

    1953   The mental health of the Hutterites. *Scientific American* 189:31–37.

Edgerton, Robert B.

    1970   Method in psychological anthropology. In *Handbook of method in cultural anthropology,* ed. R. Naroll and R. Cohen, pp. 338–352. Garden City, N.Y.: Natural History Press.

    1971   *The individual in cultural adaptation.* Berkeley and Los Angeles: University of California Press.

1974   Cross-cultural psychology and psychological anthropology: One paradigm or two? *Reviews in Anthropology* 1:52–65.

Eggan, Dorothy

1961   Dream analysis. In *Studying personality cross-culturally,* ed. B. Kaplan, pp. 551–577. New York: Harper & Row.

Ekman, Paul

1973   Cross-cultural studies of facial expression. In *Darwin and facial expression,* ed. P. Ekman, pp. 169–222. New York: Academic Press.

Ekman, Paul, and Wallace V. Friesen

1975   *Unmasking the face.* Englewood Cliffs, N.J.: Prentice-Hall.

Ember, Melvin

1978   Size of color lexicon: Interaction of cultural and biological factors. *American Anthropologist* 80:364–367.

Endleman, Robert, ed.

1967   *Personality and social life.* New York: Random House.

Erikson, Erik H.

1958   *Young man Luther.* New York: Norton.

1963   *Childhood and society.* 2d ed. New York: Norton.
(1950)

1969   *Gandhi's truth.* New York: Norton.

1975   *Life history and the historical moment.* New York: Norton.

Evans, Richard I.

1967   *Dialogue with Erik Erikson.* New York: Harper & Row.

Fanon, Frantz

1965   *The wretched of the earth.* New York: Grove.

Fenichel, Otto

1945   *The psychoanalytic theory of neurosis.* New York: Norton.

Fisher, S., and R. P. Greenberg

1977   *The scientific credibility of Freud's theories and therapy.* New York: Basic Books.

Flügel, J. C.
    1950   *The psychology of clothes.* London: Hogarth Press.

Fogelson, R. D., ed.
    1976   *Contributions to anthropology: Selected papers of A. I. Hal-
            lowell.* Chicago: University of Chicago Press.

Foster, George M.
    1965   Peasant society and the image of limited good. *American
            Anthropologist* 67:293–315.

Foulks, E. F.
    1972   *The Arctic hysterias of the North Alaskan Eskimo.* An-
            thropological Studies No. 10. Washington, D.C.: Ameri-
            can Anthropological Association.

Fox, Robin
    1962   Sibling incest. *British Journal of Sociology* 13:128–150.
    1967   *Kinship and marriage.* Baltimore: Penguin.

Fox, Robin, and Usher Fleising
    1976   Human ethology. *Annual Review of Anthropology* 5:265–
            288.

Frake, Charles O.
    1962   The ethnographic study of cognitive systems. In *An-
            thropology and human behavior,* pp. 72–85. Washington,
            D.C.: Anthropological Society of Washington.

Frank, Jerome D.
    1963   *Persuasion and healing.* New York: Schocken.

Franklin, Karl J.
    1963   Kewa ethnolinguistic concepts of body parts. *Southwest-
            ern Journal of Anthropology* 19:54–63.

Freedman, Daniel
    1974   *Human infancy: An evolutionary perspective.* Hillsdale,
            N.J.: L. Earlbaum Associates.

Freud, Anna
    1946   *The ego and the mechanisms of defense.* London: Hogarth
            Press.

Freud, Sigmund

   1950   *Totem and taboo.* New York: Norton.
   (1913)

   1952   *On dreams.* New York: Norton.
   (1901)

   1959   *Group psychology and the analysis of the ego.* New York:
   (1921) Norton.

   1961   *Civilization and its discontents.* New York: Norton.
   (1930)

Fromm, Erich

   1941   *Escape from freedom.* New York: Farrar and Rinehart.

Garson, Barbara

   1977   *All the livelong day.* New York: Penguin.

Geertz, Clifford

   1973   *The interpretation of culture.* New York: Basic Books.

Gladwin, Thomas, and Seymour B. Sarason

   1953   *Truk: Man in paradise.* Viking Fund Publications in An-
           thropology No. 20. Chicago: University of Chicago
           Press.

Glenn, M., and R. Kunnes

   1973   *Repression or revolution: Therapy in the United States today.*
           New York: Harper & Row.

Gluckman, Max, ed.

   1964   *Closed systems and open minds: The limits of naivety in social
           anthropology.* Chicago: Aldine.

Goffman, Erving

   1959   *The presentation of self in everyday life.* Garden City, N.Y.:
           Anchor.

   1961a   *Encounters.* Indianapolis: Bobbs-Merrill.

   1961b   *Asylums.* Garden City, N.Y.: Anchor.

   1963   *Stigma.* Englewood Cliffs, N.J.: Prentice-Hall.

   1967   *Interaction ritual.* Garden City, N.Y.: Anchor.

   1969   *Strategic interaction.* Philadelphia: University of Pennsyl-
           vania Press.

1971   *Relations in public.* New York: Basic Books.

1974   *Frame analysis.* New York: Harper & Row.

1979   *Gender advertisements.* New York: Harper & Row.

Goodenough, Ward H.

1957   Cultural anthropology and linguistics. In *Report of the 7th annual roundtable on linguistics and language study,* ed. P. L. Garvin, pp. 167–173. Georgetown: Georgetown University Press.

Gorer, Geoffrey

1955   *Exploring English character.* New York: Criterion Books.

1964   *The American people.* New York: Norton.
(1948)

Gorer, Geoffrey, and John Rickman

1962   *The people of Great Russia.* New York: Norton.
(1949)

Graves, Nancy B., and Theodore D. Graves

1978   The impact of modernization on the personality of a Polynesian people. *Human Organization* 37:115–135.

Hallowell, A. Irving

1955   *Culture and experience.* Philadelphia: University of Pennsylvania Press.

Harner, Michael J., ed.

1973   *Hallucinogens and shamanism.* New York: Oxford University Press.

Harris, Marvin

1964   *The nature of cultural things.* New York: Random House.

1968   *The rise of anthropological theory.* New York: Crowell.

Hay, Thomas H.

1976   Personality and probability: The modal personality of the Tuscarora revisited. *Ethos* 4:509–524.

Henry, Jules, and Melford E. Spiro

1953   Psychological techniques: Projective tests in field work. In *Anthropology today,* ed. A. L. Kroeber, pp. 417–429. Chicago: University of Chicago Press.

Hewitt, John P.

 1976   *Self and society.* Boston: Allyn and Bacon.

Holloman, Regina E.

 1974   Ritual opening and individual transformation: Rites of passage at Esalen. *American Anthropologist* 76:265–280.

Hsu, Francis L. K., ed.

 1961   *Psychological anthropology.* Homewood, Ill: Dorsey.

 1972   *Psychological anthropology.* New ed. Cambridge: Schenkman.

 1973   Prejudice and its intellectual effect in American anthropology. *American Anthropologist* 75:1–19.

Hull, Clark L.

 1943   *Principles of behavior.* New York: Appleton-Century.

Hunt, Robert, ed.

 1967   *Personalities and cultures.* Garden City, N.Y.: Natural History Press.

Hymes, Dell, ed.

 1964   *Language in culture and society.* New York: Harper & Row.

Inkeles, Alex

 1961   National character and modern political systems. In *Psychological anthropology,* ed. F. Hsu, pp. 172–208. Homewood, Ill.: Dorsey.

Inkeles, Alex, et al.

 1967   Modal personality and adjustment to the Soviet sociopolitical system. In *Personality and social life,* ed. R. Endleman, pp. 210–221. New York: Random House.

Izard, C. E.

 1971   *The face of emotion.* New York: Appleton.

Jacobs, Melville

 1959   *The content and style of an oral literature.* Viking Fund Publications in Anthropology No. 26. Chicago: University of Chicago Press.

James, William

  1952 *Principles of psychology.* Chicago: Encyclopedia Brittanica.
  (1880)

Kaplan, Bert

  1954 A study of Rorschach responses in four cultures. *Papers of the Peabody Museum, Harvard University,* vol. 42.

Kaplan, Bert, ed.

  1961 *Studying personality cross-culturally.* New York: Harper & Row.

Kaplan, Bert, and Thomas F. A. Plaut

  1956 *Personality in a communal society.* Lawrence: University of Kansas Publications, Social Science Studies.

Kardiner, Abram, with Ralph Linton

  1939 *The individual and his society.* New York: Columbia University Press.

Kardiner, Abram, with Ralph Linton, Cora DuBois, and James West

  1945 *The psychological frontiers of society.* New York: Columbia University Press.

Kardiner, Abram, and Lionel Ovesey

  1951 *The mark of oppression.* New York: Norton.

Kardiner, Abram, and Edward Preble

  1963 *They studied man.* New York: Mentor.

Katcher, Aaron, and Joan Katcher

  1967 The restructuring of behavior in a messianic cult. In *Personality and social life,* ed. R. Endleman, pp. 500–514. New York: Random House.

Kaufman, I. Charles

  1975 Learning what comes naturally: The role of life experience in the establishment of species typical behavior. *Ethos* 3:129–142.

Kelly, George A.

  1963 *A theory of personality.* New York: Norton.

Kennedy, John G.

1966 "Peasant society and the image of limited good": A critique. *American Anthropologist* 68:1212–1225.

Kiev, Ari

1972 *Transcultural psychiatry.* New York: Free Press.

Kluckhohn, Clyde

1957 *Mirror for man.* New York: Premier Books.

1962 *Culture and behavior,* ed. R. Kluckhohn. New York: Free Press.

Konner, Melvin J.

1976 Maternal care, infant behavior and development among the !Kung. In *Kalahari hunter-gatherers,* eds. R. B. Lee and I. DeVore, pp. 218–245. Cambridge: Harvard University Press.

Kroeber, Alfred L.

1952 *The nature of culture.* Chicago: University of Chicago Press.

Kuhn, Thomas S.

1962 *The structure of scientific revolutions.* Chicago: University of Chicago Press.

Lang, Kurt

1964 Alienation. In *A dictionary of the social sciences,* eds. J. Gould and W. L. Kolb, pp. 19–20. Glencoe, Ill.: Free Press.

Langer, Walter C.

1973 *The mind of Adolf Hitler.* New York: Signet.

Lee, Dorothy

1959 *Freedom and culture.* Englewood Cliffs, N.J.: Prentice-Hall.

Leighton, Alexander, et al.

1963 *Psychiatric disorder among the Yoruba.* Ithaca, N.Y.: Cornell University Press.

LeVine, Robert A.

1973   *Culture, behavior, and personality.* Chicago: Aldine.

1974   *Culture and personality: Contemporary readings.* Chicago: Aldine.

Lévi-Strauss, Claude

1963   *Totemism.* Boston: Beacon Press.

1966   *The savage mind.* Chicago: University of Chicago Press.

Lewis, Oscar

1951   *Life in a Mexican village.* Urbana: University of Illinois Press.

Lifton, Robert Jay

1961   *Thought reform and the psychology of totalism.* New York: Norton.

1970   *History and human survival.* New York: Random House.

Lindesmith, A. R., and Anselm L. Strauss

1950   A critique of culture-personality writings. *American Sociological Review* 15:587–600.

Linton, Adele, and Charles Wagley

1971   *Ralph Linton.* New York: Columbia University Press.

Linton, Ralph

1930   *The study of man.* New York: Appleton-Century-Crofts.

1945   *The cultural background of personality.* New York: Appleton-Century-Crofts.

Loehlin, J. C., Gardner Lindzey, and James N. Spuhler

1975   *Race differences in intelligence.* San Francisco: W. H. Freeman and Company.

Lomax, Elizabeth, et al.

1978   *Science and patterns of child care.* San Francisco: W. H. Freeman and Company.

Lurie, Alison

1976   The dress code. *New York Review of Books,* November 25, pp. 17–20.

Lynch, Kevin
    1964   *The image of the city.* Cambridge: MIT Press.

MacCannell, Dean
    1976   *The tourist.* New York: Schocken.

McClelland, David C., et al.
    1978   Making it to maturity. *Psychology Today* 12:42–53; 114.

MacCorquodale, K., and P. E. Meehl
    1948   Hypothetical constructs and intervening variables. *Psychological Review* 55:95–107.

Madariaga, Salvador de
    1928   *Englishmen, Frenchmen and Spaniards.* London: Oxford University Press.

Mahler, M. S., Fred Pine, and A. Bergman
    1975   *The psychological birth of the human infant.* New York: Basic Books.

Malinowski, Bronislaw
    1955   *Magic, science and religion.* Garden City, N.Y.: Anchor.
    1961   *Argonauts of the western Pacific.* New York: Dutton.
    (1922)

Maquet, Jacques
    1978   Castaneda: Warrior or scholar? *American Anthropologist* 80:362–363.

Marcuse, Herbert
    1955   *Eros and civilization.* Boston: Beacon Press.

Marx, Karl
    1904   *A contribution to the critique of political economy.* New York:
    (1859)   International Library.

Mead, George Herbert
    1934   *Mind, self and society.* Chicago: University of Chicago Press.

Mead, Margaret

1930   An ethnologist's footnote to *Totem and taboo*. *Psychoanalytic Review* 17:297–301.

1932   An investigation of the thought of primitive children with special reference to animism. *Journal of the Royal Anthropological Institute* 62:173–190. (Reprinted in Hunt 1967.)

1942   *And keep your powder dry*. New York: Morrow.

1949   *Coming of age in Samoa*. New York: Mentor.
(1928)

1953a   *Growing up in New Guinea*. New York: Mentor.
(1930)

1953b   *National character*. In *Anthropology today*, ed. A. L. Kroeber, pp. 642–667. Chicago: University of Chicago Press.

1956   *New lives for old*. New York: Morrow.

1959   *An anthropologist at work: Writings of Ruth Benedict*. Boston: Houghton Mifflin.

1963   *Sex and temperament in three primitive societies*. New York:
(1935) Apollo.

1972   *Blackberry winter*. New York: Morrow.

1974   *Ruth Benedict*. New York: Columbia University Press.

Merton, Robert K.

1957   *Social theory and social structure*. Rev. ed. Glencoe, Ill.: Free Press.

Métraux, Rhoda, and Margaret Mead

1954   *Themes in French culture*. Palo Alto, Calif.: Stanford University Press.

Milgram, Stanley

1974   *Obedience to authority*. New York: Harper & Row.

Miller, Daniel R., and Guy E. Swanson

1966   *Inner conflict and defense*. New York: Schocken.

Miller, Neil, and John Dollard

1941   *Social learning and imitation*. New Haven: Yale University Press.

Minturn, Leigh, and William Lambert
   1964   *Mothers of six cultures.* New York: Wiley.

Morgan, Lewis Henry
   1877   *Ancient society.* Chicago: Kerr.

Munroe, Robert L., and Ruth Munroe
   1975   *Cross-cultural human development.* Monterey, Calif.: Brooks-Cole.

Murdock, George P.
   1949   *Social structure.* New York: Macmillan.
   1957   World ethnographic sample. *American Anthropologist* 59:664–687.

Murphy, Gardner
   1947   *Personality: A biosocial approach to origins and structure.* New York: Harper & Brothers.

Murphy, Gardner, and Lois B. Murphy, eds.
   1968   *Asian psychology.* New York: Basic Books.

Murray, Frank B., ed.
   1972   *Critical features of Piaget's theory of the development of thought.* New York: MSS Information Corporation.

Naroll, Raoul, and Ronald Cohen, eds.
   1970   *A handbook of method in cultural anthropology.* Garden City, N.Y.: Natural History Press.

Needham, Rodney
   1965   Review of *Lucien Lévy-Bruhl,* by Jean Cazenueve. *American Anthropologist* 67:1291–1292.

Needler, Martin C.
   1971   *Politics and society in Mexico.* Albuquerque: University of New Mexico Press.

Neisser, Ulrich
   1976   *Cognition and reality.* San Francisco: W. H. Freeman and Company.

O'Nell, Carl W.

1976   *Dreams, culture, and the individual.* San Francisco: Chandler & Sharp.

Opler, Marvin K., ed.

1959   *Culture and mental health.* New York: Macmillan.

Orlansky, Harold

1949   Infant care and personality. *Psychological Bulletin* 46:1–48.

Orwell, George

1954   *A collection of essays by George Orwell.* Garden City, N.Y.: Anchor.

Paul, Robert A.

1976   Did the primal crime take place? *Ethos* 4:311–352.

Penfield, Wilder

1975   *The mystery of the mind.* Princeton: Princeton University Press.

Pettit, Philip

1975   *The concept of structuralism.* Berkeley: University of California Press.

Phillips, Herbert P.

1965   *Thai peasant personality.* Berkeley: University of California Press.

Piaget, Jean

1971   *Genetic epistemology.* New York: Norton.

1973   *The child and reality.* New York: Grossman.

Piers, Gerhart, and Milton Singer

1953   *Shame and guilt.* Springfield, Ill.: Charles C Thomas.

Piker, Steven

1966   The image of limited good: Comments on an exercise in description and interpretation. *American Anthropologist* 68:1201–1211.

Pitt-Rivers, Julian A.

1960–1 "Interpersonal relations in peasant society": A comment. *Human Organization* 19:180–183.

Polanyi, Michael

1964 *Personal knowledge.* New York: Harper & Row.

Powers, William T.

1973 *Behavior: The control of perception.* Chicago: Aldine.

Price-Williams, D. R.

1975 *Explorations in cross-cultural psychology.* San Francisco: Chandler & Sharp.

Price-Williams, D. R., W. Gordon, and M. Ramirez

1969 Skill and conservation. *Developmental Psychology* 1:769.

Radin, Paul

1957 *Primitive man as philosopher.* 2d rev. ed. New York: (1927) Dover.

Redfield, Robert

1953 *The primitive world and its transformations.* Ithaca, N.Y.: Cornell University Press.

1955 *The little community.* Chicago: University of Chicago Press.

Rickers-Ovsiankina, M. A.

1977 *Rorschach psychology.* 2d ed. Huntington, N.Y.: Krieger.

Rieff, Philip

1961 *Freud: The mind of the moralist.* Garden City, N.Y.: Anchor.

1966 *The triumph of the therapeutic.* New York: Harper & Row.

Riesman, David

1954 *Individualism reconsidered.* Garden City, N.Y.: Anchor.

Riesman, David, with Nathan Glazer and Reuel Denney

1961 *The lonely crowd.* New Haven: Yale University Press. (1950)

Róheim, Géza

    1943   *The origin and function of culture.* Nervous and Mental
            Disease Monographs No. 69. New York.

    1974   *The riddle of the sphinx.* New York: Harper & Row.
    (1934)

Rohrer, John H., and Munro S. Edmonson, eds.

    1964   *The eighth generation grows up.* New York: Harper
            Torchbooks.

Rosch, Eleanor, et al.

    1975   *Basic objects in natural categories.* Working Paper No. 43.
            Berkeley: Language Behavior Research Laboratory.

Sapir, Edward

    1921   *Language.* New York: Harcourt, Brace.

    1949   *Culture, language and personality.* Berkeley: University of
            California Press.

Saucier, J.-F.

    1972   Correlates of the long postpartum taboo: A cross-
            cultural study. *Current Anthropology* 13:238–249.

Schachtel, Ernest G.

    1959   *Metamorphosis.* New York: Basic Books.

Schachter, Stanley, and Jerome Singer

    1962   Cognitive, social, and physiological determinants of
            emotional states. *Psychological Review* 69:379–399.

Scheflen, Albert E.

    1974   *How behavior means.* Garden City, N.Y.: Anchor.

Scott, James C.

    1976   *The moral economy of the peasant.* New Haven: Yale Uni-
            versity Press.

Segall, Marshall H., Donald T. Campbell, and Melville J. Herskovits

    1966   *The influence of culture on visual perception.* Indianapolis:
            Bobbs-Merrill.

Sennett, Richard, and Jonathan Cobb

    1973   *The hidden injuries of class.* New York: Vintage.

Serpell, Robert

1976   *Culture's influence on behavior.* London: Methuen.

Shirley, R. W., and A. Kimball Romney

1962   Love magic and socialization anxiety. *American Anthropologist* 64:1028–1031.

Shweder, Richard A.

1977   Likeness and likelihood in everyday thought: Magical thinking in judgments about personality. *Current Anthropology* 18:637–658.

Siegler, Miriam, and Humphrey Osmond

1974   *Models of madness, models of medicine.* New York: Harper & Row.

Simmel, Georg

1950   *The sociology of Georg Simmel.* Trans. by Kurt H. Wolff. New York: Free Press.

Singer, Milton

1961   A survey of culture and personality theory and research. In *Studying personality cross-culturally*, ed. B. Kaplan, pp. 9–90. New York: Harper & Row.

Sisk, John P.

1970   *Person and institution.* Notre Dame, Ind.: Fides Books.

Slater, Philip L.

1970   *The pursuit of loneliness.* Boston: Beacon Press.

Smith, Hedrick

1977   *The Russians.* New York: Ballantine.

Spain, David H.

1972   On the use of projective tests for research in psychological anthropology. In *Psychological anthropology.* New ed., ed. F. Hsu, pp. 267–308. Cambridge: Schenkman.

Spindler, George D., ed.

1978   *The making of psychological anthropology.* Berkeley: University of California Press.

Spiro, Melford E.

1951   Culture and personality: The natural history of a false dichotomy. *Psychiatry* 14:19–46.

1958   *Children of the kibbutz.* Cambridge: Harvard University Press.

1965   Religious systems as culturally constituted defense mechanisms. In *Context and meaning in cultural anthropology,* ed. M. E. Spiro, pp. 100–113. New York: Free Press.

1976   A. Irving Hallowell (an obituary). *American Anthropologist* 89:608–611.

Spiro, Melford E., and Roy G. D'Andrade

1958   A cross-cultural study of some supernatural beliefs. *American Anthropologist* 60:456–466.

Spradley, James P., ed.

1972   *Culture and cognition: Rules, maps and plans.* San Francisco: Chandler.

Srole, Leo R., et al.

1962   *Mental health in the metropolis: The Midtown Manhattan study.* vol. 1. New York: McGraw-Hill.

Stephens, William N.

1962   *The Oedipus complex.* Glencoe, Ill.: Free Press.

Stoetzel, Jean

1955   *Without the chrysanthemum and the sword.* New York: Columbia University Press.

Sugerman, A. Arthur, and Ralph E. Tarter, eds.

1978   *Expanding dimensions of consciousness.* New York: Springer.

Szasz, Thomas S.

1961   *The myth of mental illness.* New York: Dell.

Tart, Charles

1978   Altered states of consciousness: Putting the pieces together. In *Expanding dimensions of consciousness,* eds. A. A. Sugerman and R. E. Tarter, pp. 58–78. New York: Springer.

Tocqueville, Alexis de

1954   *Democracy in America.* 2 vols. New York: Vintage.
(1830)

Tolman, Edward Chace

1958   Cognitive maps in rats and men. In *Behavior and psychological man, selected essays of E. C. Tolman,* pp. 241–264.
Berkeley: University of California Press.

Triandis, Harry, et al.

1971   Cross-cultural psychology. In *Biennial review of anthropology,* ed. B. J. Siegel, pp. 1–84. Palo Alto, Calif.: Stanford
University Press.

Turner, Roy, ed.

1974   *Ethnomethodology.* Baltimore: Penguin.

Tyler, Stephen A., ed.

1969   *Cognitive anthropology.* New York: Holt, Rinehart and
Winston.

Tylor, Edward B.

1889   On a method of investigating the development of institutions applied to laws of marriage and descent. *Journal of the Royal Anthropological Institute* 18:245–269.

1958   *Primitive culture.* 2 vols. New York: Harper & Row.
(1871)

Vayda, Andrew P., ed.

1969   *Environment and cultural behavior.* Garden City, N.Y.:
Natural History Press.

Wagner, Roy

1975   *The invention of culture.* Englewood Cliffs, N.J.:
Prentice-Hall.

Wallace, Anthony F. C.

1952   The modal personality structure of the Tuscarora Indians as revealed by the Rorschach test. *Bureau of American Ethnology Bulletin No. 150.* Washington, D.C.: Smith-
sonian Institution.

1958   Dreams and the wishes of the soul. *American Anthropologist* 60:234–248.

1965   Driving to work. In *Context and meaning in cultural anthropology,* ed. M. E. Spiro, pp. 277–292. New York: Free Press.

1966a   Review of *The revolution in anthropology* by I. C. Jarvie. *American Anthropologist* 68:1254–1255.

1966b   *Religion: An anthropological view.* New York: Random House.

1970   *Culture and personality.* 2d ed. New York: Random
(1961)   House.

Watts, Alan W.

1969   *Psychotherapy East and West.* New York: Ballantine.

White, Leslie A.

1949   *The science of culture.* New York: Grove Press.

Whiting, Beatrice, ed.

1963   *Six cultures: Studies of child-rearing.* New York: Wiley.

Whiting, Beatrice, and John W. M. Whiting

1974   *Children of six cultures.* Cambridge: Harvard University Press.

Whiting, John W. M.

1941   *Becoming a Kwoma.* New Haven: Yale University Press.

1964   Effects of climate on certain cultural practices. In *Explorations in cultural anthropology,* ed. W. H. Goodenough, pp. 511–544. New York: McGraw-Hill.

Whiting, John W. M., et al.

1966   *Field guide for a study of socialization.* New York: Wiley. (First published in B. Whiting 1963).

Whiting, John W. M., and Irvin L. Child

1953   *Child training and personality: A cross-cultural study.* New Haven: Yale University Press.

Whiting, John W. M., Richard Kluckhohn, and Albert Anthony

    1958   The function of male initiation ceremonies at puberty. In *Readings in social psychology*, 3d ed., eds. E. Maccoby, T. Newcomb, and E. Hartley, pp. 359–370. New York: Holt.

Whyte, Lancelot Law

    1960   *The unconscious before Freud.* New York: Basic Books.

    1974   *The universe of experience.* New York: Harper & Row.

Williams, Raymond

    1976   *Keywords.* New York: Oxford University Press.

Wills, Garry

    1971   *Nixon agonistes.* New York: Signet.

Wilson, E. O.

    1975   *Sociobiology: The new synthesis.* Cambridge: Belknap Press.

Witkin, H. A.

    1967   A cognitive style approach to cross-cultural research. *International Journal of Psychology* 2:233–250.

Wolf, Arthur P.

    1970   Childhood association and sexual attraction: A further test of the Westermarck hypothesis. *American Anthropologist* 73:503–515.

Wolman, Benjamin B., ed.

    1973   *Handbook of general psychology.* Englewood Cliffs, N.J.: Prentice-Hall.

Woodworth, Robert S.

    1948   *Contemporary schools of psychology.* Rev. ed. New York: Ronald Press.

Wrong, Dennis H.

    1961   The oversocialized conception of man in modern sociology. *American Sociological Review* 26:183–193.

Wundt, Wilhelm
   1916   *Elements of folk psychology.* New York: Macmillan.

Wylie, Philip
   1946   *Generation of vipers.* New York: Rinehart.

Young, Frank W.
   1965   *Initiation ceremonies.* Indianapolis: Bobbs-Merrill.

Index

ABEL, T., 89, 224
ABERLE, D., 62, 66
Abstract thinking, 26–27, 238
Adaptation:
　behavioral, 188, 213
　environmental, 154–156
　individual, 87, 91
　psychosocial, 180–182
Adolescence, crisis of, 75
ADORNO, T., 113
Aggression, 21, 150, 166
Alienation, 188
ALTHUSSER, L., 188
Ambivalence, 200
　See also Taboo
American culture, 23, 73, 78, 198, 244
Americanism, 121
American Journal of Psychiatry, 81
American national character, 119–126
American People, The, 119–121, 127
Anal zone, 34, 150, 173
And Keep Your Powder Dry, 119
Animal phobias, 44, 46
Animism, 25
Animistic thinking, 25, 78
ANTHONY, A., 156
Anthropology, definition of, 1
Apache, 153, 160
Apollonian pattern, 69
AQUINAS, T., 19
Arapesh, 79, 160
ARONSON, E., 8, 22
ARTHUR, R. J., 203

Authoritarian personality, 112–113, 115
Authority, attitudes to, 120, 165
Autism, 170
Autonomous character, 124
Autonomy, 173
Avoidance learning, 143, 159
AYRES, B., 151

Balinese Character, 128
Banalysis, 246
BANFIELD, E., 191
BARASH, P., 188
BARKER, R. G., 212
BARNOUW, V., 203
BARRY, H., 193
BARTLETT, F., 27
Basic personality structure
　approach, 1, 57, 85–93, 105, 109, 129, 145, 150, 175, 196
Basic trust, 173
BATESON, G., 51, 128, 182, 246
BEALS, R., 220
Becoming a Kwoma, 143
BEFU, H., 112
Behavior:
　as index of personality, 210
　systems of, 150
Behaviorism, 3, 63, 141–143
BENEDICT, R., 60, 62, 65–74, 79, 86, 88, 102, 108, 110–112, 123–124, 131, 137, 157, 180, 191, 228, 250
BENNETT, J., 133
BERGMAN, A., 219

BERLIN, B., 233
BERNE, E., 204, 207
BERRY, J., 239
Betsileo, 89–91
BETTELHEIM, B., xii, 168–172, 174, 179, 204, 219, 250
Birth order, 190, 194
BLUMER, H., 201
BLURTON JONES, N., 213
BOAS, F., 26, 28–29, 63–67, 75, 86, 227
BOCK, P. K., 17, 20, 22, 45, 116, 154, 157, 222, 231, 241
BODLEY, J., 7, 19
Body parts, 231–232
BORNSTEIN, M., 234
Bourgeoisie, 187
BOURGUIGNON, E., 203
BOWLBY, J., 219
BPS: *See* Basic personality structure approach
BRAIN, J., 157
BRONFENBRENNER, U., 118–119, 190–191
BROWN, N. O., 44, 200, 249
BUKHARIN, N., 186–187
BUMSTEAD, B., 121
BUMSTEAD, D., 121
Bureaucratic personality, 193
BURLING, R., 230, 233–234
Burmese, 180–181
Bushman (!Kung), 217–218

CALOGERAS, R., 168
CAMPBELL, D., 15
Canalization, 23
CANCIAN, F., 192
Carpentered-world hypothesis, 15
CARSTAIRS, G. M., 127
CASTANEDA, C., 220–221
Castration anxiety, 46
CAUDILL, W., 39
Causal assumption, 134
Causal relationships, 87–91, 144, 149, 156–157, 213
CAZENUEVE, J., 27
CHAPPLE, E., 108
Character, 57, 58
    See also Megalomaniac character; National character; Paranoid character; Personality

Character and Personality (journal), 81
CHEIN, I., 182
Chicago, University of, 197, 245
CHILD, I., 89, 144–145, 149–153, 170, 208
Childhood experience, 20, 104, 237, 159, 240
Childhood and Society, 172, 175
Child and Reality, The, 236
Children of Bondage, 195
Children of Crisis, 178
Children of the Dream, 171
Children of Six Cultures, 210–211
Child training, 20–22, 77
    future orientation of, 118
    and growth, 161
    and motivation, 21
    See also Socialization
Child Training and Personality, 144, 149, 152, 170
Chrysanthemum and the Sword, The, 110–111
Civilization and Its Discontents, 38, 48
Class conflict, 186–187
Climate, 20
Cloacal birth, theory of, 179
COBB, J., 188
Cognition, 24–29
    universals of, 237–238
Cognition and Reality, 241
Cognitive anthropology, 29, 227–246
Cognitive development, 235–241
Cognitive maps, 239–241
Cognitive style, 238–239
COHEN, R., 153
COHEN, Y., 156
COLBY, B. N., 100
COLE, M., 237, 239
COLES, R., 178, 250
Collective representations, 27
Color blindness, 11–12
    terminology, 12, 232–234
Columbia University, 65, 85–86, 245
Comanche, 86
Coming of Age in Samoa, 74
Componential analysis, 229–231
Concentration camp, 168–169

Conditions of work, 187–193
Configurationalist approach, 1, 57, 63–80, 85, 87, 105, 109, 115, 144, 166
Conflict:
  psychic, 32, 37, 53, 165, 176
  value, 125–126
Congruence theory, 137–138
CONKLIN, H., 228, 235
Consciousness:
  altered states of, 208
  alternative states of, 219–224
  class, 186
  false, 186
Conservation, concept of, 236–237
Continuity assumption, 21, 132, 144, 197, 204, 207, 219
COOLEY, C. H., 197
Correlational method, 145–153, 157, 170, 193, 202, 207, 245, 250
COSTIGAN, G., 54
COULT, A. D., 220
Critique of Political Economy, 186
Cross-cultural approach, 1, 58, 85, 129, 131, 141–162
  See also Correlational method
Crowding, 216–218
Cultural change, 86, 95, 243
Cultural wholes, 67–68
Culture, Behavior, and Personality, 137, 181
Culture and Personality, 133
Culture and Personality School, 49, 57–59, 74, 85, 94, 131, 136, 165, 185, 204
  approach of, 60, 177, 203
  assumptions of, 107, 112, 132–136, 138, 162, 193
  crisis in, 131–141, 144, 162
Culturology, 2
CUMMING, E., 203
CUMMING, J., 203

D'ANDRADE, R., 153, 224
DARWIN, C., 9, 46, 73, 80, 181, 189, 213
DASEN, P. R., 236
DAVIS, A., 194–196
DAWKINS, R., 189

Deception, 198–199
Defense mechanisms, 35–36, 53, 167, 240
  culturally constituted, 181
DEMENT, W., 224
Democracy in America, 119
Denial, 35, 168–169
DENNEY, R., 121
Dependency, 169
  fear of, 126
DEVEREUX, G., 39, 223–224, 250
DILTHEY, W., 68
Display rules, 213, 215
Distribution of personality types, 101, 181
Dobu Islanders, 68, 70, 72, 123, 191
DOLLARD, J., 85, 141–143, 166, 194–196, 240
DOUGLAS, J., 201–202
Dramaturgical analysis, 199–200
DRAPER, P., 217–218
Dreaming, 222–224
Dreams:
  interpretation of, 37–38
  manifest and latent content of, 37
  as wish fulfillment, 38
DRIVER, H., 154
Drugs, psychotropic, 221–222
DuBois, C., 85, 93–96, 99, 105, 137
DUMONT, L., 127, 128
DURKHEIM, E., 26, 197
Dynamic theory, 32, 34, 37, 53

EATON, J. W., 202
EDGERTON, R., 99, 137, 193, 212, 246
EDMONSON, M., 194–196, 249
EGGAN, D., 222–224
Ego, integrative functions of, 170–171, 174–175, 196
Eighth Generation, The, 194
EKMAN, P., 213–215
EMBER, M., 153, 234
Emotion, 245
  ambivalence of, 170–171
  and culture, 23, 95
  facial expression of, 213–215

Encounters, 200
ENDLEMAN, R., 72, 171, 181, 193–194, 248
Englishmen, Frenchmen, and Spaniards, 127
Enlightenment, Age of, 7
Epidemiology, 202–203
Equality, 120, 124, 128
ERIKSON, E. H., 9, 39, 46, 92, 113–114, 128, 137, 168, 170, 172–178, 196, 217, 249
Eros, 33–34
Escape from Freedom, 112
Ethnomethodology, 201
Ethnosemantics, 228–235
Ethology, 200, 207, 212–219
Ethos (journal), 79
EVANS, R., 113
Evolution:
  cultural, 25, 91, 168
  theory of, 7, 12, 73, 213
Exogamy, 44
Experimental method, 145
Explanations of behavior, 58, 250
Exploration, Age of, 7
Exploring English Character, 127

Fairy tales, 171–172
FANON, F., 18
FENICHEL, O., 34, 36, 51, 52
FERENCZI, S., 179
Fetishism:
  breast, 121
  clothing, 51
Field-dependence, 239
FISHER, S., 53
Fixation, 153, 173
FLEISING, U., 213
FLÜGEL, J. C., 39, 49–52
FOGELSON, R., 82
Folk psychology, 25
Folk taxonomy, 234–235
FORD, C. S., 142
Fore, 214–215
Forgetting, 33
FORTUNE, R., 73
FOSTER, G. M., 191–192, 240
Four Families (film), 128

FOX, R., 48, 158–161, 213
FRAKE, C., 228–229, 240
Frame Analysis, 200
FRANK, J., 224
FRANK, L. K., 108
FRAZER, J., 26–27, 31, 227
Free association, 37
FREEDMAN, D., 219
FREUD, A., 36, 169
FREUD, S., 1, 21, 29, 31–49, 52–54, 57, 73–74, 120, 137, 149, 158–160, 162, 166, 167, 171, 177, 197–200, 223, 225, 238, 249, 250
FRIESEN, W., 215
FROMM, E., 39, 92, 112, 137, 166
Frustration and Aggression, 142
Functionalism, 80, 86, 108
Future of an Illusion, The, 38

GALTON, F., 153
Galton's problem, 153–154, 162
GANDHI, M., 128
Gandhi's Truth, 177
GARFINKLE, H., 201
GEERTZ, C., 9
Generation of Vipers, 119
Genital zone, 34
Geographic bias, 154, 162
Gestalt psychology, 61–63, 66, 68
Gestalt therapy, 207
GLADWIN, T., 17, 20, 103–105
GLAZER, N., 121
GLUCKMAN, M., 2
GOFFMAN, E., 198–201
Golden Bough, The, 26
GOODALL, J., 25
GOODENOUGH, W., 228
GORDON, W., 237
GORER, G., 39, 114–117, 119–121, 127, 137
GORKY, M., 115
GREENBERG, R. P., 53
Group Psychology and the Analysis of the Ego, 38, 48–49
Growing Up in New Guinea, 74
Guardian spirit, 65–66
Guilt, 47, 110, 165, 175, 190
  shared, 200

HALLOWELL, A. I., 17, 81–82,
    100–102, 136, 180, 228
HARING, A. D., 82
HARLOW, H., 215
HARNER, M., 221–222
HARRIS, A., 178
HARRIS, M., 3, 18, 63, 80
HARTMANN, H., 169
Harvard University, 154, 219
HAY, T., 101
HENRY, J., 99
HERSKOVITS, M., 15
HEWITT, J., 201
Hidden Injuries of Class, The, 188
History and Human Survival, 178
HITLER, A., 112–114
HOBBES, T., 8
HOLLOMAN, R., 224
Home for the Heart, A, 169
Homo hierarchicus, 128
Hopi, 223–224
Horizontal–vertical illusion, 15–16
HRAF (Human Relations Area
    Files), 142, 151–152, 158
HSU, F. L. K., 57, 125–127, 136
HUGHES, E. C., 197
HULL, C., 141–142
Human nature, 8–9, 31
Human Relations Area Files
    (HRAF), 142, 151–152, 158
Hutterites, 202–203
HYMES, D., 228
Hypothesis testing, 142, 144–145,
    161, 162, 170, 208–211
Hypothetical construct, 92, 149

Identification, 35, 45, 99, 155–156
    with aggressor, 169, 176
    primary role, 195–196, 249
Identity, 113–114, 172, 177, 196
Illness, explanations of, 90,
    149–151
Image of the City, The, 240
Image of limited good, 191–192,
    240
Individual differences, 2, 54, 79,
    188
Individual and His Society, The, 86,
    89

Individualism, 124–125, 187, 244
Information, control of, 198
Initiation rites, 67, 155–157
Initiative, 175, 217
INKELES, A., 112, 118, 137
Inner-directed character, 122
Instincts, 33–34
Institute of Human Relations
    (Yale), 141–142
Institutions, primary and
    secondary, 87–88, 94, 150,
    166
Integration:
    of culture, 61, 67, 82, 91–92
    of personality, 58, 195–196
Intelligence and culture, 242–245
Interaction:
    mother–infant, 215–219
    social, 136, 197, 204, 212
    symbolic, 201
Interactionist approach, 185,
    196–204, 207, 249, 250
Interpretation of Dreams, The, 37
Introjection, 35
Isomorphism, 111, 115
IZARD, C., 214

JACOBS, J., 179
JAMES, W., 26
Jivaro, 221
JONES, E., 39
JONES, REV. JIM, 224
Journal of Abnormal and Social
    Psychology, 81
Judges, use of, 151–152, 211
Judgment of emotion, 214–215
JUNG, C. G., 38

KAPLAN, B., 81, 133, 135
KARDINER, A., 23, 85–96, 105, 124,
    137, 145, 150, 155, 167, 175,
    196
KATCHER, A., 224
KATCHER, J., 224
KAUFMAN, I. C., 215–217
KAY, P., 233
KENNEDY, J. G., 192
Kewa, 231–232
Kibbutz, Israeli, 160, 171

KIEV, A., 203
Kinship terms, 230–231
KLUCKHOHN, C., 4, 39, 99,
    108–109, 117–119
KLUCKHOHN, R., 156
KOFFKA, K., 62
KÖHLER, W., 62
KONNER, M., 218
KROEBER, A. L., 48, 49, 172
KUHN, T., 246
Kwakiutl, 68, 72, 75, 88–89, 123
Kwoma, 143–144, 208

Laboratory of Human
    Development (Harvard), 154
LAING, R. D., 249
LAMBERT, W., 208
LANG, K., 188
LANGER, W. C., 113
Language, 4, 17, 62, 67, 212
Language Behavior Laboratory
    (Berkeley), 233
Latency period, 34, 45, 165
Learning environment, 208–211
LEARY, T., 219
LEE, D. D., 22, 82, 227–228, 249
LEIGHTON, A., 203
LeVINE, R., 39, 99, 135, 137–138,
    180–182, 222
LÉVI-STRAUSS, C., 44, 237–238
LÉVY-BRUHL, L., 27, 29, 31, 227
LEWIS, O., 191
Life-history interview, 4, 93–95,
    118, 121, 127, 193
LIFTON, R. J., 125, 224
LINDESMITH, A., 133–135
LINDZEY, G., 243
LINNAEUS, C., 20
LINTON, A., 86
LINTON, R., 85–91, 94, 131
Little Hans, 46
LOEHLIN, J., 243
LOMAX, E., 132
Lonely Crowd, The, 121–124
Longitudinal studies, 132, 196
Love magic, 154
LURIE, A., 49
LYNCH, K., 240–241

MacCANNELL, D., 241
McCLELLAND, D., 137, 196
MacCORQUODALE, K., 92
MADARIAGA, DE, S., 127
MAHLER, M., 219
Male envy of female functions,
    170, 179
MALINOWSKI, B., 26, 80, 154, 160,
    227
Manus (Admiralty Islands), 76–78
MAQUET, J., 220
MARCUSE, H., 36
Marginality, 196
MARX, K., 9, 137, 186–188
Material interests of ruling class,
    186, 189
Materialist approach, 185,
    186–189, 192, 203–204
Mazeway, 240
MEAD, G. H., 197–198
MEAD, M., 9, 29, 60, 65, 66, 73,
    74–81, 108, 110, 114, 119,
    127, 128, 137, 144, 217
Mediation theory, 137, 149
MEEHL, P. E., 92
Megalomaniac character, 70–71,
    114
MEKEEL, H. S., 172
Memory, 32–33
Mental illness:
    attitudes to, 72, 203
    myth of, 249
    rates of, 202
MERTON, R., 193
MÉTRAUX, R., 89, 127, 224
MILLAR, J., 18
MILLER, D., 193
MILLER, N., 142–143, 240
Mind of Primitive Man, The, 28
MINTURN, L., 208
Modal class, 101
Modal personality approach, 1, 57,
    85, 93–96, 105, 128, 132–133,
    250
Modes of behavior, 173–174
Modes of conformity, 121–123
MORGAN, L. H., 18, 25
Moses and Monotheism, 38, 177

Mothers of Six Cultures, 208
Motivation, 17–24
MP: *See* Modal personality approach
Müller–Lyer illusion, 14–16, 234
Mundugumor, 79
MUNROE, R., 162
MUNROE, R. L., 162
MURDOCK, G. P., 141–143, 145
MURPHY, G., 23, 97–99, 197, 239, 248, 249
MURPHY, L. B., 248
MURRAY, F., 236
MURRAY, H., 99
Myth, interpretation of, 179–180, 238
Mythical thought, 238, 247

NAROLL, R., 153
National character, 1, 20, 58, 107, 129, 134, 144
    American, 108, 119–126
    Balinese, 128
    English, 108, 127
    German, 112–114
    Hindu, 127–128
    Japanese, 109–112
    Russian, 114–119
Nature of Cultural Things, The, 3
Navajo, 153, 232
Need for achievement, 22, 100, 192, 194
NEEDHAM, R., 27
NEEDLER, M., 129
Needs, 17
Neo-Freudian approach, 1, 49, 165–183
Neurosis, 36–37, 186, 207
    and culture, 38–39, 150, 166, 177
New Lives for Old, 77
NIETZSCHE, F., 69, 70
NIXON, R., 120
Nonverbal communication, 76, 77, 128, 219
Normality, relativity of, 72, 250
Null hypothesis, 146–147

Obedience, 89–90
    delayed, 47, 165
OBERHOLZER, E., 94, 98, 101
Objective method, 145
Objectivity assumption, 135–136
Obligation, 111
Observations of behavior, 207, 210–211, 245
    reliability of, 211
Obsessional neuroses, 40–41
Oedipus complex, 44–46, 53–54, 89, 113, 165, 169
Ojibwa, 81, 102
Old Ones of New Mexico, The, 178
O'NELL, C. W., 224
OPLER, M. K., 203
Optical illusions, 14–16, 234
Oral zone, 34
Organization of diversity, 103, 133
ORLANSKY, H., 132
ORWELL, G., 2, 53
OSMOND, H., 249
Other-directed character, 122
Overdetermination, 182
Oversocialization, 166, 190
OVESEY, L., 196

Paranoid character, 70
Patterns of Culture, 66–73, 86, 123
Peasant personality, 191–192
PENFIELD, W., 33
Pennsylvania, University of, 85
People of Alor, The, 93–96, 99, 105, 134
Perception, 10–17, 63
    tests of, 13–14, 24
Perceptual cycle, 242
Perceptual skills, 12
Perceptual world, 11
Personality, 4, 57–58, 79, 204, 211, 219
Personality and Psychotherapy, 142
PHILLIPS, H., 191
PIAGET, J., 235–238
PIERS, G., 110
PIKER, S., 192
PINE, F., 219
Plains Indians, 68–70

PLAUT, T., 203
POLANYI, M., 182
PORTEUS, S., 94
Porteus maze test, 93–94
Positionalist approach, 185,
    189–196, 204
Potlatch, 71
POWERS, W. T., 11
PREBLE, E., 92
*Presentation of Self in Everyday Life,
    The*, 198
PRICE-WILLIAMS, D., 14, 80, 222,
    225, 237, 243–245, 250
Primal horde, 46–47, 120
Primate behavior, 167, 215–217
Primitive thought, 24, 26–27, 31
    See also Cognitive anthropology
Principles of Psychology, 26
Projection, 35, 87, 150
Projective assumption, 134–135
Projective system, 88
Projective tests, 19, 96–105,
    134–135, 193–194
Protein deficiency, 156
Psychedelic anthropology,
    219–220
Psychiatry (journal), 81
Psychoanalytic Anthropology
    School, 29, 31–54, 162,
    182–183, 203, 237
Psychohistory, 177–178, 250
Psychological anthropology, 1, 57,
    250
Psychology:
    class, 186–187, 197
    common-sense, 2–3
    cross-cultural, 236–237, 246
    definition of, 1
    See also Behaviorism; Gestalt
        psychology
Psychology of Clothes, The, 49–52
Psychopathology of Everyday Life, The,
    198
Psychosexual stages, 34, 173–175
Pueblo Indians, 68, 69, 75, 123,
    133
Pursuit of Loneliness, The, 125

Racism, 9, 20, 67, 165
RADCLIFFE-BROWN, A. R., 80

RADIN, P., 29
RAMIREZ, M., 237
Rationalism, 187
Reaction formation, 36
Recognition of motive, social, 22
REDFIELD, R., 67
Regression, 35–36, 169
REIK, T., 92
Rejection of parents, 120
Relations in Public, 200
Renunciation, instinctual, 45
Replication of uniformity, 133
Repression, 34, 35, 159, 171, 183
Resentment of authority, 126
Resistance, psychic, 45–46, 53–54
Retentive mode, 173, 176
Return of repressed, 165–183
RICKERS-OVSIANKINA, M., 95
RICKMAN, J., 116–117
Riddle of the Sphinx, The, 167
RIEFF, P., 54, 249
RIESMAN, D., 121–124, 126
Ritual learning, 224
RIVERS, W. H. R., 14–15, 31
ROBERTS, J. M., 158
ROE, A., 193–194
RÓHEIM, G., 39, 92, 137, 166–168,
    223
ROHRER, J., 194–196, 249
ROMNEY, A. K., 153–154
RORSCHACH, H., 97
Rorschach test, 81, 93, 17–99,
    100–102, 133, 135, 194
ROSCH, E., 235
ROUSSEAU, J. J., 8
RUSSELL, B., 5

Samoa, 74–76, 144
Sampling, 101, 117, 145, 146, 150,
    151, 158, 161, 162
SANTAYANA, G., 250
SAPIR, E., 58–62, 63–64, 66, 73, 74,
    79, 85, 95, 131, 142, 181, 228,
    250
SARASON, S., 20, 103–105
SAUCIER, J.-F., 157
Savage mind, 1, 8
Savage Mind, The, 238
Savage passions, 18, 54
SCHACHTEL, E. G., 32

SCHACHTER, S., 22
SCHEFLEN, A., 219
Scientific thought, 24, 238
Scientists, personality of, 193–194
SCOTT, J. P., 192
SCRIBNER, S., 237, 239
Security, 89–90, 122, 167, 193
SEGALL, M., 15–16
Self, as social product, 197–198, 204
Selfish Gene, The, 189
Self-reliance, 125–126
Semantic domains, 228–235
SENNETT, R., 188
Sentence completion test, 97
Separation, 216, 219
SERPELL, R., 239, 241, 248
Sex and Temperament in Three Primitive Societies, 74, 78–79
Sexual anxiety, 151, 154
Sexual behavior, 150, 166
SHAKESPEARE, W., 19–20
Shallowness of feeling, 76, 217
Shamanism, 221–222, 225
SHIRLEY, R. W., 153–154
Shona, 244
SHWEDER, R., xii, 247
Sibling incest, 158–161
SIEGLER, M., 249
SIMMEL, G., 197–198
SINGER, J., 22
SINGER, M., 110
Sioux, 175–176
SISK, J., 182
Situation:
  definition of, 198
  influence of, 168–169, 197–201, 204, 207, 218
Six Cultures, 208
Six Cultures project, 158, 208–211, 219
SLATER, P., 124–125
Sleeping arrangements, 156
Social Darwinism, 9
  See also Sociobiology
Socialization:
  of adults, 192
  anxiety, 150–154
  differential, 190
  theory of, 143, 166

See also Child training
Social Learning and Imitation, 142
Social Meanings of Suicide, 201
Social patterning, 66
  See also Configurationalist approach
Social psychiatry, 203
Social role, 192–199
Social Structure, 143
Social structure and motivation, 28, 189
Social Structure and Personality School, 1, 185–204
Sociobiology, 188–189
SPAIN, D., 99
Special senses, 16–17
SPENCER, H., 9
SPENGLER, O., 68
SPINDLER, G., xi, 131
SPIRO, M. E., 23, 81, 99, 135, 136, 137, 153, 160, 171, 180–181, 249
SPUHLER, J., 243
STEPHENS, W., 156
Stereotypes:
  contradictions in, 8, 10, 17, 108
  and prejudice, 8, 12, 114, 136
Stigma, 199–200
STOETZEL, J., 111
STRAUSS, A., 133–135
Study of culture at a distance, 109
Study of Man, The, 86
Sublimation, 36, 166–167, 179
SUGERMAN, A., 222
Suicide, 111, 160, 201–202
SULLIVAN, H. S., 81
Superego, 32, 48, 94, 197
Superstructure, 187
Swaddling hypothesis, 52, 114–118
SWANSON, G., 193
Symbolic Wounds, 170
Symbolism:
  in culture, 61
  in dreams, 37
Synthesis, 141, 180–181, 245–246, 250
SZASZ, T., 249

Taboo, 39–43, 77, 88–89, 143
  and ambivalence, 40–43, 158

Taboo (continued)
  definition of, 39
  food, 151, 238
  incest, 158–161
  postpartum, 156
  topics, 29
TACITUS, 107
Tanala, 89–90
TART, C., 81
TARTER, R. E., 222
TAT (Thematic Apperception
  Test), 99–100, 104–105, 194
Tchambuli, 79
Teachings of Don Juan, The, 220
Temperament, 72
  and sex roles, 78–80
Thanatos, 33
Thematic Apperception Test
  (TAT), 99–100, 104–105, 194
Themes:
  in American life, 120
  in French culture, 127
  in Trukese personality, 104
THEOPHRASTUS, 107
THOMAS, W. I., 197
Thresholds, 19
THUCYDIDES, 107
TOCQUEVILLE, DE, A., 107, 119
TOLMAN, E. C., 239
Totemism, 25, 39, 43–48
Totemism and Exogamy, 26
Totem and Taboo, 38, 39–48, 88,
  167, 171, 200
Tradition-directed character, 122,
  191
Traits:
  cultural, 63–66, 145–146, 156
  personality, 58
Transcultural psychiatry, 248
Transvestism, 51
TRIANDIS, H., 13
Trobriand Islanders, 160
Truk, Man in Paradise, 103–105
TURNER, R., 201
Tuscarora, modal personality of,
  100–103
Twice Born, The, 127
Two Worlds of Childhood, 118
TYLER, S., 228, 230

TYLOR, E. B., 25, 145

Umwelt, 10
Unconscious processes, 33
Uniformity assumption, 64, 107,
  112, 132–133, 158, 185, 191,
  204
Uses of Enchantment, The, 171–172

Variability, kinds of, 116–117, 133,
  152, 157, 181, 210
VAYDA, A. P., 20
Völkerpsychologie, 25

WAGLEY, C., 86
WEBER, M., 192
WEIL, R. J., 202
WERNER, O., 232
WERTHEIMER, M., 62
WESTERMARCK, E., 158–160
WHITE, L. A., 2, 137
WHITING, B., 208, 210–211
WHITING, J., 89, 141–145,
  149–153, 155–158, 166, 170,
  181, 208–211
WHYTE, L. L., 33, 224
WILLS, G., 52, 120, 125
WILSON, E. O., 188
Wisconsin, University of, 85
Wit and Its Relation to the
  Unconscious, 53
WITKIN, H. A., 238–239
WOLF, A., 160
WOLMAN, B., 17, 58
WOODWORTH, R., 63
WRIGHT, H. F., 212
WRONG, D., 166
WUNDT, W., 25–26, 28, 31, 38, 42,
  62, 227
WYLIE, P., 119

Yale University, 85, 141–142, 245
Yaqui, 220
YOUNG, F. W., 157
Young Man Luther, 178
Yurok, 175–176

Zuni Pueblo, 68, 88–89